RUNNER'S *WORLD*

COMPLETE
BOOK OF
RUNNING

RUNNER'S WORLD

COMPLETE BOOK OF RUNNING

EVERYTHING YOU NEED TO KNOW TO RUN FOR FUN, FITNESS, AND COMPETITION

EDITED BY AMBY BURFOOT

EXECUTIVE EDITOR, RUNNER'S MAGAZINE
AND WINNER OF THE 1968 BOSTON MARATHON

Rodale Press, Inc.
Emmaus, Pennsylvania

Library of Congress Cataloging-in-Publication Data

Burfoot, Amby.
   Runner's world complete book of running : everything you need to know to run for fun, fitness, and competition / by Amby Burfoot.
      p.   cm.
   Includes index.
   ISBN 0–87596–354–4 hardcover
   1. Running.   2. Running—Training.   I. Runner's world (Emmaus, Pa. : 1987) II. Title.
GV1061.B78   1997
796.42—dc21
                                                                        96–53296

   ISBN 1–57954–186–0 paperback

Distributed to the book trade by St. Martin's Press

        8 10 9   hardcover
   4 6 8 10 9 7 5   paperback

Visit us on the Web at www.runnersworldbooks.com, or call us toll-free at (800) 848-4735.

─── OUR PURPOSE ───

*We inspire and enable people to improve
their lives and the world around them.*

Notice

The information here is designed to help you make decisions regarding your fitness and exercise program. It is not intended as a substitute for professional fitness and medical advice. As with all exercise programs, you should seek your doctor's approval before you begin.

Runner's World Complete Book of Running **Editorial Staff**

EXECUTIVE EDITOR, *Runner's World* Magazine: Amby Burfoot

EDITOR: John D. Reeser

CONTRIBUTING WRITERS: Liz Applegate, Gordon Bakoulis, Dan Bensimhon, Amby Burfoot, Martin Dugard, Joe Ellis, Jeff Galloway, Tom Hall, John Hanc, Joe Henderson, Hal Higdon, Dave Kuehls, Doug Kurtis, Jerry Lynch, Ken McAlpine, Linda Miller, Gretchen Reynolds, Joan Samuelson, Mark Will-Weber, Bob Wischnia

PERMISSION COORDINATOR: Kelly Elizabeth Coffey

COPY EDITORS: Amy K. Kovalski, Karen Neely

COVER DESIGNER: Charles Beasley

BOOK DESIGNER: Stan Green/Green Graphics

ILLUSTRATOR: Robert Frawley

MANUFACTURING COORDINATOR: Patrick T. Smith

OFFICE MANAGER: Roberta Mulliner

OFFICE STAFF: Julie Kehs, Mary Lou Stephen

OFFICE MANAGER, *Runner's World* Magazine: Patricia Erickson

Rodale Health and Fitness Books

VICE-PRESIDENT AND EDITORIAL DIRECTOR: Debora T. Yost

EXECUTIVE EDITOR: Neil Wertheimer

DESIGN AND PRODUCTION DIRECTOR: Michael Ward

RESEARCH MANAGER: Ann Gossy Yermish

COPY MANAGER: Lisa D. Andruscavage

STUDIO MANAGER: Stefano Carbini

BOOK MANUFACTURING DIRECTOR: Helen Clogston

CONTENTS

Part 5. Building Strength, Endurance, and Speed

Part 6. The Mental Side of Running

Part 7. Cross-Training

Part 8. The Marathon

INTRODUCTION

Hello. And welcome to what I hope you'll find to be the most informative and friendly running book ever published. From the very beginning of this book project, I have had two simple goals: to gather the best, most helpful running advice available and to present it in the clearest, most user-friendly manner.

You can be certain of the quality of the information, because the topics have all been covered over the years in the pages of *Runner's World* magazine, the world's leading running magazine for more than 30 years. I'll talk more about the friendly side of this book in a few paragraphs.

Since 1966, *Runner's World* magazine has led the way in every key area of how-to journalism about running: from training programs to shoe buyer's guides to nutrition. *Runner's World* has covered the sport—the Olympics, the Boston Marathon, and so on—but it has devoted many more pages to advice articles than to anything else. There's a basic reason for that: Running is a participatory sport, not a fan sport. For the most part, we are doers, not watchers.

When I began gathering material for this book, I included chapters only on those subjects that I knew you would like because readers of the magazine had already responded by the thousands to similar articles. There are no duds here. I can almost guarantee that every chapter will strike a chord with you. After all, every chapter has been reader tested and approved by runners much like you.

And who am I who claims to know so much about *Runner's World* and its readers? First of all, I've been executive editor of *Runner's World* for the past 10 years. Before that, I was one of the magazine's feature writers for another 10 years. For two decades, I've read every word that has gone into the magazine and every word of response from readers.

I've also been running for more than 30 years. In 1968 I even won the Boston Marathon. But that's not nearly so important as the fact that I'm still running enthusiastically and healthily today. So what if I'm not fast anymore? That doesn't bother me. I run for recreation, stress relief, weight control, camaraderie, health, challenge, and many other reasons.

I suspect that these are many of the same reasons you run. Or, if you're a beginner, these are the things that you would like to achieve by taking up a running program.

Throughout the pages of this book, you'll find me always at your side, because I've written a brief introduction and summary to the chapters. This is where the book gets its friendly, chatty style. Or at least that's the way I hope you'll feel.

I know that when I visit a museum or historical site, I enjoy having a guide. Guides provide information, which is important, but the best guides also add a certain liveliness to the basic facts. They elevate an educational experience and turn it into entertainment. If they have fun, you have fun.

That's what I've tried to do with my introductions and summaries. They've been fun for me to write, and I hope you'll enjoy reading them. The chapters provide the core information you're most interested in, but I hope you find that my additional comments add perspective and analysis.

As your tour guide, there's one other important role I'd like to fulfill. I want to be your cheerleader. I want to encourage you every step of the way. I want you to know that running is the best fitness sport in the world, that the payoffs from a running lifestyle are greater than you can possibly imagine, and that you can do everything that's described in this book. Even a marathon.

Let me address the last issue first, because some of you are no doubt already scoffing that you could never run a marathon. Maybe not. But Oprah Winfrey did, so maybe you could. And even if you decide that you don't want to run marathons, many of the workouts and other advice in the Marathon section can improve your vigor and your endurance. So read the section and adapt the principles in each chapter to fit your own needs.

The beauty of running is that it's so simple, so adaptable, and so positive. Any healthy person can run. (And many others, despite assorted physical and mental handicaps, have also succeeded.) You learned to walk when you were a child, right? Well, running is nothing more than glorified walking. You can do it.

You might not run fast. And you might not run far. But you can do it. And even if you have to mix walking with your running, you'll lose weight, lower your blood pressure, reduce the stress of daily life, and feel a surge of energy.

And those are only the physical benefits. The mental benefits include lowered risk of depression and increased creativity. Many runners take up the sport because they want to lose a few pounds or decrease their inherited risks of heart disease. They continue running for the way it clears their minds every day.

Running is the ultimate individual sport. It doesn't matter how fast or slow you are relative to anyone else. You set your own pace and you measure your own progress. You can't lose this race because you're not running against anyone else. You're only running against yourself, and as long as you *are* running, you are winning.

Ultimately, I hope that's the message you will get from this book. The advice is all here. Your cheerleader is at your side. You can hardly go wrong. So lace up those running shoes and get on with it.

Amby Burfoot
Executive Editor, *Runner's World* Magazine

1

BEGINNING RUNNING

CHAPTER 1

THE FIRST OF MANY MILES

A Surefire Plan to Keep You Running

All running programs for beginners are the same: They move you from walking, which anyone can do, to running, which anyone can do if they have the determination. The difference between walking and running isn't speed or biomechanics. It's determination.

If you have the determination to stick with the following program, you'll soon be a runner. Trust me. It won't be long before you learn that I'm right.

The beginning of your life as a runner just might be the most exciting time in your entire running career. Of course, you won't necessarily realize that at the time. It may take months or years before you can look back and see what you've achieved. But rest assured—you will.

Getting started . . . first steps . . . the beginning of a great adventure. In many ways, beginning to run is a declaration of personal independence. A statement that says, "In a world that confronts me with mechanical convenience and idle luxury at virtually every turn, I have decided, nonetheless, to improve my physical fitness."

Later, of course, you realize that running offers so much more than a flatter stomach, more muscle tone, and a longer and more energetic life. For most of us, body and soul both tune in to this stimulating activity we call running. Running strengthens the body while it soothes the soul.

So what are you waiting for? The sooner you get started, the better.

WALK BEFORE YOU RUN

More than a few training programs—especially the New Year's–resolution variety—are doomed almost before they start. Why? Because the schedules are overly ambitious and complex. Or, in direct contrast, they are completely lacking in a goal.

The first step for an exercise program (after you get a medical exam) is to ask yourself, what's realistic for me? Think "simple." Think "goal." Think "long term."

Unless you are coming from a strong (and recent) background in another physically demanding sport (such as cycling, martial arts, tennis, basketball, soccer, or cross-country skiing), don't jump right into a running program. Instead, begin with a run/walk program. An excellent goal for a run/walk program is four workouts per week, with each one lasting 20 to 30 minutes.

"If you're just beginning a fitness program, the best way to start is with walking," says Budd Coates, health promotions manager at Rodale Press in Emmaus, Pennsylvania, and four-time Olympic Marathon Trials qualifier. "Continuous walking will slowly prepare your legs for running and will also help you develop a consistent daily routine." Dozens of other programs begin the same way.

Coates recommends that a person with absolutely no running background get started with eight straight days of walking: first, four days of 20 minutes, then four days of 30 minutes. (For more information, see "Ease into This Running Program" on page 6.)

After that initial break-in period, introduce 2 minutes of running, alternating with 4 minutes of walking. Do this five times for a total of 30 minutes per workout. The runs should be slow jogs, not the kind of sprints that you did back in your teens when you played high school sports.

"The biggest mistake that beginning runners make is they tend to think in mile increments—1 mile, 2 miles, 3 miles," says Coates. "Most of them aren't ready for that. They need to think in minutes of running, not miles.

"The other major mistake is that beginners try to run too fast," adds Coates. "They get completely out of breath, their leg muscles scream, and, naturally, running isn't fun under those circumstances. So they get discouraged and quit. Instead, they need to begin at a pace that is about the same as a fast walk."

The talk test is a simple way to judge your pace. Aim to run at a comfortable pace that lets you talk with a training partner. Don't go any faster. Comfort is far more important than speed.

After 10 weeks Coates's program brings the beginning runner to a complete 30-minute run, without walking. Once you can comfortably run 30 minutes without stopping, then you can think in terms of miles per week. A reasonable goal is 9 to 14 miles, with three days of running and four days of rest, some of which might include some alternative exercise such as swimming, cycling, or strength training.

THE BEST PLACES TO RUN

One of the first questions that beginners ask is, where should I begin my running? It's probably not best to start on the street right outside your door, though certainly many runners do, if for no other reason than convenience.

If you can, start on a well-maintained track at your local school or a path in a public park. Grass can be good, too, but make certain the field is cut close and even. A treadmill at the local health club can also supply a smooth beginning.

Running on a smooth, soft surface is the key, so even if you're relegated to the roads, try to run on the silt along the road's edge. Avoid roads with a steep camber to them; these can throw off your foot-plant, leading to sore muscles and injuries. Whenever possible, choose blacktop roads over concrete (concrete is harder), and always run *against* oncoming traffic. This makes you more visible to the driver (especially if you're wearing light or reflective clothing) and allows you to spot threatening situations before they develop.

Sidewalks may offer better safety from traffic, but concrete's hardness can provoke shinsplints and other aches and pains common to the beginning runner. Also, sidewalks often force you to run up and down the edges at intersections—not a great way to develop your running rhythm.

Although admittedly not always the most exciting locale, the track has its advantages, especially for the beginner. First, it's flat and soft. You can also judge exactly how far you have been running and at what pace. This constant feedback helps you progress with minimal risk and also makes it easy to chart your progress.

When you're running on the track, it makes good sense to run in the outer lanes and occasionally—perhaps every two or three laps—switch direction. Running on the tighter inside lanes and in the same direction can put unnecessary wear and tear on joints and tendons, especially if you're not accustomed to running the turns. Also, if there are advanced runners conducting timed sessions on the track, it's considered proper etiquette to leave the inside lanes open for them.

Eventually, you will encounter hills. You won't consider them a friend at first, but they can actually help you improve your fitness. Physically, running hills builds muscular and cardiovascular strength. Mentally, hills add a challenging touch to an advanced workout and therefore can be a good weapon against boredom. But both uphills and downhills add entirely new and taxing elements to your running program.

Olympic Marathon gold medalist Frank Shorter once referred to hills as speedwork in disguise. Treat hills as such; you'll probably be ready to run a hilly course about the same time you might be ready to attempt an introductory pace/speed session on the track. Therefore, avoid hills in the very early stages of your training program and introduce them in very small doses (and sizes) after you have logged more than a month of flat running at a comfortable pace.

If you do eventually add hills to a program as you advance beyond the beginner stage, start with some slight rollers; save the mountains for the future. Be particularly careful to avoid pounding

Ease into This Running Program

The following running schedule was created by Budd Coates, health promotions manager at Rodale Press in Emmaus, Pennsylvania, and four-time Olympic Marathon Trials qualifier. Each spring Coates leads a corporate running program for beginners that takes nonrunners and, in 10 weeks, gets them to the point where they can run 3.5 miles without stopping. Follow this schedule, and you can do the same.

Before you start this schedule, get your legs ready with eight days of walking: Walk for 20 minutes a day for the first four days, then increase to 30 minutes a day for four more days. Now you're ready to begin with week 1.

Each week of the program, do your run/walk workouts on Monday, Wednesday, Friday, and Saturday. Take a rest day or an easy walk on Tuesday, Thursday, and Sunday.

Week 1

Run 2 minutes, walk 4 minutes.
Complete 5 cycles.

Week 2

Run 3 minutes, walk 3 minutes.
Complete 5 cycles.

Week 3

Run 5 minutes, walk 2½ minutes.
Complete 4 cycles.

on the descents. As with flat running, hills that feature grass and soft paths are preferable to hard surfaces.

Regardless of where you walk and run, do some light stretching before you begin the workout. Stretching reduces muscle tightness and allows for a more comfortable stride action.

THE NEXT LEVEL: RACING

The late running philosopher George Sheehan, M.D., once noted that the only difference between a jogger and a runner was an entry blank. There's much truth to that statement. Most local races contain a number of runners who are lined up primarily to finish the

Week 4

> Run 7 minutes, walk 3 minutes.
> Complete 3 cycles.

Week 5

> Run 8 minutes, walk 2 minutes.
> Complete 3 cycles.

Week 6

> Run 9 minutes, walk 2 minutes.
> Complete 2 cycles, then run 8 minutes.

Week 7

> Run 9 minutes, walk 1 minute.
> Complete 3 cycles.

Week 8

> Run 13 minutes, walk 2 minutes.
> Complete 2 cycles.

Week 9

> Run 14 minutes, walk 1 minute.
> Complete 2 cycles.
> *Note:* After completing week 9, if you feel tired, repeat this week of training before moving on to week 10.

Week 10

> Run 30 minutes.

course, even if just slightly faster than they might run the same route during a typical training jaunt.

The point is, if you're curious about racing—and you sense improved fitness in your training runs—try it. It's natural to feel anxiety over where you might place or how fast you will (or won't) run, but recognize such thoughts as the self-imposed barriers that they are.

What's the best way to start? Look for a local, relatively low-key race. For example, sometimes a competitive race—a 10-K—is accompanied by a 2-mile fun run. Start with the fun run. In a year's time you might well progress to the longer, more-challenging race, but the 2-mile distance is perfect for testing the waters.

Also, pick a flat course and shoot for a day that's likely to feature pleasant weather conditions—particularly low heat and humidity. Convince a training partner to do the race with you to share support and the experience. Women may want to try one of the growing numbers of women's-only races such as the "Race for the Cure" series that promotes breast cancer awareness.

In your first race, be careful, above all else, not to start too fast. The excitement and adrenaline that you feel will tend to make you run faster than your accustomed pace, but you won't notice it. At least, not at first. Then, after a half-mile or so, you might realize that you're gasping for breath and your legs are beginning to feel like anchors. To avoid this, concentrate on total relaxation at the start and during the early going. Breathe comfortably, settle into a moderate pace, and enjoy yourself.

There's an old running maxim that holds for everyone from beginners to Olympic champs: If you start too slow, you can always pick it up later; but if you start too fast, your goose is cooked. It takes most runners several races to find their perfect pace—a pace that spreads out their reserves equally over the full distance.

WATCH OUT FOR THE BUG

With the possible exception of the very beginning of your running program, the next most dangerous time for a novice runner is just after that first race—especially if the initial racing experience is a successful and enjoyable debut.

The danger, of course, comes from being bitten by the racing bug. The temptation for some runners is suddenly to race every weekend, but this multiplies the possibility of injury or burnout.

Along the same lines, beware of "marathon fever." Some novice racers run a couple of local 5-K events and, flush with excitement, jump right into training for a mega-marathon, such as New York City

Do's and Don'ts for Beginners

Running is a simple activity, but the following guidelines will help you succeed at it.

1. Don't begin a running program without a full medical exam.

2. Don't attempt to train through an athletic injury. Little aches and pains can sideline you for weeks or months if you don't take time off and seek medical advice.

3. Do dress correctly. If it's dark, wear white or, better yet, reflective clothing. If it's cold, wear layers of clothing, gloves or mittens, and a wool ski cap to retain heat. Sunblock, sunglasses, a baseball cap, and white clothing make sense on hot days.

4. Don't run in worn-out shoes (check them for broken-down heels or very smooth areas where you push off on your strides). Don't run in shoes that are designed for other sports, such as basketball or tennis sneaks.

5. Do tell someone where you'll be running and when you expect to return. Carry some identification and a quarter for a phone call.

6. Do some light stretching exercises prior to your run/walk workouts to reduce muscle tightness and increase range of motion. You should do even more stretching after the workout.

7. Do watch out for cars, and don't expect drivers to watch out for you. Always run facing traffic so that you can see cars approaching. When crossing an intersection, make sure you establish eye contact with the driver before proceeding.

8. Do include a training partner in your program, if possible. A training partner with similar abilities and goals can add motivation and increase the safety of your running.

9. Don't wear headphones when running outside, whether you're training or racing. They tune you out from your surroundings, making you more vulnerable to all sorts of hazards: cars, bikes, skateboards, dogs, and criminals.

10. Don't run in remote areas, especially if you are a woman running alone. If you don't have a partner, run with a dog or carry a self-defense spray. Don't approach a car to give directions, and don't assume all runners are harmless. (For more information on safety, send a request—along with a self-addressed, stamped envelope—to: Road Runners Club of America, 1150 South Washington Street, Suite 250, Alexandria, VA 22314.)

or Los Angeles. Resist the temptation. The marathon has been around since the ancient Greeks. It will still be there when your running has progressed to the point that your first marathon experience can be an enjoyable run. It doesn't do you any good to enter a marathon that reduces you to a survival crawl punctuated by self-doubt and tagged with the postscript "I'm never running one of these things again!"

Instead, prepare for the transition to marathoning with a gradual introduction of weekly or biweekly long runs. A long run, by definition, is what's long for *you* in relation to your present level of training. For runners training for their first marathon, the long run might start in the 10- or 12-mile range and gradually progress over several months to distances approaching 20 miles.

Also, some race experience at the 10-mile, 20-K, and half-marathon distances can serve as dress rehearsals for the big one. Both the long runs and the race distances between 10-K and 26.2 miles will prepare you mentally and physically for the marathon challenge.

You don't have to finish a marathon, however, to be a runner. There are lots of great runners who never run 26.2 miles. A runner is someone who runs; it's that simple—and that grand. Be that someone. Be yourself. Be your own runner, whether the challenge is four times around the junior high school track or qualifying and running in the Boston Marathon.

> *The key to success with a running program for beginners is to start slow and stay slow. Speed kills. Don't even think about it. Patience rewards, so stick with it, stick with it, stick with it.*
>
> *A few years ago I taught a running program for beginners in which I told my students over and over again that they should run as slowly as possible. "Don't breathe hard," I said. "Stay comfortable. Don't worry about how you look and don't worry about how fast anyone else in the class is running. Just go slow."*
>
> *A couple of people in the class seemed to be struggling, so I asked if they were sure that they were running slowly enough. "No problem," they gasped. "This is real comfortable."*
>
> *I knew they were pushing too hard, but that's a hard thing to tell someone, so I asked if I could take their pulses. After only 10 seconds of counting their pulses, I was able to inform them that they were running at about the same effort level as an Olympic champion. One of them was running at a pulse rate of*

170 beats per minute. (Most beginning runners should be between 120 and 140, depending on many variables, including age.)

Armed with an objective measure, I was able to convince my students to relax and slow down. They did, they stuck with the program, and eight weeks later they graduated from the class.

You'll graduate, too, to whatever goals you seek, so long as you concentrate on slow and steady. Remember the tortoise and the hare? You want to be a tortoise.

CHAPTER 2

ON THE ROAD WITH OPRAH

How Running Changed Her Life

In November 1994, when Oprah Winfrey sneaked into the Marine Corps Marathon in Washington, D.C., and successfully completed the 26.2-mile distance in a heavy rain, she became the biggest running story in America since President Jimmy Carter collapsed in a road race in 1979. She was on TV, she was in the daily newspapers, she was on the front page of the National Enquirer *and the other tabloids, and she recounted the story on her own* Oprah Winfrey Show.

Why did she create such a stir? Because Oprah Winfrey was the last person the American media expected to run a marathon. When she did it, and did it without stopping to walk a single step of the way, she proved that essentially anyone can be a successful runner. Her inspirational success motivated tens of thousands of other Americans, especially American women, to take up running and get in shape themselves.

In March 1993 Bob Greene received a phone call from Oprah Winfrey. At the time, Greene was head of the exercise program at Telluride Ski Resort in Colorado. Six months earlier, he had led Winfrey, who has a home in Telluride, on several strenuous mountain hikes.

Now she was calling to ask him to move to Chicago to become her personal trainer. Greene hesitated. "I like to sit down with potential new clients to make sure they're serious," he recalls. "With Oprah, that wasn't possible. Still, it was *Oprah* asking." So, he agreed.

Like everyone, Greene, an exercise physiologist, knew about Oprah and her yo-yoing weight-loss problems. Seven years earlier, in front of a national TV audience, she had told the story of her successful weight-loss diet. But within months the pounds had crept back on. She now weighed 222 pounds and didn't seem able to lose more than a pound or two, despite her adherence to a low-calorie, low-fat diet.

Greene had to wonder about Oprah's commitment to an exercise program. Five minutes into their first session, however, he knew he'd made a good choice. "I could tell she was completely determined," he says. "And she never wavered."

Both Oprah and Greene had the same original goal: healthy weight loss. But how? "I made a decision from the very beginning to center Oprah's exercise program around running," Greene says. "There were other options, including swimming or cycling. But if you want quick weight-loss results, as Oprah did, running is the best."

GETTING DOWN TO BUSINESS

At their first training session, Oprah and Greene walked about 2½ miles. Slowly. "I wanted to assess her condition," Greene says. He found her healthy enough to begin mixing jogging and walking within a few days. Her initial pace worked out to about 17 minutes per mile. But two weeks into her program, Oprah was running and walking 3 to 4 consecutive miles at that pace.

Scheduling these workouts was not easy. Five days a week Oprah would rise at 5:00 A.M. to run before taping her show. Each afternoon, she would climb onto a stair-climbing machine for 45 minutes, followed by a half-hour or so of weight training. "That might be too aggressive a program for some people," Greene admits, "especially the two-a-day training sessions. But I wanted to get her metabolism revved up."

By early summer Oprah was on a roll. "She was achieving a steady, sustainable, 8- to 10-pound weight loss every month," Greene says, "and she didn't have to change her diet." There was one brief setback. "About three weeks into our program, Oprah noticed that she'd actually gained weight, not lost it, which is a common phenomenon for people who start a serious exercise program," Greene says. "But that weight rolls right off after another week or so. Unfortunately, many people quit exercising as soon as the weight comes on. It's a convenient excuse."

Oprah did not quit. "She was so excited, because she soon began seeing dramatic results," Greene says. "The body abides by the laws of physics. The more weight you lose, the faster you run. And the faster you run, the more weight you lose."

By July 1993 Oprah was running 5 to 6 miles a day at a 10- to 11-minute-per-mile pace. By midsummer, she had lost more than 40 pounds. It was time to race.

"I believe in using races as motivators," Greene says. "Sometimes it's hard to keep going on an exercise program if you don't have a goal in sight." He had hoped to find a 10-K for Oprah to enter but couldn't locate one that matched her busy weekend schedule. Eventually, he decided to be more ambitious, so in August 1993 he entered Oprah in the America's Finest City Half-Marathon in San Diego. Oprah completed the distance in a respectable 2:16.

With her finisher's medal triumphantly in hand, Oprah began pressing Greene to come up with a new challenge. "At one point she told me that she had always loved watching the marathon in Chicago," he says. "She'd cheer for the runners going past and think, 'I'd like to do that someday.' "

Greene downplayed the idea. First, he told her, she should concentrate on reaching her goal weight of 150 pounds. She was so close. And on November 10, 1993, she made it. That same morning, for the first time ever, she completed her 5-mile run at an 8-minute-per-mile pace. "I was so proud of her," Greene remembers. "Sometimes people will say to me, 'Oprah's got it easy because she has a personal chef and a personal trainer.' But that's baloney. No one can run for you. She was on the track every morning. She worked herself as hard as any athlete I've seen. She deserved the results she achieved."

A New Goal

From that day on, the focus of Oprah's training program shifted dramatically. She had achieved her weight-loss goal. She had even run a half-marathon. What was left? "Obviously, we wanted to maintain the weight loss, first and foremost," Greene says. "But we also knew that Oprah was ready to begin running more seriously. We decided to move from a weight-loss program to a training program. We decided that in 1994 she'd run a marathon."

So, beginning in January 1994, Oprah stepped up her training. Curiously, she began by running less, but this was part of the plan. "We stopped the two-a-day workouts," Greene says. "I even cut back somewhat on her mileage. Instead, I put her on a much more intensive strength-training regimen, because I knew training for a marathon would be hard on her body. I wanted to make sure that her joints were strong and healthy."

By midsummer 1994, Oprah was running as much as 50 miles a week, which included long-distance runs on weekends. At times, she complained. "This is such a struggle," she'd say to Greene. To which he answered, "No, it's not. It's a daily renewal."

His message took hold, and Oprah stuck to the program. Three months later she completed the Marine Corps Marathon without walking a single step. "I'll never forget mile 25 of that race," Greene says. "I turned around to watch her. She was looking great, passing people. She was just so pumped. There were tears in her eyes, and I thought, this is it. This symbolizes everything from 222 pounds to where she is now. It was just so moving.

"She could have quit months before the marathon. She certainly had enough legitimate excuses. But she didn't. I like to think her progress and her commitment will show millions of other people that they can improve their lives, too. Maybe they won't run a marathon, but they can run a 5-K. Or they can lose the weight that they've been wanting to get rid of. It's just so inspiring to watch someone transform herself, and that's what Oprah has done. She's a runner now for life."

Totally by chance, I happened to attend the Marine Corps Marathon that Oprah ran. I wasn't entered or expecting to run, but when I learned that Oprah was going to go the distance, I decided to join her.

I stood near the 3-mile mark at the Pentagon, in a pouring rain, and waited to see if I could find Oprah amidst the 15,000 other runners in the field. It wasn't difficult. Before spotting her myself, I heard other spectators yelling, "There she is. There's Oprah."

When she went past, I joined in just behind her. She was running with a friend, while Greene ran just in front of her. The National Enquirer, *always on the case, also had assigned two quite-fit reporters to go the distance at Oprah's side.*

I've run more than 50 marathons and written far more than 50 stories about marathons and marathoners, but I've never experienced anything as astounding and inspirational as Oprah, up close and personal, as she ran the marathon distance. Despite the distractions of thousands of spectators and other runners constantly calling out her name or coming up to slap her on the back, she never lost her concentration, her good spirit, or her determination.

She achieved her goal because she had trained hard, and she trained hard because she never stopped believing in herself. If Oprah can run a marathon, anyone can be a successful (and healthy and weight-reducing) runner.

All you have to do is believe.

CHAPTER 3

STEP INTO GOOD SHOES

A Guide to Buying Your Most Important Piece of Gear

The great thing about running is that you only need one piece of equipment. The bad thing is that the equipment, your running shoes, is so important that it gets buried under millions of dollars of hype, advertising, and confusing technobabble.

For more than two decades, Runner's World *magazine has helped consumers decipher and unravel that confusion with semiannual reviews of the best new training shoes. In addition, the magazine publishes simple guides to help readers make the right shoe selections.*

A couple of decades ago, the world was a simpler place, and so were running shoes. Today, simple, canvas sneakers are as dead as Elvis, which isn't necessarily a bad thing. In just about every way, today's shoes are a whole lot better—more durable, more protective, and more comfortable—than ever before.

The one bad thing: They're also much more complicated. Why? Because running, while it's a simple sport that almost everyone can do, forces your feet and legs through a fairly complex series of movements.

With all the high-tech running shoes available today and all the special features that each shoe claims to have, picking the right pair can be a daunting task. Just follow the steps below, and you'll be able to find the best shoes for you.

STEP 1: LEARN ABOUT PRONATION

Running is a complex biomechanical process in which, generally speaking, you strike the ground first on the outside of your heel. Next, your foot rolls downward and inward slightly as it meets the ground. And lastly, the heel lifts from the ground, and you push off from the ball of the foot to move forward.

The rotation of the foot downward and inward when you land on the ground is called pronation, and it's a completely natural and normal process. That's worth repeating: pronation is a natural, normal process. Everyone should pronate to some degree.

Pronation is a good thing in that it helps the foot absorb the shock of impact.

Some runners, however, overpronate. That is, their feet roll too far inward. This is a common problem that can lead to injuries, particularly of the lower leg and knee. Some runners supinate (or underpronate); their feet roll inward only a little after contact. These runners are said to have "rigid" feet that don't absorb shock very well. This, too, can lead to injury over time.

STEP 2: FIGURE OUT YOUR FOOT TYPE

Most runners can determine whether they are supinators, overpronators, or normal pronators by checking their arch heights. "The arch determines how your feet and legs will function when you run," explains Joe Ellis, D.P.M., a podiatrist from La Jolla, California, and author of *Running Injury-Free*.

"Our studies show that 50 percent of runners have normal arches, while 25 percent have high arches and the remaining 25 percent have low arches," says John W. Pagliano, D.P.M., a podiatrist in private practice in Long Beach, California.

But how do you figure out your arch height? The easiest way is with the "wet test."

Wet the bottom of your bare foot, then make a footprint on a flat, dry surface—a piece of white paper laid on a hardwood floor works well to show the shape of your foot.

If your footprint is very full and wide and shows no arch, you have a low arch and a flat foot. If the print shows your entire foot with a moderate curve where the arch rises off the ground, you have a normal arch. And if the footprint is very slight and curved, showing mostly the ball and heel of your foot but very little of the middle of your foot, you have a high arch.

Here's what your footprint tells you about your degree of pronation.

- A flat foot means you may have a tendency to overpronate.

- A normal foot means you probably are a normal pronator.

- A high-arched foot means you may be a supinator.

STEP 3: GET THE RIGHT SHOE

Your foot type and degree of pronation determine the characteristics that you'll need in a running shoe. One of the most important characteristics to look for is shape. You can see the shape most clearly by looking at the bottom of the shoe.

In general, running shoes come in three shapes—straight, semicurved, and curved—which correspond to the three types of footprints revealed by the wet test. Most experts believe that overpronators should wear a shoe with a straight shape, supinators should wear a shoe with a curved shape, and normal pronators should wear a shoe with a semicurved shape. There are a few other characteristics to consider.

If you have flat feet and overpronate, you need a shoe that will prevent your foot from rolling in too far, that is, a motion-control shoe. Many motion-control shoes have a straight shape that gives maximum support to your foot. Also look for a firm rather than a soft midsole, a dual-density midsole with the denser material along the inner edge of the shoe to prevent excessive pronation, and a firm heel counter to minimize rear-foot motion. (See "Anatomy of a Running Shoe" for a diagram and definitions of the parts of a running shoe.)

If you have high-arched feet and supinate, your feet don't absorb shock very well, so you need a cushioned shoe. Also, you want a shoe that allows your feet to roll inward, since this helps absorb shock. "Cushioned shoes tend to be less supportive and work with the foot rather than try to control it," says Dan Norton, a shoe designer who has worked at several of the major running-shoe companies. You want a shoe with a soft, cushioned midsole and a curved or semicurved shape that permits foot motion as you run.

If you have normal arches and pronate normally, you're lucky. You don't need to search out a shoe with special features. You might want to begin by considering shoes that lie somewhere between the motion-control and cushioned types. Manufacturers often refer to such shoes as stability shoes. These shoes, which often have a slightly curved shape, don't control foot motion as much as motion-control shoes.

How much should you pay? Good question. Any shoe costing $60 or more, no matter who manufactures it, should provide the primary features and protection you need. Step up to $80, and you'll get more durability, more features, and more quality.

Spend the money. A good pair of running shoes should last for 400 to 500 miles and is the only critical purchase you have to make.

STEP 4: VISIT A SPECIALTY RUNNING STORE

Even if you have followed all the steps outlined here, it pays to go to a specialty running store. The knowledgeable people who work in these stores will be able to tell you if you're a special case who needs extra attention when it comes to shoe selection.

Anatomy of a Running Shoe

As running shoes have gotten more complicated, so has the terminology used to describe them. The glossary below will help you understand the basic parts of a running shoe.

Upper: The part of the shoe that wraps around and over the top of the foot. It's most of what you see when you look at a running shoe.

Heel counter: A firm cup that is encased in the upper and surrounds the heel. It controls rear-foot motion.

Outsole: The undersurface of the shoe, usually made from carbon rubber.

Midsole: The most important part of a shoe, it is the cushioning layer between the upper and the outsole. It is usually made of ethylene vinyl acetate (EVA), polyurethane (a synthetic rubber that's heavier and longer-lasting than EVA), or a combination of the two. Dual-density midsoles have a firmer material on the inside of the shoe. This helps limit pronation. Many shoe companies also put patented technologies in their midsoles, such as gel and high-tech plastics.

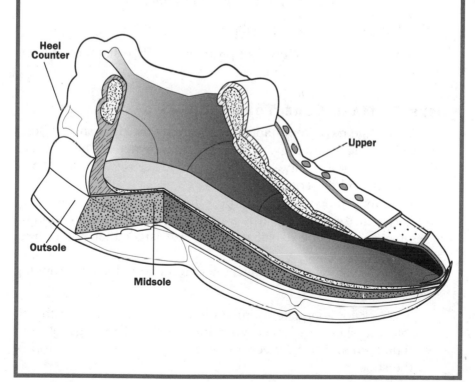

Whatever your needs, you'll want help to find the shoe model that works best for you.

Here are some tips for a successful shopping trip.

• For best fit, shop in the late afternoon when your feet are at their largest, because your feet will expand during running.

• Wear the socks that you'll wear when you run. If you don't have any, buy some before trying on shoes.

• Make sure that the salesperson measures both of your feet. Most of us have one foot slightly larger than the other, and you should be fitted for the larger foot.

• Before you try on any shoes, the salesperson should talk to you about your running, in order to guide you to appropriate shoe models.

Following are the questions that the salesperson should ask.

• How long have you been running?

• How much mileage are you running?

• Where do you do most of your running?

• How much do you weigh?

• Are you aware of any foot problems, such as flat feet or over-pronation or supination?

STEP 5: MAKE SURE YOUR SHOE FITS

This is the most important step in finding the right shoe. "Don't worry about the technology," says Bob Cook, owner of The Runner's Edge, a running specialty store in Farmingdale, New York. "Worry about the fit and the comfort."

A running shoe that fits will be snug but not tight. Buying running shoes that are too small is a common problem. Your running shoes may need to be a half to a full size larger than your street shoes.

Use the following guidelines to determine whether a running shoe fits you properly.

• Check for adequate room at the top by pressing your thumb into the shoe just above your longest toe. The edge of your thumb should fit between the end of your toe and the top of the shoe.

• Your heel should fit snugly into the rear of the shoe and should not slide up and down as you walk or run.

• The upper (the part of the shoe that wraps around and over the top of the foot) should fit snugly and hold your foot securely, but it should not irritate or press too tightly on any area of your foot.

• Take the shoes for a test run. Most specialty running stores allow—even encourage—you to run down the street or around the block so that you can feel the shoes in action.

Use these guidelines in trying out a few different models. Then decide on the pair that fits the best and feels the most comfortable. And if you get them home and find some problems with them as you begin your running program, take them back. "If you have any problems—heel slippage, a burning sensation in the balls of your feet once you start running—bring 'em back," says Dick Haines, owner of Aardvark Sports Shop in Bethlehem, Pennsylvania. "Remember, there are lots of good shoes out there. We'll find one that's right for you."

And a word for the future: Once you've found a shoe that works for you, stick with it. New models will always tempt you, but keep in mind that the right running shoes help you avoid injury. So, if your shoes fit well and feel good, and you don't have any problems with injuries, stick to a sure thing.

Now, lace up those new running shoes and head out on your path to better fitness.

With dozens of different companies and models to choose from, and exciting new shoes hitting the market every day, selecting your pair of running shoes remains a tough choice. I've found that the process is much simpler if you follow these guidelines.

Stick with proven shoes. New shoes are like new cars and new computers. You should keep away from them for a couple of years until the bugs are all worked out.

Talk to other runners and knowledgeable retail salespeople. Virtually every office and neighborhood in America has experienced runners with a collective knowledge of running shoes. Ask them what shoes they have had good luck with. Evaluate how these runners' needs are similar to or different from your own needs.

When you get your new shoes home, wear them first on short runs. After you're confident that they're broken in and don't cause any blisters or other abrasions, you can use them on longer runs.

Wear your running shoes for running only. They weren't intended for basketball or mowing the lawn, and they'll give you more miles of comfortable, injury-free running if you only use them for running.

Keep your shoes as dry as possible. Whether they're damp with sweat or wringing wet after a workout in a downpour, they'll recover fastest and best if air-dried. (And they won't stink.) Don't put your shoes in the clothes dryer, which is too hot. A small fan does an excellent job of drying out shoes.

Remember that your shoes need replacement after 400 to 500 miles. Even if you don't see much cosmetic deterioration, the shoes' midsoles will have lost their cushioning and resiliency. It's time for a new pair.

CHAPTER 4

UNEXPECTED PLEASURES

*A Lifetime of Running Brings More Than
Good Health*

*In 1968 I was lucky enough to win the Boston Marathon, so
most people quite naturally assume that that's my proudest
achievement in running. It's not. Yes, I feel very proud and fortunate to be able to call myself a Boston Marathon winner, but
there's one other thing that I've done in running that gives me
even more pride.*

*After completing my first high school cross-country season
in 1963, I decided to run the biggest road race in my home
state, Connecticut. That race is called the Manchester Thanks-
giving Day Turkey Trot, and it has been run more or less con-
tinuously since the mid-1920s.*

*I ran it in 1963, and in 1964, and in 1965, and . . . well,
you get the picture. I ran it every year. Literally every year. I have
not missed the Manchester Turkey Trot once since 1963. I've
run it more than 30 years in a row, and I hope to rack up many
more runs at Manchester.*

*Along the way, I won the race nine times, but I don't con-
sider that nearly as important as the fact that I have started and
finished it every year. In running, consistency is everything. This
chapter, by Hal Higdon, senior writer for* Runner's World *magazine (who's been running even longer than me), will tell you
what you can do to be as consistent in your running as I have
been in my racing at Manchester.*

The goal of any beginning running program should be contin-
uing. First you get in good enough shape to be able to run for 30
minutes at a time. Then you move on to another running goal. Then
you continue doing it for the rest of your life.

A running program that lasts only a month or two is like an
exercise bicycle that gets shunted away to the garage after a couple
of months: hardly worth the effort. On the other hand, a running
program that you continue practicing for years, and even decades,
wiil provide rewards for that entire time.

Of course, during a lifetime of running, we go through phases that range from enthusiasm to ennui. We pursue goals. We achieve triumphs. We suffer defeats. Injuries sometimes plague us. Boredom hits. Seasons change. The weather is too cold or too hot or just right. We need to find something that will keep us going.

In his days at the University of Oregon, former Olympic coach Bill Bowerman pioneered a training plan that calls for hard days of training followed by easy days. Most runners today follow some variation of that plan in their weekly routines. But in a broader sense, that philosophy can extend to your lifetime training plan: Hard weeks can be followed by easy weeks, hard months by easy months, hard years by easy years, hard decades by easy decades. As we pass through our twenties, thirties, forties, fifties, and onward through our sixties and beyond, we change our training patterns. We may compete or we may not. But we run on.

I, too, have experienced different phases in my more than 40 years of running. I ran in high school track but devoted as much energy to playing touch football with the guys and flirting with the girls. Only after graduating from college did I begin to mature as a runner. I had good years and bad years. Then I spent a long period away from serious running until the masters movement came along and collected me.

In all those years, an occasional injury forced reductions in training, but since 1952 I've taken only three two-month breaks from running. Through it all, I learned one important lesson: When training through the seasons of your life, you don't always need to run at your peak. You don't need to struggle to be in top shape all the time. You don't have to race a 10-K, then a marathon, then another 10-K, and on and on.

You can let yourself relax, then get excited about running again. It's also better sometimes to plan "down" seasons or years, rather than be forced by injuries to take a break from hard training. I have taken several breaks from hard training and racing, and they have kept me running all these years.

According to studies on what happens when you stop training by Edward Coyle, Ph.D., at the University of Texas at Austin, fitness declines by 50 percent in three weeks. That doesn't mean that you should be afraid to skip three weeks of running. Dr. Coyle didn't claim that you lose your fitness permanently by stopping your training; you simply put it aside for a while. Fitness can be won back. It may take a while to regain your past peak if you relax your training, but you can do it.

During a visit of mine to Russell Pate, Ph.D., director of the

Human Performance Laboratory at the University of South Carolina in Columbia, he commented that the key forms of training—speedwork, hill training, long runs, and rest—need to be part of any successful training program, but the way they are pieced together will vary across a training year and probably, to some extent, across a career as well.

"One thing we don't know nearly as much about as we would like," commented Dr. Pate, "is whether or not there are certain stages in life when certain forms of training are most effective and have the most lasting impact on a person." There may be particular periods when speedwork is appropriate, other times when you should run long, and still other times when you should maintain a steady routine of casual jogging.

The discussion with Dr. Pate reminded me of something the late running philosopher George Sheehan, M.D., once said: "Everybody is an experiment of one." Different people have different responses to training and different demands on their time. During certain periods running can be an important part of a person's lifestyle; at other times it may be best to put aside running temporarily or reduce it to a recreational level.

MAKING IT HAPPEN

Your approach to training has an important effect on how you come through the up and down phases of running. By following a few principles of balanced training and racing, running will remain an important and enjoyable activity throughout your life.

Set long-term goals. Take time to look past next weekend's race to determine future goals, not only for this and next year, but for years to come. At the end of each year, I review my training diary to assess my successes and failures. I also set goals for the coming season and beyond. A running goal might be to relax one year so that I can run hard the following year.

Figure out your baseline of training. Just as you set a heart monitor to beep if your pulse rate falls below a certain level in training, you can also determine a baseline for your training. Set a certain level of miles or hours that you will run each week whether you are preparing for a race or not. If your training falls below that, you know you should get more serious about running.

Determine your top level of training. You cannot train your hardest month after month and expect to maintain your motivation and high race performance. Monitor your running through your training log and, after a certain period of high-intensity training, back off and follow a more moderate program for as long as you need. You'll avoid injury and mental and physical fatigue.

Don't ignore pain or injury. Listen to your body. When it hurts, it's telling you to slow down or stop running entirely. Don't train or cross-train through every injury. Use the time off from running to reacquaint yourself with your family or to concentrate on other activities. You will lose some fitness, but that fitness can be easily regained. And remember, over the period of a lifetime, the weeks or months lost will prove inconsequential. In fact, it's more likely that the rest will prove beneficial if it provides for fuller, stronger recovery.

Look into cross-training. Too much cross-training can develop muscles antagonistic to those you use in running, but that doesn't mean you should avoid other activities such as cycling, swimming, or weight lifting. They may provide just the mental break you need from your running schedule.

Set your sights on a marathon. One value of a marathon is that it forces you to focus your training on a specific goal, using a steady increase in mileage to achieve that goal. This can make all the difference during those times when you want to keep running steadily but may need a little extra motivation. If you don't want to run a marathon, consider training for a half-marathon or other event that requires you to follow a schedule.

Cut back your food when you cut back training. When you back off on your training, you may need to back off on your eating as well. If you continue to eat as much as you did during peak training, you will gain weight because you won't be matching calories burned with calories consumed. Abandon those creamy desserts and between-meal snacks. When you return to high-level training, you'll find it much easier to reach top form if you stay close to your racing weight.

Be thankful for age groups. We should all now turn and nod thankfully in the direction of San Diego, where a quarter century ago an attorney named David Pain invented masters track, which resulted in age-group racing for the young and old. Every five years, as we move to another age bracket, a whole new world of competition opens up with new personal records to achieve. And toward the end of each five-year period, we can find an excuse to relax, take time off, or learn the value of humility as younger runners nudge ahead of us. Age-group competition provides new goals and rewards for an entire lifetime of running and racing.

Hal's tips provide just about all the guidelines you'll ever need to continue running for a long time. I'll add just one of my own: Don't get discouraged.

As far as I'm concerned, a positive attitude is the most important attribute any runner can have. You'll need it often. Every runner has bad days, every runner has occasional injuries, and every runner eventually slows down (take it from someone who has slowed down a lot).

But as long as you maintain a positive attitude, you'll find ways to overcome the obstacles and continue running. After all, running offers countless rewards. It's simply up to you to find the ones that have the most meaning for you.

2
NUTRITION

CHAPTER 5

FUELING UP FOR A PEAK PERFORMANCE

Tapering Your Eating Is as Important as Tapering Your Training

Before a big race, runners set aside a period of time, called the taper, that can last from two days to two weeks. The idea is to rest, get strong, and get psyched for the upcoming race. Training wears you down somewhat; the taper allows you to recover and then catapult forward to the high level of performance you hope to achieve on race day.

Tapering involves far more than just reducing your daily training. Another important factor is changing your diet. Indeed, the biggest advances in sports nutrition during the last two decades have been those that have focused on prerace nutrition.

Nearly everyone has heard about carbohydrate loading, the cornerstone of any pre-event nutrition plan. But a thorough nutritional taper involves much more than just the Ps—pasta, potatoes, and pancakes. There are also the Fs—fats, fiber, and fluids, for example. In this chapter, Liz Applegate, Ph.D., nutrition editor for Runner's World *magazine, deals with all these topics and many more.*

When race day nears, whether it's a 5-K or a marathon, you adjust your training by decreasing your mileage, getting in some extra speedwork, and then tapering the last few days beforehand.

But do you know how to adjust your diet? Improper fueling before a race can result in a lackluster performance. By planning a *nutritional* taper as carefully as you do your training taper, you can stoke up to race your best.

The following guide will tell you when, what, and how much to eat and drink before your next race.

SETTING THE STAGE

Before you taper, estimate your daily calorie needs by allotting between 17 and 26 calories per pound of body weight, depending on your training intensity. This comes to approximately 2,500 to 4,000 calories for a 150-pound runner. Carbohydrate intake should be at least 60 percent of your total calories.

Keep the fat percentage down to 20 to 25 percent of total calories, with protein at 15 to 20 percent per day. If you're running a marathon, begin your nutritional plan seven days beforehand; for 5-K and 10-K races, four days before is fine.

Since you'll be tapering your training, do the same with your diet. To avoid gaining weight, you need to bring your calorie intake down about 100 calories for every mile you deduct from your training during your taper. At the same time, you want carbohydrate intake to be sufficient to keep your stores of glycogen (a complex carbohydrate that your body uses for quick energy) full for race day.

As always—but especially now—go for low-fat, high-carbohydrate foods such as whole-grain cereal, bread, and pasta, along with vegetables and plenty of fruit. Consider taking a multivitamin/mineral supplement that supplies 100 percent of the Daily Value of key vitamins and minerals to ensure adequate intake, particularly if you tend to eat processed or packaged foods that may fall short on good nutrition.

During the sixth and fifth days before a marathon, continue monitoring and adjusting calorie and carbohydrate intake, making sure not to stuff yourself but still eating enough so that you don't feel hungry. It's especially important now to keep your meal times regular and not to miss meals.

HITTING A STRIDE

For shorter races such as 5-Ks and 10-Ks, begin your nutritional taper four days before the race. Remember to cut back slightly on calorie intake as you back off on mileage these few days before the race. Since shorter races (less than an hour) don't tax glycogen stores nearly as much as marathons do, carbohydrate intake is not as crucial. Nevertheless, you'll want to keep carbohydrate intake at about 60 percent of total calories, or roughly 450 grams of carbohydrates per day.

For marathoners, this is the time to begin increasing your carbohydrate intake to about 65 percent or more of total calories, which amounts to almost 500 grams per day. If you don't have the appetite for that much pasta and potatoes, try liquid sources of carbohydrates, such as fruit juices or sports drinks. And as you boost carbohydrate intake, cut back slightly on fat and protein.

At three days before the race, you've pared down your training, and you may be starting to feel a little sluggish. That's because your body responds to the training taper and the flood of carbohydrates by packing the muscles with more glycogen than usual. And since water gets tucked away with the glycogen in the muscles, you may gain a little weight. Don't worry about it. In the marathon in particular, any water you can store before the race will pay many dividends during the course of those 26.2 miles.

Marathoners should keep in mind that eating 500 grams of carbohydrates a day requires you to be a fat-sleuth, as too much fat will, in effect, crowd out needed carbohydrates.

THE HOMESTRETCH

During the two days before a race, many runners break down nutritionally. Often this happens because they need to travel to a race, which changes their routine, making it hard to stay on a steady eating schedule. Plus, when they do eat, they have less control over what they consume and how it's prepared than they have at home. It's tougher to stay on top of fluid needs as well. (Beware of the dehydrating effects of travel, particularly in airplanes.)

Try to minimize these pitfalls by planning ahead. If you're traveling, find out about restaurants and food stores near your hotel. At home or away, take along nonperishable high-carbohydrate items such as sports bars, granola bars, sports drinks, cereals, and dried fruit. These are great for augmenting your diet and keeping your carbohydrate consumption up.

Since heavy sweat loss during longer races leads to dehydration, you'll want to "fluid-load" starting two days before your race. Drink plenty of liquids throughout the day, making sure that your urine color is clear or pale yellow, not dark amber. (This is a simple but effective measure of adequate hydration status.) Taking in sports drinks at this time is a good way to get both fluids and carbohydrates.

The last few days before your race, you'll want to keep away from certain items. Beware of alcohol, especially if you're running a longer race. Alcohol interferes with glycogen and carbohydrate metabolism in the liver, which will shortchange your endurance. It also acts as a diuretic, that is, it accelerates dehydration.

At this late stage, limiting high-fiber foods such as bran cereals, beans, and some vegetables will help those runners who suffer from bowel problems during running. Stick with foods that agree with you.

On the day before the race, be sure to rest, eat (without overstuffing), and drink plenty of fluids. Provided you have been eating enough and sticking to high-carbohydrate fare that is modest in fat and protein, your glycogen stores will be at their peak by the end of this day. Snack frequently throughout the day and stay with familiar foods. And just to be safe—especially if you're on the road—carry your own water bottle and "go to the well" often to stay hydrated.

Give careful consideration to the meal you eat the night before racing. It should include 800 to 1,000 calories, and—as you know by now—it should be high in carbohydrates and low in fat and protein. Avoid beans, broccoli, and other gas-causing foods, especially if they normally give you problems. Keep alcohol to a strict minimum or skip it altogether. Finally, the night before is not the time to experiment with new foods; the result of the experiment could be diminished performance (or, worse, stomach distress) the next day.

RACE DAY

A good rule of thumb: Eat a light meal the morning of your race, no matter how early it starts. Taking in carbohydrates, particularly before longer races, provides more energy for muscles.

Your prerace meal should be eaten 2 to 4 hours before starting time and should consist of at least 200 grams of carbohydrates, which works out to about 800 calories' worth. To speed digestion, select foods and beverages that are low in fat and fiber. Don't worry about swings in blood sugar levels, as research shows this doesn't decrease performance.

Bagels, raisins, bananas, sports drinks, pasta, and rice make great prerace foods. But if the thought of eating in those prerace morning hours doesn't sit well with your stomach, consider a liquid meal such as a sports drink, a high-carbohydrate beverage, or a nutritional supplement drink.

These may even help you in a nonmarathon race. One study has shown that sprint performance at the end of a 15-K race was improved in runners who consumed a sports drink an hour before race time.

During the race itself, be sure to stay adequately hydrated. Use those water stops. In longer races, you'll need to replenish with carbohydrates as well. This helps maintain glycogen stores.

On the course, plan to drink from one-half to three-quarters cup every 10 to 20 minutes, depending on weather conditions and your rate of perspiration. As for carbohydrates, consume about 25 grams of carbohydrates per 30 minutes for races that last over an hour. Stick with bananas, orange slices, sports drinks, or other quickly digested sources. With experience, you'll find out what food or drink works best for you.

THE POSTRACE PLAN

Postrace refueling won't improve your time, but it's essential for quick recovery. For starters, drink plenty of fluids, about 2 cups for every pound of sweat you lose. Glycogen stores also need rebuilding. And remember, too, that your muscles are most receptive to carbohydrate replenishment during the first hour or so after exercise.

Take in 50 to 100 grams of carbohydrates within the first 15 minutes after your race. Start with liquids first; switch to more solid items when your stomach allows you.

Following a long race, aim to consume 600 grams (or 2,400 calories) of carbohydrates in the next 24 hours. Pace yourself at about 50 grams every 2 hours, on average. One study showed that including protein with carbohydrates in those first postrace meals improves the glycogen resynthesis. (According to the study, the optimal ratio was about 3 grams of carbohydrate to 1 gram of protein.) Therefore, a postrace meal of cereal with milk, or maybe some rice with a small portion of chicken, would provide the right carbohydrate/protein combination.

You don't have to be a runner for long before you'll have your first workout that's cut short by stomach distress. The same goes for racing. Start entering races and, far too soon, you'll have one that's ruined by stomach cramps or nausea. This is virtually a universal experience among runners; few escape it.

Fortunately, we do learn. And one of the first and most important things we learn is to stick with simple, tried-and-true foods that we eat almost every day. The night before one of my first Boston Marathons, I was struck by an uncontrollable urge for apple butter. I satisfied the urge that evening but paid a heavy price the next day during the marathon; the apple butter forced me to make several pit stops en route.

You can bet that I have never eaten apple butter again before a race. Instead, I concentrate on foods that are part of my normal diet—pasta, rice, toast, and bagels. These are healthy foods that fuel my muscles rather than knot my stomach. You must certainly have similar foods that you feel comfortable eating every day. These foods, as long as they are carbohydrate-packed, are the ones you should concentrate on for your prerace meals.

CHAPTER 6

THE LOWDOWN ON FATS

New Thinking about Dietary Bad Guys

Many people, for some reason, think that runners are different from average individuals. I tend to think that we are the same— only we runners are somewhat more attuned to our bodies, our physical performances, and our nutritional needs. One area in which we're much like everyone else is in our concern for fatty foods in the diet.

Many runners run at least in part to lose weight or maintain a healthy weight. These runners also, according to many studies, watch their food intake closely. They don't count on running solely for weight-control magic. They know that they should also follow a low-fat diet that's full of performance-boosting, carbohydrate-rich foods.

At the same time, they understand that it's counterproductive to be obsessive about limiting fatty foods. Some daily fat intake, after all, is an essential part of the diet. The trick is in finding the right balance.

This balance gets even tougher to find when, every once in a while, a new study or theory comes out in favor of increased fat consumption for improved endurance. Is this hocus-pocus or a great new way for you to enjoy tasty foods and run better at the same time? In this chapter, Liz Applegate, Ph.D., nutrition editor for Runner's World *magazine, will help you understand these issues and answer the questions you have.*

Every once in a while, you probably read somewhere that runners should be adding more fat to their diets. The claim may even be made that additional fat consumption can improve your running performance.

This notion flies in the face of that most ingrained of dietary rules—the tenet that a diet low in fat and high in carbohydrates produces optimum health and performance. Yet in one study, runners ran longer and even showed a boost in maximal oxygen capacity (max VO_2, which measures the greatest volume of oxygen that can be dispatched to your muscles during exercise) after following a diet of 38 percent fat calories, compared to the usual high-carbohydrate meal plan.

But hold on to your pasta coupons, runners. The jury on fat burning is still out. In order to better understand the study and its implications, here are some basics of fuel burning.

THE LOWDOWN ON FUEL BURNING

Whether you're plopped in an armchair or out on the road, your body burns two basic fuels: fats and carbohydrates. Fats, tucked away in fat cells and also "muscle-bound" within muscle fibers, provide more energy than an equal amount of carbohydrates.

Sounds promising, doesn't it? But you need lots of oxygen for fat burning, whereas carbohydrates can supply energy at a lower oxygen cost. Low-intensity workouts such as walking, during which oxygen supply is plentiful, rely heavily on fat as fuel, often burning up to 60 percent of total calories from fat supplies. At a slow walk, only 40 percent of calories come from carbohydrates.

This ratio shifts as exercise intensity increases. A brisk 10-K run, for example, uses 70 percent carbohydrate and 30 percent fat. This has led some people to believe, mistakenly, that slow exercise burns more fat than harder exercise. Not true. Only the percentage of fat burned is higher.

At a slow walk, for example, you might burn 200 total calories in an hour, 60 percent from fat. Sixty percent of 200 is 120, the number of fat calories you would burn. Running for an hour, you might burn 600 total calories, 30 percent from fat. Thirty percent of 600 is 180, the number of fat calories you would burn.

Interestingly, endurance exercises such as running or bicycling can also improve your muscles' ability to burn fat. This is good news, as our fat stores are abundant (more than 60,000 calories' worth in the average runner), whereas our carbohydrate stores are few (less than 2,000 calories on average). Once you are fit, you will still be burning more carbohydrates than fats during your 10-K, but fats will play a somewhat larger role. Result: the conservation of precious carbohydrates.

The composition of your diet also influences fuel burning, as dietary fat can prompt your fat-burning machinery to work more efficiently. Studies show that athletes who eat high-fat diets of 50 to 60 percent fat calories are able to rely more on fat as fuel during exercise than athletes who eat low-fat, high-carbohydrate diets.

Finally, a higher-fat diet also results in a kind of "fat loading" of the muscles. Microscopic droplets of muscle-bound fat normally exist within the muscle fibers; this fat serves as fuel for exercising muscles. There is far less fat store here than in the body's fat tissue, but muscle-bound fat is more readily used during exercise. Endurance exercise depletes the small fat droplets, and it takes about seven days for rebuilding. These microscopic fat stores are more quickly depleted in runners who eat a high-carbohydrate diet than in runners on high-fat fare.

The significance of this isn't yet known, but some researchers believe that during exercise, runners on high-carbohydrate diets must rely on fat supplied from fat tissue. This source is slower to respond with its energy than muscle-bound fat, so more glycogen (a complex carbohydrate that your body uses for quick energy) must be burned as fuel while the muscles await fat's arrival. In other words, eating a high-carbohydrate diet means less muscle-bound fat is available, so the body turns to carbohydrates to make up that deficit.

A Runner's Sampler

Here's a day's menu that supplies more than 300 grams of carbohydrates and just under 30 percent fat calories.

Breakfast

- 4 whole-grain pancakes (with 2 teaspoons margarine and 2 tablespoons syrup)

- ¾ cup fresh, sliced kiwifruit and strawberries with ¼ cup nonfat vanilla yogurt

- 8 ounces nonfat milk

Lunch

- Chicken sandwich made with 2 ounces roasted chicken breast, 2 teaspoons pesto spread, 2 slices fresh tomato, 2 tablespoons bean sprouts, 2 slices whole-wheat bread

- ¾ cup bean and cucumber salad (with 1 tablespoon vinaigrette dressing)

- 1 banana

THE PERFORMANCE CONNECTION

How all this translates to performance is not yet clear. Exercise physiologists, nutritionists, and athletes know that carbohydrates— not fats—are king when it comes to distance running. It's known that carbohydrate stores fizzle out during long bouts of exercise.

That's why it's recommended that you consume a preworkout meal rich in carbohydrates, then refuel with carbohydrate-rich sports drinks during exercise. Since fats are slow to digest, you certainly don't want to be downing hot dogs or other fatty foods just before or during a workout.

That said, let's look at a study that was mentioned earlier. Researchers from the State University of New York (SUNY) at Buffalo measured the effects of high-fat versus high-carbohydrate diets on the performance of highly trained, collegiate middle-distance runners. The runners spent one week on a high-fat diet composed of

---

- 2 oatmeal cookies

- 8 ounces iced tea

Snack

- 1 whole-wheat pita pocket with 1 tablespoon peanut butter and 3 tablespoons raisins

- 8 ounces orange-cranberry juice mixed with sparkling mineral water

Dinner

- 4 ounces grilled salmon (brushed with 1 tablespoon ginger–canola oil marinade)

- ½ cup fresh corn and black bean salsa

- 1 cup cooked black beans topped with plain low-fat yogurt

- 1½ cups mixed greens salad (with 2 teaspoons olive oil and vinegar dressing)

- 1 cup peach frozen low-fat yogurt sprinkled with chopped walnuts

Total calories: 2,800

38 percent fat and 50 percent carbohydrate calories. They spent a second week on a high-carbohydrate diet of 15 percent fat and 73 percent carbohydrate calories. At the end of each week, the runners were tested on a treadmill for max VO_2, a good measure of fitness level. The runners also did a run-to-exhaustion treadmill endurance test.

While on the high-fat diet, the runners' max VO_2 was 11 percent greater than when they were on the high-carbohydrate diet; high-fat dieters also lasted 9 percent longer on the endurance run. The researchers theorize that the higher-fat diet improved performance by enhancing the runners' ability to burn fats for fuel. (In effect, the fat forced their fat-burning systems to work more efficiently.) Another possibility is that the week of higher-fat eating may have "loaded" those small droplets of muscle-bound fat, which could then serve as an accessible fuel source during the run.

Now, a strong word of caution. The SUNY researchers themselves realize that this study has many limitations and that conclusions cannot be drawn until follow-up work is done. The design of the study, for example, was not well-controlled in certain aspects and may have biased the results. And since the researchers did not actually test for the presence of muscle-bound fat droplets, their conclusions about them as a fuel source are speculative.

The results are intriguing, however, and have attracted the attention of researchers, athletes, and the media. W. Michael Sherman, Ph.D., assistant professor in the department of exercise physiology at Ohio State University in Columbus, agrees that the study is exciting, but that any conclusions at this point are premature. "Perhaps all this means is that endurance athletes should eat training diets that they enjoy and that are moderate in fat—about 30 percent," says Dr. Sherman. "Athletes should also be sure to consume carbohydrates before, during, and soon after exercise."

Hold Off on High Fat

Too much scientific evidence places fat at the center of health problems such as cancer, heart disease, and obesity to justify a high-fat diet. So for good health and top performance, stick with a diet made up of 30 percent fat calories or less. How low you go below 30 percent depends on your own needs and experiences. Some athletes, for example, feel best, perform best, and maintain their weight best with a 20 percent fat-calorie diet.

Remember also that a 30 percent fat-calorie diet is, in fact, a moderately high-carbohydrate diet. Certainly, it provides ample carbohydrates for most runners.

From the mid-1970s to the mid-1990s, carbohydrates ruled as absolute monarch to the runner's dietary world. Then in the mid-1990s, fats seemed to get their day in the sun as a result of studies from the SUNY Buffalo exercise physiology lab, the popularity of a diet launched by the book The Zone, *by Barry Sears, Ph.D., and several successful energy bars.*

The vast majority of sports nutritionists and researchers, however, have not accepted the fat-burning hypothesis, nor have I. The most compelling reason to stick to a low-fat, high-carbohydrate diet is the health reason. There's no denying that too much fat consumption leads to a variety of health ills. And since most runners run primarily for their health, why adopt a regimen that is counterproductive?

Of course, some runners also dream of faster marathon times. (I'm one of them.) These runners might want to experiment with several days of fat loading before they switch to the final three days of carbohydrate loading prior to a marathon. It may be possible to boost both fat fuels and carbohydrate fuels before a long endurance event.

CHAPTER 7

FOR MEN ONLY: 10 TRUTHS

How to Maximize Your Running Potential

Twenty-five years ago, before the first wave of the running boom, men apparently had almost no interest in nutrition. That was something for women to worry about—whether through reading recipes or shopping for the family or preparing meals. Men simply didn't care about these kinds of things.

By coincidence, the running boom coincided with the health and nutrition boom and the rise in feminism. Now, men have to care about food whether they want to or not. They often have to shop at the grocery store and prepare meals for themselves and their children.

Fortunately, many of today's men, especially runners, care very much about their diets. They understand that men, more than women, are ravaged by heart disease and other illnesses linked to diet as well as other lifestyle factors (like exercise). They also know that diet makes a difference in performance—both how they feel throughout the day and week and how they race on weekends. This chapter addresses many of the nutrition issues that are most important to men and provides tips to help male readers make even better food and cooking decisions.

I don't worry about my diet," says one high-ranking male triathlete. "I'm sure I get what I need," he continues, "because I eat a lot."

But, like so many other men, he may not be adequately fueling his performance and health with this "garbage-disposal" eating method. Men often think that they are free of any special dietary concerns and sometimes don't realize that their diets do make a difference. Diet can affect a man's running and his sexual performance. It can determine the length of his life span and reduce his risk of getting diseases such as prostate cancer. Here are 10 things that every man should do to improve his diet.

1. Eat your way to better sex. Many runners enjoy a better sex life than sedentary folks. Reports suggest that regular exercise improves self-image, which boosts sexual desire and enjoyment.

   But an athlete can also tell you that sex is often the last thing on his mind. This can happen because of lower male hormone levels that occur following exhaustive workouts. Training for 2 hours a day (or, for that matter, training for 40 minutes after a long, stressful day in the office) may not only squelch your desire but it can also lead to weight loss, which can further lower testosterone levels. So check your training mileage, track your sleep and fatigue levels, and make sure that you keep your weight steady by eating frequently—five to six small meals a day, if necessary.

Though no food is a proven aphrodisiac, the mineral zinc, found in oysters, meats, and whole grains, is essential for sperm production and male sexual functioning. (In rare situations, low zinc intake may contribute to impotence.) Adequate vitamin C intake may also contribute to healthy sperm cell production.

2. Take care of your prostate. One in 10 men will get cancer of the prostate—the small gland situated just below the bladder, responsible for producing seminal fluid. Risk factors include family history and race (African-Americans have a 40 percent greater risk than whites do), but accumulating research suggests that diet plays a part, too. Eating a high-fat diet, particularly when the fat comes from animal products, can greatly increase your risk.

   Other research shows that certain foods may protect the prostate. Japanese men, for example, have a much lower prostate cancer risk than Europeans do. This may be attributable to the popularity in Japan of soybean-based foods such as tofu. Soybeans contain isoflavones, which have been shown to protect against cancer; other beans such as lentils and peas also contain cancer-fighting isoflavones.

3. Knock out stress. A hectic lifestyle means stress, and stress can mean health problems. Studies show that emotional stress can lead to higher levels of artery-clogging low-density lipoprotein (LDL) cholesterol, increasing the risk of heart disease in men. Stress can also aggravate asthma symptoms and a host of digestive problems. Fending off all these ravages of stress requires a comprehensive approach. You need to monitor your sleep patterns and the amount of tension-busting free time you give yourself.

   Also, be sure that you get plenty of fiber and keep your alcohol and caffeine intake to a moderate level. (Too little fiber and too much caffeine both can cause digestive problems.) Eating plenty of fresh vegetables, fruits, whole grains, and fiber-filled breakfast cereals will help you get the recommended 25 grams of dietary fiber a day.

4. Avoid muscle loss. Okay, so you aren't bodybuilding's Mr. Universe. As a runner, you wouldn't want to be. Yet heavy-duty marathon training can lead to muscle tissue loss, and that isn't good either. Studies have shown that endurance training of about 2 hours a day breaks down muscle tissue that is then used for energy by working muscles, particularly when stores of glycogen (a complex carbohydrate that your body uses for quick energy) have run low. Because of this, some endurance athletes see a drop in body weight and a loss of muscle over a few months of heavy training.

   Eating sufficient calories, carbohydrates, and protein daily will help stave off this wasting. You need anywhere from 450 to 600 grams of carbohydrates a day. This means eating more than 12 servings of grains and at least 4 servings each of vegetables and fruits daily. Endurance training pushes protein needs to 25 to 50 percent more than the Daily Value, or 70 to 90 grams total a day. You can meet this requirement with regular servings of fish, beans, cooked grains, poultry, and other lean meats.

5. Re-energize after you run. Whether you run in the morning or squeeze your miles in later, what you eat afterward may determine the quality of your next workout and your energy level for the rest of the day. During training, glycogen stores diminish. Rebuilding these stores soon after exercise is crucial, as that's when muscles are their hungriest.

   Munching on a carbohydrate-rich food is a good idea, but studies suggest that a combination of carbohydrates and protein about 30 minutes after hard running can rebuild glycogen stores better than carbohydrates alone. This combo may also speed muscle recovery. Based on these studies, you should consume 80 to 100 grams of carbohydrates and 15 to 40 grams of protein after exercising. This is equivalent to eating either a tuna sandwich with a banana and an apple, or a hefty bowl of breakfast cereal with skim milk and sliced strawberries.

6. Go easy on the booze. You have probably heard that drinking some alcohol is good. That's true. Men who consume modest amounts of alcohol—one or two drinks daily—have a lower risk of heart disease, the leading cause of death in men. The drink of choice is red wine because it contains phenol, a substance that prevents LDL cholesterol from getting stuck on artery walls.

   But too much alcohol can interfere with carbohydrate metabolism. Alcohol also adversely affects vitamins (particularly the B vitamins, such as B_6 and thiamin) and minerals in the body by accelerating both their breakdown and their rate of loss in the urine. Finally, alcohol, because it's a diuretic (like coffee and tea), can shortchange performance by increasing water loss from the body. Therefore, if you do drink, keep it to one or two drinks per day.

7. Eat steadily throughout the day. With your busy schedule, occasionally skipping breakfast or missing lunch is inevitable. But this will drag your performance down—both at the job and during your workout. Studies show that reading comprehension and math computations falter in people who go without eating for 4 or more hours, whereas eating every 3 hours or so may enhance cognition by fueling the brain with a steady supply of carbohydrate energy. Attempting to run on an empty stomach may also squash your performance during long workouts, since going without food for 4 or more hours begins to eat away at glycogen stores.

    Try to eat something every 3 hours to stay at peak energy levels. Take along easy-to-tote foods such as sports bars, dried fruit, pretzels, and sports drinks for an energizing snack, whether you're at work or motoring down the freeway.

8. Become acquainted with your kitchen. Men often go for take-out food rather than prepare their own meals, but this can bump up fat intake and leave out performance-boosting carbohydrates. Fixing your own meals allows you to choose the ingredients so that you can keep meals low in fat and loaded with vitamins and minerals.

    You don't have to become a gourmet cook or spend all your time in the kitchen. Pick up a copy of *Prevention's Quick and Healthy Cooking* at your newsstand or try some of the many low-fat, ready-to-use food products available. These save time and still deliver good taste and nutrition. Look for jarred pasta sauces, canned black beans, and frozen, vegetable-filled potpies.

9. Try new foods. Like cross-training, cross-eating adds needed variety to your life—in this case, nutritional variety. Men frequently eat fewer food items than women. Existing on a few dietary staples like bagels, bananas, and sports bars may leave you short on the fiber, vitamins, and minerals that are crucial for health and performance.

    You can expand your nutrient repertoire by trying a new food each week, or by getting in the habit of sampling new grains or pasta dishes at your local gourmet deli. Go for more variety at each meal by, for example, including two steamed vegetables and two grain foods (like rice and whole-grain bread) instead of a single source of each. Having more foods at each meal will also help control portion sizes, which may keep you from overloading on fat or sodium from one particular food.

10. Strengthen your immunity. Staying healthy means building a strong immune system. Exercise can help boost the number of germ-fighting cells in the body, and eating the right foods helps, too. Adequate intake of protein, zinc, iron, and vitamins C and E, to name a few, is critical for a strong immune system. For example, too little zinc depresses the number of immune cells, which are needed to fight off bacterial infections. Studies of elderly people have shown that immune response improves with vitamin and mineral supplementation. So stay well by eating a variety of fruits, vegetables, whole grains, and lean protein sources. If you don't routinely eat the nutrient-packed foods that you know you should, consider taking a multivitamin/mineral supplement that provides 100 percent of the Daily Value of key vitamins and minerals.

Men, here's the bottom line: If we want to live a long, healthy, vibrant life, we have to pay attention to what we eat. And the best way to do this, I believe, is to take advantage of all the foods available to us. Meat and potatoes (heaped with butter) may have worked for the dawn-to-dusk farm workers of a century ago, but they don't make sense any longer, at least not in large quantities.

It makes a lot more sense to graze on four or five modest meals a day than to gorge on two or three. It makes more sense to eat baked or broiled fish or poultry than fat-laden red meats. It makes more sense to consume a variety of fruits and vegetables than lots of cheeses and sauces. In general, the more different kinds of foods in your diet, the healthier that diet is.

Runners, of course, can never wander too far from the best carbohydrate food groups: grains and cereals. Bread, rice, and pasta are low-fat foods that provide fast energy, fiber, and a host of B vitamins. If you can build a diet around these key foods and supplement it with a wide sampling of fruits and vegetables, you'll have a nutrition foundation that will lead to great health, energy, and longevity.

CHAPTER 8

TOMORROW'S BEVERAGES TODAY

Sports Drinks Are Packing More Than Just Liquid Refreshment

The development of sports drinks has been without question the biggest change (and improvement) in sports nutrition in the last 30 years. It seems impossible to imagine now, but athletes were once told to avoid water during competitions. They were told that water would give them stomach cramps and perhaps nauseate them.

Today, no one has any problems with drinking water and other fluids during sports competitions ranging from marathons to Little League games. The water bottle is as much a part of sports as the baseball cap.

Virtually all the best research on sports drinks has been done on runners. It started 30 years ago (I know—I was a guinea pig in the first experiments) and has continued into the present. And every year we have learned more about sports drinks. Most of the best and latest information is summarized in this chapter.

Not too many years ago, the state of the art in fluid replacement was a swig from the nearest garden hose. No longer. Thanks to the many new sports drinks on the market, the art of rehydration has been raised to new heights.

The drinks replace lost water and electrolytes, which you can sweat away at a rate of 8 ounces every 15 minutes when exercising heavily in hot conditions, and they can recharge your muscles with glycogen (a complex carbohydrate that your body uses for quick energy). This combination gives you more zip during your long runs and also helps you recover better after workouts.

The future is even more exciting. Soon, sports drinks may be able to prevent muscle fatigue. You could never get that kind of help from a garden hose.

BETTER THAN PLAIN WATER

This isn't to say that plain water is a total washout for fluid replacement, but sports drinks do have their decided advantages, and here's why.

You absorb them faster. Yes, quaff a sports drink on the run, and its vital fluids will get to your working muscles more quickly than if you were to drink an equal amount of plain water. This is because most sports drinks contain between 4 and 8 percent carbohydrate plus small amounts of sodium, which speed the passage of the water through the walls of the stomach.

Speed of fluid replacement is crucial for optimal running performance. Fail to replace these losses, and you risk shutting down not just your body's cooling system but eventually your muscles as well.

They're full of minerals. You do more than replenish just water with a sports drink. You also replace the minerals that get lost with that water—sodium, chloride, and potassium, for example, all crucial contributors to optimal running performance. Most sports drinks supply between 50 and 100 milligrams of sodium per 8-ounce serving. While this isn't enough to replenish all the sodium you lose, it makes a very valuable contribution. The danger of replacing none of the lost sodium can be a condition known as hyponatremia, in which the body's sodium levels fall so low as to cause nausea, cramping, extreme fatigue, convulsions, and in some cases even death.

They'll boost your energy. A good sports drink can even give you energy during a long, hard run. When you run long, you whittle away at your body's glycogen stores, and a sports drink, unlike water, can help replenish glycogen. Some of the formulations contain mixtures of sugars such as sucrose or dextrose for this purpose, while others use starches in a liquid form such as maltodextrin or glucose polymers. Both types appear to replace lost glycogen equally well, so don't feel you need to choose your sports drink on this basis.

The amount of carbohydrate you use in refueling is more important than the type. Try to pace your intake on the run so that you'll be consuming between 30 and 60 grams of carbohydrate (about three 8-ounce cups) for every hour you run. Then take in another 50 grams or so within 15 to 30 minutes of completing your workout. Finally, you should aim to consume another 50 grams of carbohydrate in a sports drink or food/drink combination (bagel and beverage, for example) after that.

They taste good. Not only do the carbohydrates in sports drinks replace lost glycogen but they also help the drinks taste good, which is yet another advantage of performance beverages over water. And not purely for reasons of pleasure. If you're like one group of runners studied, you're probably drinking only about half as much as you should to replace all the fluid you lose on a run. A good-tasting sports drink will encourage you to consume more.

This may be especially true for older runners. Research suggests that the ability to perceive thirst may diminish with age. A group of runners 65 and older reported feeling less thirsty, and consequently drank less, than a group of runners ages 19 to 25 following a similar bout of exercise in the heat. So drink up, seniors, and reach for a good-tasting sports drink if that's what it takes to make you do it.

THE NEXT GENERATION

As good as the current sports drinks are, some are getting even better by including suspected performance enhancers such as chromium and choline. Studies indicate that athletes who exercise heavily may not be getting enough of these important minerals, chromium especially, which intense exercise appears to deplete.

Since endurance athletes tend to eat a lot of refined carbohydrate foods such as pasta, white bread, white rice, and sugary snacks, which are poor chromium sources, some nutritionists fear that these athletes may be especially at risk for chromium deficiencies. More research is needed to determine exactly how well chromium is used by the body when consumed during exercise.

A futuristic formulation may soon be available with the trace mineral choline. Choline is involved in the neurological processes responsible for muscular contraction. Researchers hypothesize that low levels of this chemical may contribute to the onset of muscular fatigue.

A group of runners who had just completed the Boston Marathon were studied by Richard Wurtman, Ph.D., of the Massachusetts Institute of Technology in Cambridge. He found a 40 percent drop in their choline levels. Subsequently, Dr. Wurtman gave the runners supplemental choline an hour before and then again halfway through a 20-mile run. Sure enough, with the choline, 7 of the 10 runners ran an average of 5 minutes faster for 20 miles. Dr. Wurtman theorizes that fatigue may be due in large part to low levels of choline that reduce the efficiency of muscular contractions. As with chromium, more research is needed to confirm choline's effectiveness.

In addition to the experiments with chromium and choline, some sports drinks have gone crystal clear in the wake of consumer distaste for artificial coloring. Many ecologically minded manufacturers also are distributing their sports drinks in recyclable plastic containers.

Some sports drinks are even "chilling out" in the frozen foods section of your local supermarket. The manufacturers of Power Burst, for example, have teamed up with the Frozfruit Corporation to create a frozen performance-enhancer on a stick for an especially refreshing postrun boost.

I have become a believer, though it hasn't been easy. As I mentioned above, I was involved in some of the earliest research studies with a then-little-known product named Gatorade. In 1968, Gatorade hadn't yet evolved to its present, quite-moderate formula, and scientists didn't know how much a runner should drink .

As a result, during three straight days of 2-hour-long runs on a treadmill in a laboratory, I was force-fed too much Gatorade that was too strong. I didn't enjoy it. In fact, I was nauseated most of the second hour. To this day, the memory of those experiments makes it hard for me to drink as much fluid while running as I probably should.

Nonetheless, I do drink because I have closely followed the last 30 years of research on Gatorade and similar products, and it's very compelling. The drink makers have figured out how to reduce the glucose and salt levels to a lower concentration, which makes the drinks both palatable and at the same time very effective. While water can keep you hydrated, only a sports drink can keep you hydrated, well-fueled, and salt-balanced, all of which are important. Three things at once. I figure that's a pretty good deal.

CHAPTER 9

SAY GOOD-BYE TO MEAT

How to Switch to a Vegetarian Diet

In their search for the perfect diet, runners are willing to explore many alternatives, including some considered extreme. One, the vegetarian diet, used to be thought the eating pattern of certain religious fanatics. Today, as it continues to increase in popularity, vegetarianism is seen as an unusually simple, sound, and healthful diet—and one that many runners find attractive.

There are many reasons for a strong link between running and vegetarianism. These range from ethics to a concern for the environment to a desire to consume a pure, natural diet that provides plenty of nutrients without a lot of cholesterol and fatty foods.

At the same time, runners are concerned about their performances, which leads them to wonder if a vegetarian diet is sufficient to provide the energy and endurance they need. After all, we tend to imagine vegetarians as emaciated individuals who sit around in the lotus position all day meditating about one thing or another. This may be a great way to achieve personal enlightenment, but what will it do for your 10-K time? The information in this chapter will answer this and similar questions.

If you have ever thought about becoming a vegetarian, you've probably had many doubts. Perhaps you question how you will perform on a vegetarian regimen or how you will take in adequate protein from plant sources alone. Still you must answer the biggest question—is a vegetarian lifestyle right for you?

To begin with, there are two basic types of vegetarianism. Vegans are vegetarians who eat no red meat, chicken, fish, or animal products such as milk, cheese, and eggs. Lacto-ovo vegetarians eat no red meat, chicken, or fish but do consume milk, cheese, and eggs. Now for the nutritional questions that haunt many would-be vegetarians.

How healthful are vegetarian diets? Various studies show that most vegetarians are less likely than most meat-eaters to contract a variety of chronic diseases such as heart disease or to become obese. Risk of colon cancer is also lower in vegetarians than in meat-eaters, probably because vegetarian diets tend to be higher in fiber and lower in fat than diets that include meat. And foods such as tofu and other soybean products, which are staples in most vegetarian diets, may have cancer-fighting powers.

Of course, diet isn't the only variable in these studies. Vegetarians, as a whole, tend to take better care of themselves than meat-eaters. More meat-eaters smoke, abuse alcohol or drugs, or lead sedentary lives than vegetarians and, as a result, tend to experience more chronic illnesses.

But vegetarian diets can be problematic, too. A lacto-ovo vegetarian meal made with high-fat cheeses, for instance, isn't particularly healthful. And a diet that contains some meat (5 to 6 ounces a day) can be as low in fat and high in fiber as many vegetarian diets. Regardless of the eating style you choose, you must watch your fat and fiber intake for optimum health and performance.

How do I combine vegetarian dishes properly to take in adequate protein? Protein is made up of amino acids, some of which your body requires but cannot manufacture on its own. So meat-eaters and vegetarians alike must take in amino acids through food.

The protein found in beef, chicken, fish, eggs, and milk (animal protein) contains all the amino acids you need, in the right proportion, whereas the protein found in rice and beans (vegetable protein) does not. When grains and beans are combined, however, they provide the perfect mix of amino acids. So vegetarians must pair grains such as wheat, rice, corn, barley, and millet with legumes or beans such as lentils, pinto beans, and soybeans within the same meal. This guarantees that they are supplying their bodies with the proper amino acid profile. Any combination of grains and beans will do.

To figure serving sizes, consider that a 3-ounce serving of meat (about the size of a deck of cards) contains roughly 21 grams of protein. To replace this with a vegetarian source of protein, you must eat a generous cup of cooked beans with a cup of cooked grain. One cup of cooked lentils served over a large square of corn bread, for instance, is a great substitute for a 3-ounce serving of cooked chicken.

Is getting enough protein a problem, particularly during heavy training? Meeting your protein needs can be challenging on a vegetarian diet. But if you take care to combine grains with cooked beans or add milk, cheese, and eggs to your diet occasionally (once a day for women, several times a week for men), you should have no trouble. Keep in mind, however, that runners need more protein than sedentary people—roughly 25 percent more than the Daily Value or about half a gram of protein for every pound of body weight.

Let's say that you weigh 150 pounds. You would need to take in 75 grams of protein per day, or 10 to 12 servings of grain products (breads, pasta, or rice); 2 cups of cooked beans or bean products such as hummus (which is made from garbanzo beans), tofu (soybean curd), or miso (soybean paste); and a serving or two of nuts such as whole almonds or nut products such as peanut butter. Eating dairy products such as 2 servings of skim or 1 percent milk along with low-fat cottage cheese will help you meet your protein needs, as will adding eggs or egg whites to casseroles, soups, or stir-fried dishes.

Protein Sources

Here are 20 vegetarian foods that provide good ways to get protein.

Food	Calories	Fat (grams)	Protein (grams)
Black beans, 1 cup cooked	227	1	15
Bread (whole-grain), 2 slices	140	2	6
Brown rice, 1 cup cooked	232	1	5
Corn, 1 cup cooked	178	2	6
Corn bread, 2-inch square	130	4	3
Corn tortilla	67	1	2
Cottage cheese (1%), 1 cup	164	2	28
Egg, 1 large	75	2	6
Egg white, 1 large	16	0	3
Garbanzo beans, 1 cup cooked	285	3	12
Kidney beans, 1 cup cooked	225	1	15
Lentils, 1 cup cooked	231	1	18
Milk (1%), 1 cup	120	2	11
Pasta, 1 cup cooked	200	2	7
Potato, baked with skin	220	1	5
Refried beans, 1 cup cooked	270	3	16
Split peas, 1 cup cooked	231	1	16
Tempeh, ½ cup	165	6	16
Tofu, ½ cup	183	11	20
Yogurt (nonfat), 1 cup	127	0	13

Will eating a vegetarian diet boost my endurance?
Perhaps. Various studies have shown that training diets that provide
at least 600 grams of carbohydrates per day—a quota that's easy to
meet with heaping plates of rice and beans—boost endurance. But
rice, beans, bread, and pasta, which are all rich in carbohydrates, are
also big on volume. As a result, your stomach may fill up well before
your muscles do. That could help you lose a few pounds, which
might be just what you need short-term. But over the long-term, it
could lead to fatigue and breakdown.

Will I miss out on certain key nutrients by eating a vege-
tarian diet? In a word, yes. Vitamin B_{12}, for instance, isn't found in
plants. Some fermented bean products such as miso and tempeh
contain vitamin B_{12}, but they are not reliable sources. So vegetarians
must go out of their way to eat foods such as packaged cereal and
soy products that are supplemented with the vitamin.

The same is true for iron and zinc. Most plant foods are paltry
providers of both minerals, and the iron and zinc they do contain
aren't readily absorbed into the body. So vegetarians must take care
to consume iron-rich foods, especially since heavy exercise might
prompt iron loss. Some good selections are dried fruit, beans, chard
greens, and kale, and a multivitamin/mineral supplement that provides 100 percent of the Daily Value for iron and zinc.

As for calcium, vegans have a tough time getting enough. They
must substitute soy milk, soy yogurt, or tofu (which is made with
calcium carbonate) for dairy products and eat broccoli, bok choy,
collard greens, and other leafy greens daily to take in all of the
calcium that they can.

Are there any health risks associated with eating a vege-
tarian diet? Although the research isn't conclusive, some studies
suggest that vegetarian diets may lower the levels of sex hormones
in female and male athletes. For instance, many amenorrheic women
runners (women who don't have regular menstrual cycles) are
vegetarians. This has led some scientists to postulate that lower
estrogen levels caused by low-fat, high-fiber vegetarian diets are at
the root of amenorrhea. Other scientists suspect that the low iron
and zinc intakes of many vegetarian runners lead to amenorrhea.
Either way, estrogen levels sink, and the risk of osteoporosis rises.

A similar situation appears to develop in male athletes. In one
study, a group of male endurance athletes (runners, rowers, and
cyclists) were divided into two groups, each of which trained similarly. One group, however, ate a lacto-ovo vegetarian diet, while the
other ate a diet that supplied the same amount of protein but from
animal sources. After six weeks, blood levels of testosterone in the

vegetarian athletes had dropped 35 percent. Although dips in testosterone levels pose no health risk, they may depress sexual drive. Whether these levels would return to normal after a period of time on the vegetarian diets wasn't tested.

Do vegetarian meals take a long time to prepare? They don't have to. Simply take advantage of frozen vegetarian entrées, canned black beans and refried beans, and quick-cooking pasta and brown rice.

> *During the summer between my sophomore and junior years at college, I decided to become a strict lacto-ovo vegetarian. I told friends that this was an ethical decision—that I was opposed to the needless killing of animals for human consumption. Secretly, I hoped that it would also make me run faster.*
>
> *It did. My junior year in college was my best ever and led to several outstanding years that followed. It seemed that the vegetarian diet worked for me. Or did it? In truth, there's no way to know. My new successes could have been diet-related or they could have been related to any number of other things, including a harder training schedule.*
>
> *Over the years, I have been asked more questions about vegetarianism than about any other diet topic. I always begin my answers with the above anecdote and end by saying that I don't think anyone should become a vegetarian to improve his race performances. There are too many other excellent arguments for vegetarianism to trivialize the subject with thoughts of faster times.*
>
> *Have confidence that the vegetarian way of eating is fully compatible with a runner's training and racing needs. And then decide if vegetarianism makes sense for you.*

CHAPTER 10

BURIED TREASURES

Add These Foods to Boost
Your Running Performance

*Runners believe in superfoods just as they believe in super work-
outs. They're always looking for that special food—or workout—
that will make them stronger and faster. No matter that they
know these things are improbable. They keep hoping.*

*Bee pollen. Algae. Ginseng. All have been promoted at one
time or another as ergogenic foods—that is, foods or supplements that can improve performance. And these are just a few
among many. Amino acids. Chinese herbs. Chromium picoli-
nate. The list goes on and on.*

*Reputable sports nutritionists put little stock in these sub-
stances, pointing out that anecdote and testimony, even from
famous, world-class runners, does not amount to science.
Lacking proof from rigorous experiments, these nutritionists
tend to disregard the nutritional claims made about self-pro-
claimed superfoods. That's not to say, however, that nutritionists don't believe in the power of healthy foods. They do, as this
chapter by Liz Applegate, Ph.D., nutrition editor for* Runner's
World *magazine, makes clear.*

Most runners know that tried-and-true food favorites such as
pasta, bagels, and baby carrots provide good health, top performance, and superior flavor. But they're not the only foods to do so.
In fact, there are dozens of lesser-known vegetables, condiments,
and entrées that have more nutritional value than you suspect.
Some, such as mayonnaise, have been falsely labeled as unhealthy
while others, such as cactus, have been pigeonholed as weird. Yet
all pack specific nutritional benefits.

Consider the following foods. Each is tasty, healthful, and, yes,
a bit different. Try sampling one or two a week, and you can perk
up your meals without sacrificing your health.

1. Baby lima beans. One cup of cooked baby limas—delicious in
   soups, stews, casseroles, and three-bean salads—contains almost

8 grams of fiber (a third of your suggested daily intake), about 30 percent of the Daily Value of iron, 15 percent of the Daily Value for zinc, and about 25 percent of the RDA for magnesium. And that's not all. The same serving size also packs all of your daily requirement of folic acid, an important B vitamin that may prevent birth defects when consumed before and during pregnancy.

2. Beer. Be it nonalcoholic or the regular brew, beer is a great source of chromium, a mineral that plays a part in processing carbohydrates for energy. Various studies suggest exercise may increase chromium losses in the urine. And since it's not clear whether chromium in supplement form can boost performance, runners need to look to their diets to supply 50 to 200 micrograms of natural chromium a day. A tall, cold one is a good place to start (and finish): One 12-ounce beer provides about 60 micrograms of chromium.

3. Blackberry fruit spread. Blackberries are particularly rich in fiber (just 1 cup of fresh berries provides more than 6 grams of fiber), but they're a seasonal fruit. Fortunately, you can get blackberry preserves anytime. Swirl this tart treat, which is also rich in fiber and vitamin C, into plain low-fat yogurt or use it as a topping for pancakes, toast, or bagels.

4. Blackstrap (dark) molasses. Okay, it looks like sludge, but it packs a powerful nutritional punch. While most sweeteners offer little more than calories (regular table sugar, for instance, provides 46 calories per tablespoon but no essential vitamins or minerals), a tablespoon of blackstrap molasses provides about 20 percent of the Daily Value of iron, and 580 milligrams of potassium—about 20 percent of the Daily Value. Pretty good for a sweetener. Use blackstrap molasses to top off a bowl of hot cereal or as a substitute for a portion of the sugar used in baking muffins or cookies. (For instance, if a recipe calls for 1 cup of sugar, try using ½ cup with 3 to 4 tablespoons of blackstrap molasses.)

5. Cactus. Packed with potassium and vitamin C, a 1-cup serving of this delicacy provides about 20 percent of the Daily Value for calcium and iron. In addition, one study showed that people with diabetes who eat cooked cactus have improved control over their blood glucose levels and, as a result, are able to minimize health problems such as poor vision and bad circulation

that typically occur with the disease. Stick cactus in soups and stir-fry dishes and serve it as an exotic accompaniment to more common main dishes.

6. Canned chili. Have you checked out the canned chili aisle in the grocery store? "Lite" chili is in, and it's low in fat and high in performance-boosting protein.

7. Canned clams. Most runners eat lots of refined grains and very little meat. As a result, they often fall short of the Daily Value for zinc (15 milligrams), which helps fight infection, repairs wounds, and contributes to the growth of new blood cells and other tissues. To meet your Daily Value for zinc (150 percent of it, to be specific) and pick up 140 percent of the Daily Value for vitamin B_{12}, munch on a 3-ounce serving of clams right out of the can. Add clams to marinara sauce and eat them over pasta for a delicious, nutrient-packed meal.

8. Celery. Although celery doesn't have a nutrient report card worth writing home about (one stalk contains less than 1 gram of fiber, about 25 percent of the Daily Value for vitamin C, and a smattering of potassium and other nutrients), it does contain a special ingredient called 3-n-butyl phthalide, which may be helpful in lowering blood pressure. Research revealed that 3-n-butyl phthalide lowers blood pressure in lab animals and indicated that it may lower levels of stress hormones that can cause high blood pressure in people. Reach for celery when you need a crunchy snack or a healthful addition to soups, stews, or stir-fried food.

9. Frozen Chinese pot stickers. Easy to prepare and low in fat, too, Chinese pot stickers are the perfect accompaniment to steamed rice and vegetables. These chicken and vegetable dumplings contain lots of cancer-fighting cabbage and only about 1 gram of fat each.

10. Frozen pancakes. Check this out: Three 4-inch pancakes provide 246 calories (just under 15 percent from fat) and almost 50 grams of carbohydrate. So they're perfect for pre- or postrace carbo loading, especially when their preparation time is only seconds. Garnish a short stack with fresh fruit for added vitamins and minerals.

11. Mayonnaise. Yep—the real stuff, too. Regular mayonnaise has much more to offer than calories and fat. Along with 100 calo-

ries, a tablespoon of mayonnaise packs more than 50 percent of the Daily Value for vitamin E. That's three to four times the vitamin E found in most oils and margarines. And according to research, the oxidative damage that typically occurs with heavy endurance exercise may be prevented by taking in 200 to 400 international units of vitamin E, well above the Daily Value of 30 international units. But you don't have to drown your tuna sandwich in mayo; simply add mayonnaise to pasta salads, dressings, or sauces every once in a while.

12. McDonald's shake. These low-fat shakes contain less than 5 percent fat calories and a whole lot more. One chocolate shake provides 11 grams of protein (more than a glass of milk), 30 percent of the Daily Value for riboflavin and 30 percent of the Daily Value for calcium. Plus, 82 percent of its calories come from carbohydrate, so a shake every so often can be considered carbo loading, too.

13. Pesto. The olive oil, garlic, basil, and pine nuts that comprise pesto are a winning combination. The olive oil and garlic help depress total blood cholesterol, while basil provides plenty of magnesium and folate (the natural form of the supplement folic acid). And pine nuts pack the essential fats necessary for healthy skin and low blood pressure and may help prevent heart disease and diabetes. Add pesto to pasta, sauces, and soups for great flavor and good nutrition.

14. Refried beans. Although they sound fattening, refried beans simply aren't. At 270 calories per cup, canned refried beans contain less than 10 percent fat calories. And this is just the beginning. Each cup provides more than 6 grams of fiber (mostly water-soluble fiber, which helps lower blood cholesterol levels), about 20 percent of the Daily Value for protein, about 25 percent of the Daily Value for magnesium, 23 percent of the Daily Value for zinc, and about 15 percent of the Daily Value for calcium. Plus, fat-free versions are now on the market. Serve refried beans with corn tortillas, rice, or couscous for a high-quality, complex-carbohydrate meal.

15. Sweet potatoes. Most people reach for carrots to pack their diets with beta-carotene, but sweet potatoes are a far better source. One baked sweet potato is virtually fat-free and provides 250 percent of the Daily Value for vitamin A. (In addition to fending off cataracts, cancer, and heart disease, beta-carotene converts to

vitamin A once it is inside the body.) Whether they are baked, mashed, or added to stews, sweet potatoes are power spuds.

The best way to find your own superfoods is to sample what's available and learn what works best for you. A food that works wonders for one man or woman won't necessarily do the same for another. We are all individuals who react differently to different kinds of foods.

About a dozen years after I had begun running seriously, I sat down one evening to see if I could figure out what foods worked best for me. I was about to begin another serious training buildup, and I wanted to make sure that I was covering my nutritional bases. How could I do this? I wondered.

Simple. I wrote down a list of the foods that I ate often and next to each food put one to three check marks. Three meant that I always felt strong and energetic after eating this particular food.

I didn't know what to expect when I began this process, but it didn't take long for the results to explode off the paper at me. Rice and bananas. Sounds like a baby food combination, but in fact these were the only two foods to which I assigned three check marks. In the years since, I've added oatmeal to my list of favorite performance-enhancing foods.

Your personal-best foods probably aren't the same as mine, but you'll never know until you make yourself sit down and create a list. It's a deceptively simple process that can yield results. At least it did for me.

3

INJURY PREVENTION

CHAPTER 11

THE BIG FIVE

Preventing These Injuries Will Keep You
Ahead of the Pack

Injuries come in many shapes, sizes, and places, so it's difficult to make generalizations about how to avoid them or recover from them. Each one is unique in its own way, especially when you consider that each of us is unique. Still, certain injuries are more common than others. If you can figure out how to avoid these, you're ahead of the game.

When the Runner's World *editors decided to write about the five most common injuries, we debated them a little. We researched the subject by reviewing the medical literature. We asked each other which injuries we had incurred the most or heard our friends complain about.*

But in the end, it wasn't very complicated. Five injuries kept coming up over and over again. So we tackled them head on by asking Runner's World *senior writer Dave Kuehls to interview the experts and gather their advice. If you can avoid these five injuries, that's no guarantee that you won't develop others, but it's a big step in the right direction.*

Life used to be so much simpler. One day you came home complaining of knee pain. Mom took a look at your scraped knee, washed it, put an adhesive bandage on it, and sealed the treatment with a kiss. A few days later you forgot that your knee ever hurt.

Today, the pain in your knee is chondromalacia, an insidious wearing away of the cartilage beneath your kneecap. You go to see an orthopedic surgeon who doesn't look at all like Mom. And the prescribed treatment is not something that's over with in a minute. It's more likely to take weeks before you're running pain-free again.

Fortunately, many running injuries last only a few weeks. And most are preventable. If you run smart and do all the right things to ensure your running health—things you've heard before, such as strengthening and stretching your leg muscles, wearing proper shoes, and taking easy days or rest days when you're tired—you can avoid most running injuries or at least nip them in the bud.

That is, if you know what you're doing.

That's where this guide comes in. Below are the five most common running injuries: Achilles tendinitis, chondromalacia, iliotibial band syndrome, plantar fasciitis, and shinsplints. This guide tells you what they are and how to deal with them—everything from whether or not to run through them, to when it's time to see a doctor. And which doctor or sports-medicine specialist to see.

ACHILLES TENDINITIS

This troublesome heel pain is caused by inflammation of the Achilles tendon. The Achilles is the large tendon connecting the two major calf muscles—the gastrocnemius and soleus—to the back of the heel bone. Under too much stress, the tendon tightens and is forced to work too hard. This causes it to become inflamed (that's tendinitis) and, over time, can produce a covering of scar tissue that is less flexible than the tendon. If the inflamed Achilles continues to be stressed, it can tear or rupture.

Symptoms: Dull or sharp pain anywhere along the back of the tendon, but usually close to the heel. Limited ankle flexibility. Redness or heat over the painful area. A nodule (a lumpy buildup of scar tissue) that can be felt on the tendon. A crackling sound (scar tissue rubbing against the tendon) when the ankle moves.

Causes: Tight or fatigued calf muscles, which transfer too much of the burden of running to the Achilles. This can be brought on by not stretching the calves properly, increasing mileage too quickly, or simply overtraining. Excessive hill running or speedwork, both of which stress the Achilles more than other types of running, can also cause tendinitis. Inflexible running shoes, which force the Achilles to twist, cause some cases. Runners who overpronate (their feet rotate too far inward on impact) are susceptible to Achilles tendinitis.

Self-treatment: Stop

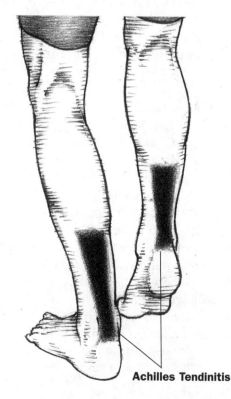

Achilles Tendinitis

running. Take aspirin or ibuprofen and ice the area for 15 to 20 minutes several times a day until the inflammation subsides.

Self-massage may also help. "I have every therapeutic machine available for the treatment of Achilles tendinitis, and the treatment of choice is massage with a heat-inducing cream or oil," says Marc Chasnov, a physical therapist in Rye Brook, New York. He suggests rubbing semicircles in all directions away from the knotted tissue three times a day.

Once the nodule is gone, stretch the calf muscles. Don't start running again until you can do toe raises without pain. Next, move on to skipping rope, then jumping jacks, and then gradually begin running again. You should be back to easy running in six to eight weeks.

Medical treatment: If your injury does not respond to self-treatment in two weeks, see a physical therapist or orthopedic surgeon. Surgery to scrape scar tissue off the tendon is a last resort and not very effective. "It usually just stimulates more scar tissue," says Chasnov.

Alternative exercises: Cycling in low gear, swimming, and pool running. No weight-bearing exercises.

Preventive measures: The best stretch for the Achilles tendon is also the simplest. Stand on the balls of your feet on stairs, a curb, or a low rung of a ladder, with your legs straight. Drop both of your heels down and hold for a count of 10. To increase the intensity of the stretch, keep one foot flat and lower the other heel. When done, switch legs.

Achilles Stretch

Strengthen and stretch the muscles in your feet, calves, and shins. Wear motion-control shoes or orthotics to combat over-pronation. Do not run in worn-out shoes. Ease into any running program. Avoid hill work. Incorporate rest into your training schedule.

CHONDROMALACIA

One of the most common knee injuries, chondromalacia is a softening or wearing away and cracking of the cartilage under the kneecap, resulting in pain and inflammation. The cartilage becomes like sandpaper because the kneecap is not riding smoothly over the knees.

Symptoms: Pain beneath or on the side of the kneecap. "It's a soreness, a nagging discomfort," says Dave Apple, M.D., an orthopedic surgeon at Piedmont Hospital in Atlanta. Pain can worsen over a year or so and is most severe after you run hills. Swelling is also present. In severe cases, you can feel—and eventually hear—grinding as the rough cartilage rubs against cartilage when the knee is flexed.

Causes: Overpronation can cause the kneecap to twist sideways. The quadriceps muscles, which normally aid in proper tracking of the kneecap, can prevent the kneecap from tracking smoothly when they are fatigued or weak. A muscle imbalance between weak quads and tighter hamstrings can also pull the kneecap out of its groove. Hill running (especially downhills) can aggravate the condition, as can running on the same side of a cambered road, or, in general, overtraining.

Self-treatment: Stop running. Ice the knee for 15 minutes, two or three times a day. Use a flexible, frozen gel pack that wraps around the knee (or, in a pinch, try

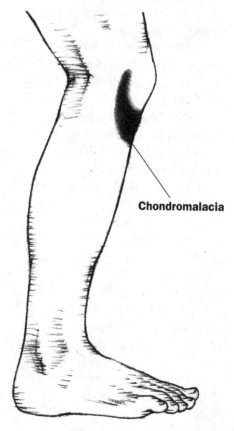

Chondromalacia

a bag of frozen vegetables). Take aspirin three times a day for 12 weeks. "Aspirin has been found to block further breakdown of cartilage," says Dr. Apple. Also try self-massage on the sore spots around the knee.

Once the pain and swelling are gone, do quadriceps strengtheners. Stand on a step or box at least 4 inches high. Keep your right quadriceps tight while you lower your left leg slowly toward the floor. Then raise the leg back up to the box and relax. Repeat 40 times with each leg. Continue increasing repetitions in increments of five every two days, all the way up to 60 reps.

Don't forget to stretch your quadriceps and hamstrings. When you start running again, you also might try wearing a rubber sleeve with a hole that fits over the kneecap, which can help the knee track better.

You should be back to easy running in four to six weeks.

Medical treatment: If chondromalacia isn't responding to the self-treatment after four weeks, see an orthopedic surgeon. He may prescribe custom-made orthotics to control overpronation. Surgery to scrape away rough edges of cartilage can alleviate some pain. Despite what you may have heard, cortisone injections won't work. "The problem is, you won't feel pain while you're crunching your knee to bits," says Dr. Apple.

Alternative exercises: Swimming, pool running, and rowing. Anything that doesn't put pressure on the knee.

Preventive measures: Stretch and strengthen your quadriceps, hamstrings, and calves. If you overpronate, consider switching to motion-control shoes with firm midsoles. Don't run in worn-out shoes. You may need orthotics. Avoid downhill running, and stay off cambered roads. If you can't, try to run on the flattest part of the road. Incorporate rest into your training schedule. Don't overdo it.

Quadriceps Strengthener

ILIOTIBIAL BAND SYNDROME

This condition results in inflammation and pain on the outside of the knee where the iliotibial (IT) band (a ligament that runs along the outside of the thigh) rubs against the femur, the large leg bone.

Symptoms: A dull ache that starts when you're a mile or two into a run, lingers during the run, but disappears soon after you stop. In severe cases, pain can be sharp, and the outside of the knee can be tender or swollen.

Causes: Anything that causes the leg to bend inward, stretching the IT band against the femur, such as bowlegs, overpronation, worn-out running shoes, or workouts on downhill or indoor, banked surfaces. A tight IT band can contribute to the injury. So can stepping up your training too quickly. Sometimes a single hard workout can cause IT band syndrome.

Self-treatment: "You usually can't run through IT band pain," says Dr. Apple. "But if you do run, back off. Cut back on speed-work, don't run down-hill, and make sure to stretch the band a couple of times a day. The main thing you have to do is restore the band's flexibility."

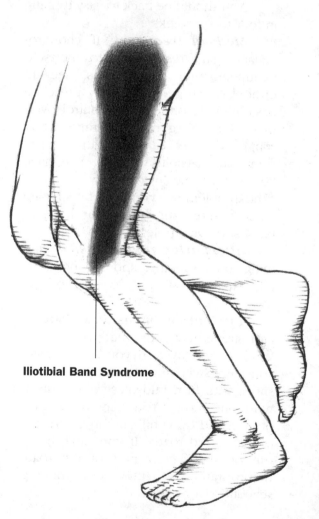

Iliotibial Band Syndrome

Perform the IT band stretch, the most common and effective IT band exercise: Stand with your right leg crossed in back of your left and extend your left arm against a wall, pole, chair, or other stable object. Lean your weight against the object while pushing your right hip to the right. Keep your right foot anchored while allowing your left knee to flex. You should feel the stretch in the iliotibial muscle in your right hip and extending down the outside of your right leg.

In addition to doing the IT band stretch, ice the knee for 15 to 20 minutes after running, try self-massage on the area, and stretch hamstrings and other leg muscles. You should be back to easy running in two to four weeks.

Medical treatment: If your IT band problem isn't responding to self-treatment after four weeks, see an orthopedic surgeon. Severe cases may call for a cortisone injection under the band to alleviate pain.

Alternative exercises: Swimming, pool running, cycling, and rowing, but not stair climbing. "Anything that doesn't put pressure on the outside of the knee is fine," says Dr. Apple.

Preventive measures: Stretch the IT band (after a workout is best). Stretch and strengthen your quadriceps and hamstrings. Warm up well before a run. Avoid hard workouts on cambered roads, downhill surfaces, or indoor tracks. Ease into any running program.

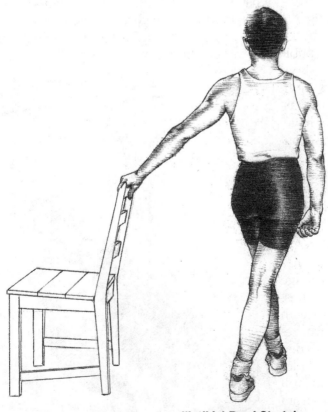

Iliotibial Band Stretch

Plantar Fasciitis

This is an inflammation of the plantar fascia, a thick, fibrous band of tissue in the bottom of the foot, running from the heel to the base of the toes. When placed under too much stress, the fascia stretches too far and tears, causing inflammation of the fascia and surrounding tissues. The tears are soon covered with scar tissue, which is less flexible than the fascia and only aggravates the problem.

Symptoms: Pain at the base of the heel. "Most people describe it as feeling like a bone bruise or a stone bruise," says Joe Ellis, D.P.M., a sports podiatrist from La Jolla, California, and the author of *Running Injury-Free.* "Plantar fasciitis is most severe in the morning when you get out of bed or at the beginning of a run, because the fascia is tighter at those times. The pain may fade as you walk or run."

Often, a runner will change stride to alleviate pain, but this only provides temporary relief. A bone spur may also develop at the heel, where the fascia has started to tear away.

Causes: Stress, tension, and pulling on the plantar fascia. Runners with tight Achilles tendons (which put more stress on the fasciae), or high arches and rigid feet, or flat feet that overpronate are most susceptible. Worn-out shoes, which allow feet to over-pronate, or shoes that are too stiff, which stretch the fasciae, can also make you more susceptible.

Self-treatment: Reduce your running. Take aspirin or ibuprofen daily. Ice the area for 15 to 20 minutes several times a day. Ice-massage the fascia. To do this, fill a paper cup with water and freeze. Peel off the paper, place the ice under your foot, and roll the foot over it, from your heel to the ball

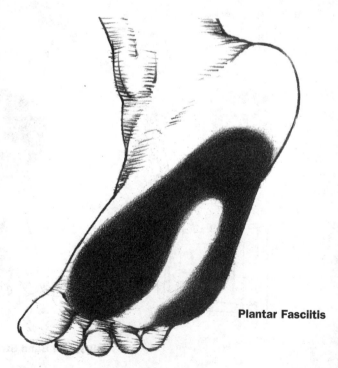

Plantar Fasciitis

of your foot and back again. A frozen-juice can works equally as well.

Medical treatment: If the injury hasn't responded to self-treatment in four weeks, see a podiatrist, who may prescribe orthotics, ultrasound, or friction massage. Surgery to detach the fascia from its insertion into the heel may be recommended if medical treatments don't help after a year. The success rate is 80 percent. Surgery to remove bone spurs usually doesn't work. "The spur isn't the problem," says Dr. Ellis. "It's a reaction to the problem."

Alternative exercises: Swimming, pool running, and cycling in low gear. After surgery, only swimming is recommended during rehabilitation.

Preventive measures: Stretch your calf muscles. Strengthen muscles of the foot by picking up marbles or golf balls with your toes or pulling a towel toward you with your toes. (Grab some of the towel with your toes and pull, then grab some more.)

To help stretch the fascia, you can perform a similar motion using a golf ball. Start with the golf ball under the base of your big toe and roll the foot forward over the ball to the base of the second toe and repeat. Do the same motion starting from each toe, always exerting enough pressure so that you feel a little tenderness.

Do the plantar fascia stretch: While sitting on the floor, with one knee bent and the same ankle

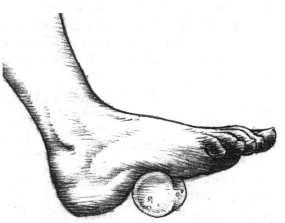

Plantar Fascia Pain Reliever

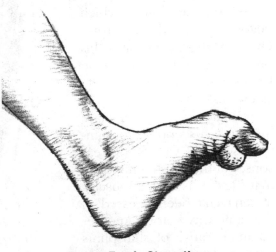

Plantar Fascia Strengthener

flexed toward you, pull the toes back toward the ankle. Hold for a count of 10. Do 10 times.

Wear orthotics if you overpronate or have flat feet. Ice the area for 15 to 20 minutes after running. Run on soft surfaces. Don't run in worn-out shoes. Incorporate more rest into your training schedule.

SHINSPLINTS

A very common and nagging injury, shinsplints are an inflammation of the tendons on the inside of the front of the lower leg. (Sports-medicine specialists don't like to use the term "shinsplints" because it commonly refers to several lower-leg injuries. This section uses it anyway but focuses on the specific problem that is the most common: tendinitis of the lower leg.)

Symptoms: An aching, throbbing, or tenderness along the inside of the shin (though it can radiate to the outside also) about halfway down, or all along the shin from the ankle to the knee. Pain when you press on the inflamed area. Pain is most severe at the start of a run, but it can go away during a run once the muscles are loosened up (unlike a stress fracture of the shinbone, which hurts all the time). With tendinitis, pain resumes after the run.

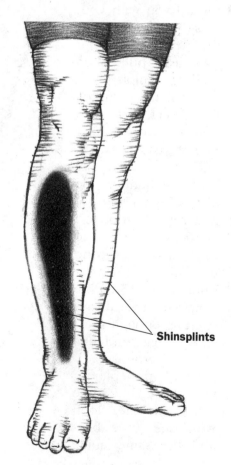

Shinsplints

Causes: Tired or inflexible calf muscles put too much stress on tendons, which become strained and torn. Overpronation aggravates this problem, as does running on hard surfaces such as concrete sidewalks.

Beginning runners are the most susceptible to shinsplints for a variety of reasons, but the most common is that they're using leg muscles that haven't been stressed in the same way before. Another common cause of shinsplints among beginners is poor choice of running shoes or running in something other than running shoes. Runners who have started running after a long layoff are also prone to shinsplints because they often increase their mileage too quickly.

Self-treatment: Many runners experience mild shin soreness, which usually can be tolerated. "If shinsplints hit you at the beginning of a season, a certain amount of running through it will help the body adapt," says David O'Brian, D.P.M., a podiatrist in private practice in Roselle, Illinois. "But if it's a persistent problem, you shouldn't run through it."

If it does persist, ice the inflamed area for 15 minutes, three times a day, and take aspirin or ibuprofen. Ice immediately after running. To hasten recovery, cut down on running or stop altogether. Recovery time: two to four weeks.

Medical treatment: If the injury doesn't respond to self-treatment and rest in two to four weeks, see a podiatrist, who may prescribe custom-made orthotics to control overpronation. Ultrasound and anti-inflammatories may also be prescribed. Surgery is rarely required.

Alternative exercises: Nonimpact exercises such as swimming, pool running, walking, and cycling in low gear.

Preventive measures: To stretch and strengthen the tendons

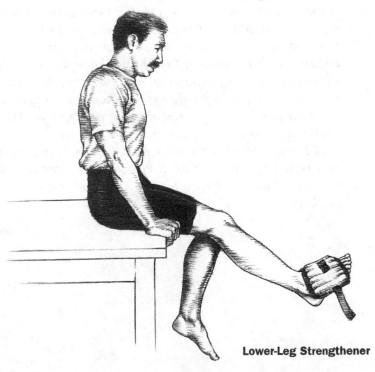

Lower-Leg Strengthener

and muscles in the front of the leg, sit on a table or chair and loop an ankle weight around your foot. Without bending your knee, move your foot up and down from the ankle. Or have a partner grasp the foot to provide resistance.

You can also strengthen the lower leg with band exercises. Anchor one end of an exercise band to a heavy object, such as the leg of a sofa. Stretch the band, then loop the free end around your forefoot. Move the foot up and down and side to side against the band's resistance to exercise different muscle groups. The band can be ordered from a doctor or bought at some sporting goods stores. Ask for "tension tubing."

Finally, make sure to wear motion-control shoes—and orthotics if your doctor says you need them. Don't run in worn-out shoes. Warm up well and run on soft surfaces. Avoid overstriding, which puts more stress on shins.

The best injury-prevention advice I know is also the most boring: rest. What's more, it leads to zany conclusions like, "If I never ran at all, I would never get injured, so maybe I should head for the couch instead of the roads."

I suppose that I've been guilty of similar black-and-white thought patterns myself. Only the thought that I had when I was younger and hungrier was "If I don't run 20 miles today, someone else will, and that person will beat me in the next race." I won lots of races in those days. I was also injured a lot. And, looking back, I wonder if I might not have won even more races by tempering my training a bit and avoiding those injuries (one of which thwarted my only real chance at the Olympic Games).

Today, I know that resting one day just makes me (and probably you) more enthusiastic about running the next day. And I understand better what judicious rest can do. It can help you recover from injuries. It can help prevent injuries. It can help you train and race better. All in all, that's a compelling package.

CHAPTER 12

THE NO-INJURIES RUNNING PROGRAM

A Foot Doctor Tells You How to Stay on Your Feet

The runner's doctor is the sports podiatrist. Running philosopher George Sheehan, M.D., was the first to discover this, just as he was the first to discover many things from the medical and philosophical sides of running. And during his life he did much to promote the ways a podiatrist could help injured runners.

This isn't to say that podiatrists are the only medically trained professionals who can help or that other physicians (especially orthopedic specialists) aren't better suited to analyze and treat certain injuries. What's more, many runners swear by their favorite chiropractor, physical therapist, or massage therapist. Still, podiatrists generally fare best in treating the many foot and lower-leg maladies that occasionally trouble runners.

At Runner's World *magazine we learned this long ago and immediately began contacting podiatrists who are also serious runners (there are many) to help us prepare articles. One of the first and best was Joe Ellis, D.P.M.—an enthusiastic runner, a great podiatrist, and a frequent contributor to* Runner's World *magazine. In this chapter, Dr. Ellis outlines a simple but effective program that can help keep you injury-free.*

Most runners know injuries. They're almost part of the game. Run long enough or hard enough, and you'll probably come down with an ache that will temporarily sideline you.

Fortunately, most running injuries are short-term. After a few days or weeks of rest, you can return to your regular routine. Still, there is a better way: Don't get injured in the first place.

Impossible, you say? Not at all. If you adopt the principles outlined on these pages, you'll have a reasonable chance of running in good health indefinitely. Ignore them, and . . . well, you know. You sow what you reap.

Carefully choose where you run. The best surfaces for running are firm but not too hard, relatively flat (without camber), and smooth (without ruts or holes). Generally, roads make fine running surfaces, but keep in mind that most are canted so that water will run off the center of the road. As you run down the road against traffic, the slant causes your right foot to pronate (roll inward) and your left foot to supinate (roll outward). So map out your routes over the flattest streets that you can find. Here's a look at other possible running venues.

Beaches: Most beaches are poor places to run. Generally, the sand is too soft and causes uneven footing, which strains and stresses your leg muscles. Also, the beach is slanted, and just as on a crowned road, your legs are forced to work unevenly—one pronating too much and the other supinating. If you can't resist a seaside jaunt, run at low tide when you can get onto packed sand and a flatter stretch of beach. Also, don't run too far in one direction; turn around to reverse the stresses on your legs.

Cinder paths: A packed cinder path can be an ideal running surface—provided it is well-maintained, not lumpy or rutted. And not wet. On rainy days a cinder trail can become muddy and slippery. Many towns and cities have fitness trails in their parks and recreation areas. Seek out one near your home.

Lawns and other grassy areas: Because they're soft, you might think that golf courses or cross-country courses would be good places to run. But the unevenness of these surfaces forces the muscles and tendons in your feet and legs to work harder than they would on a flat course and increases the possibility of injury. When you consider that more than half the population has some biomechanical abnormality, you begin to see the risks of cross-country running. It can be downright treacherous if you head out over terrain where ruts and holes lie hidden in the grass. Most runners' ankle sprains occur on cross-country courses. You're better off running on dirt trails, because you can see the rough spots and avoid them.

Sidewalks: Stay away from sidewalks unless you are running in heavy traffic and need to get off the street. Concrete is significantly harder than asphalt, and since sidewalks aren't continuous, you have to jump off and on at every corner. Furthermore, many sidewalks are cracked and uneven. If you catch your toe on a raised chunk of walk, next thing you know, you'll be nose-down against the pavement.

Tracks: Tracks offer an even surface that's firm but not too hard. The one disadvantage is that they force you to turn frequently and can strain your muscles unevenly. But if you change direction every two or three laps, you'll lessen the chances of injury. Also, run in the far outside lanes, especially during warm-ups and cooldowns. The angle of the curve is less there, so it generates reduced forces on your legs.

Outdoor tracks are almost always better than indoor tracks because they are larger and unbanked. Indoor tracks often have a steep camber, which is murder on the knees. Also, most indoor tracks are smaller and require you to run more laps per mile—meaning more turns per mile.

Be sure to warm up and cool down. When you first get up in the morning, your muscles and soft tissues are tight. In fact, at that time your muscles are generally about 10 percent shorter than their normal resting length. When you start to exercise, your muscles stretch, reaching up to 10 percent longer than resting length. This means you have a 20 percent change in muscle length from the time you get out of bed until your muscles are well warmed up.

According to basic laws of physics, muscles work more efficiently when they are longer; they can exert more force with less effort. This means, too, that longer muscles are much less prone to injury.

Make it a practice to warm up before a run or race. Pedal for a few minutes indoors on a stationary bike or jump rope for a few turns before you head down the road. If you would rather warm up on the run, begin with a walk or a slow jog and gradually move into your training pace.

Cooling down can also help you avoid injury. An easy jog after a hard workout or race has been shown to speed recovery by helping remove any lactic acid that may have accumulated. It also gently brings your muscles back to a resting state.

A good warm-up and cooldown are especially important before and after a hard workout such as intervals or a race in which you push your muscles to their limits. The extra time you spend warming up your muscles before a training run or race and cooling down afterward is worth the effort in improved efficiency and decreased likelihood of getting injured.

Stretch those muscles. Without flexibility, you are an injury waiting to happen. Tight muscles cannot go through their full range of motion. Lack of flexibility is probably the biggest cause of Achilles tendinitis and is a major factor in plantar fasciitis and shinsplints.

Although muscles in the back of your upper legs (the hamstrings) tend to be the workhorses, don't forget to stretch the muscles in the front of your legs as well. They're busy, too.

Stretching is not the same as warming up. Trying to stretch a tight muscle may cause injury. The best time to stretch is after a run, when your muscles are warm and elongated. Make stretching part of your routine every day.

When you stretch, move slowly and gradually into each position and hold it for just 2 seconds before relaxing again. Repeat each stretch 8 to 12 times. Never stretch a muscle to the point of pain. Pain indicates that you are stretching too hard or that some injury needs attention.

Schedule rest in your program. If you train hard every day, you'll wear your body down rather than build it up. You need to recover after a tough workout or a race, giving your muscles a chance to mend and stock up on glycogen for your next hard effort. This is why most experts recommend that you never schedule hard workouts two days in a row. Give yourself at least one day of easy running or rest between hard efforts. If you run fast one day, train slowly the next. If you run long one day, go short the following day. This is the "hard/easy" method of training.

Just as some people need more sleep than others, some people need more recovery. You may discover that your body performs best when you rest for two days after a hard workout. Or you may even need three easy days. Experiment with various combinations of hard and easy days and compare the merits of easy running versus rest or cross-training.

Listen to your body. Let your training schedule be your guide, but never your prison guard. One of the surest ways to become injured is to train hard on a day when you're fatigued or feeling the soreness of an injury about to happen. Even if you're following all the rules—running on a good surface, warming up, stretching, using a hard/easy pattern—other factors of your lifestyle figure into your physical well-being and level of fatigue. Stress at work or at home or lack of sleep can take a toll as well.

If you feel fatigued or overly sluggish or if you notice twinges of muscular pain, ease up on your training. If you have planned speedwork, run easy instead or take a day off altogether. You will not lose fitness over a day, or even a few days, of rest. Unfortunately, most runners have a hard time following this advice.

Let's say that you are training for a certain race and your schedule calls for a 10 percent increase in mileage this week, yet you're feeling a little twinge in your hamstrings. How do you respond? Do you go ahead and follow the schedule, or do you alter it?

You know the right answer. Yet many runners insist on adhering to the printed training schedule as if it were gospel. They refuse to deviate by a single mile from that program, since they believe that any modification will ruin their chances of running a good race. In fact, the reverse is true. They would benefit more by giving their bodies a chance to recover.

Remember, training schedules are built on the assumption that you aren't experiencing any unusual pains before, during, or after the run. If pain or fatigue does strike, don't hesitate to modify your workouts.

Open up to cross-training. Runners once took a run-or-nothing approach to their sport, and many still do, believing that other sports cannot benefit their running and may in fact hurt it. The wiser runner now explores other options, both to supplement running during periods of good health and to substitute for running during injury phases. It's a rare runner today who doesn't employ some cross-training.

Participating in another sport a couple of times a week gives your feet and legs a welcome respite from the constant pounding of running and strengthens muscles that running does not exercise. In both of these ways, cross-training can help protect you from injury.

Replace an easy run or rest day with a cross-training workout. After all, often it isn't total rest that your body needs, merely a break from the overspecialized action of running.

The more muscles you can involve in your training program, the less likely you are to sustain an overuse injury. Additionally, by working more of your major muscle groups, you improve your overall state of fitness.

If you do become injured through running and have been cross-training regularly, you will have an activity to turn to that will keep you fit while you recover. Overuse symptoms such as soreness, or injuries caused by too much shock or jarring, can be relieved through swimming or cycling. By using a stair-climber, rowing machine, or cross-country ski machine, you can take the stress off an injured area and still get an excellent cardiovascular workout.

Recover properly after races. Racing pushes the limits of your speed and endurance, and too much racing can push you beyond your ability to avoid injury. Racing is hard on your body, so you must give yourself plenty of time to recover after each event.

Occasionally, you may read or hear about someone who runs an incredible number of races—a runner who runs a marathon every week for a year, for example. It's difficult to believe anyone can do that without getting injured, but there are always some people who can beat the odds. A few people can smoke three packs of cigarettes a day and live to be 100. But that doesn't mean that you can play the odds without suffering the usual painful consequences.

Log it. Keeping a training log of your daily runs may seem compulsive or boring, but charting your distance, pace, course, the weather, and how you felt can give you an important perspective. With a running log, you can trace your progress and detect errors accurately and objectively. You can see if you have been training too little or too much.

Review your log weekly with a critical eye. Pretend it's someone else's training program and that you're checking how effective and safe it is. You may be amazed at the training errors you find. Correct these errors, and you'll become a better runner—and one more likely to stay injury-free.

REBOUNDING FROM INJURIES

If you do get injured, come back slowly. . . much more slowly than you might think.

After a layoff or an injury, your feet and legs need time to get reaccustomed to the effort of running. They have become somewhat soft and lazy, and it takes time to build them to the point where they can once again absorb the forces of running.

Furthermore, it's possible that your injury hasn't healed completely. Even though you may not feel any symptoms, the area you hurt will be weaker than it was before your injury—and more susceptible to reinjury. If you stress your body too much too soon, the same symptoms are likely to reappear.

Depending on how long your layoff was and whether or not you were able to do any cross-training to maintain fitness, you might need to return to your running program with a walk/jog regimen. Although you would rather eat asphalt than be caught walking, do it anyway. You'll still be exercising your muscles but without the hard pounding of running.

If you try to take shortcuts or cheat your body's natural timetable, you're asking for trouble. You simply cannot rush your recovery. As you become stronger, increase your weekly distance by no more than 10 percent per week. This rule applies when you're healthy, too.

Finally, be sure to eat well. During a layoff, many runners cut back on their diets to prevent weight gain. This isn't necessary. You need extra nutrients to help your body mend the injured area and fuel your training once you renew your running program. If you do gain a few pounds during your recovery period, they'll just melt away when you begin running again.

So eat. And train wisely. There's no reason why you can't continue running healthy year after year.

The question of running surfaces, which Dr. Ellis covers at the beginning of this chapter, has long fascinated me. What's the best surface to run on? If the answer was simple, then we would all take a big step forward in the battle against running injuries.

Of course, the answer isn't simple, as he explains. Every surface seems to have its pros and cons. Confusing, yes, but this situation nonetheless leads me to a tentative conclusion: Run on all surfaces. All the time. Deliberately. As part of your injury-prevention program.

The way I figure it, running on just one surface adds fuel to the overuse syndrome. Say you run on the roads every day. Every footfall is almost exactly like the one before it. The same muscles, tendons, and bones get stressed in the same way over and over again.

Whereas if you vary surfaces, the stresses vary. Now you have to be careful. New stress, such as that which comes from running on a beach, for example, can be a powerful injury mechanism. So be sure that your first beach run is a short and easy one. Don't do a hard 10-mile run.

Changing surfaces in an intelligent manner is a little like cross-training. It helps you prevent injuries by giving certain muscles and joints a rest while strengthening other muscles and joints.

CHAPTER 13

10 LAWS
OF HEALTHY RUNNING

*How a Crippling Injury Made One Runner
See the Light*

> *The author of this chapter, Bob Wischnia, has been my colleague at* Runner's World *magazine for nearly 20 years. During that time, I have learned many things about "Wish," but two stand out: I don't know anyone who loves running more than Wish, and I don't know anyone who has to be more careful about avoiding injuries.*
>
> *Wish isn't a particularly graceful runner—he's stiff and he toes out at an awkward angle. Perhaps this is the source of his problem. Or perhaps it's something totally different; running form is more of a visual thing than a good predictor of underlying issues.*
>
> *At any rate, Wish seems to get injured easily. Yet nothing detracts from his love of running. Being a reasonable guy—that is, one who wants to continue running healthy as long as he can—Wish has over the course of many years developed a program that works for him. Here, he outlines his 10 Laws of Healthy Running—a series of methods and principles that can also keep you running healthy.*

Like most of you, I'm a goal-oriented kind of runner. I need some sort of carrot to chase. A few years ago, I had all the usual time and race goals that I would arbitrarily set and then try to knock down. Then, somewhere along the way, I was the one who got knocked down.

In one way, it was the incapacitating pain from a herniated disk injury and the subsequent back operation that finally did me in. But in another, it was more an obsessive character defect: I pushed too hard in many of my workouts. Either way, after 25 years of continuous running, my life had changed.

I spent an entire winter recovering on my back and vowed that if I could ever begin running again, it would be different. It would have to be especially different in one crucial area: goals. I would have to find a new approach to goal setting—a saner one. And I have.

As I began my running rebirth after the back surgery, I decided to follow the advice of my closest friend and purge the T-word from my running vocabulary. No more "training." Same with "workout." Instead of training or working out, I would play. I had always tried to regard my running as fun; now I would go even further.

With health and fun as my only goals, I drew up my 10 Laws of Healthy Running. I've been following them for the last five years, and they have worked. I'm not faster or stronger, not setting personal records or achieving breakthroughs. I'm simply happier and healthier.

1. Work stretching into your day. I realize that nobody wants to hear any more about the value of stretching, so I won't belabor the point. I'll simply tell you that I spend 20 minutes every morning doing yoga and various other stretching exercises, and it has worked. My routine varies, but I always emphasize the abdominals, the hamstrings, the calf muscles, and the Achilles tendons.

   Like a lot of us, I've always had tight hamstrings (the group of muscles in the back of the thigh). The stiff hamstrings probably had as much to do with my back injury as anything else because they placed torque on other areas of my body such as my sciatic nerve. I've always stretched my hamstrings, but now I know that placing my leg on a fence post for 20 seconds isn't enough. These days I spend at least 5 minutes stretching each leg fastidiously. And how I do it is more important than the amount of time.

   With a jump rope or long piece of rope, I lie on my back and place the middle of the rope on the ball of one foot. Grasping each end of the rope, I slowly raise my leg, making sure to keep the knee straight and my shoulders flat on the floor. The idea is to get a deep stretch right into the belly of the hamstrings without pain. I make sure that I breathe through the stretch and don't overstretch. I stretch each leg five times in this manner and try to hold each stretch for a count of 20.

   Here's another stretch that I do for my hamstrings: I lie on the floor with my butt firmly against a wall and my legs extended up against the wall with my knees locked. I place my hands on my stomach and try to stretch my toes. It feels a little strange at first. And in the beginning it's difficult to hold this position for longer than a minute or two. But it's easy to increase the time as your body becomes used to it. The longer you do it, the more relaxing it becomes.

2. Stay with shoes that work for you. You may know me as the guy who co-authors all the shoe surveys for *Runner's World* maga-

zine. I probably have more running shoes in my closet than you have T-shirts. I have my choice of any shoe being made (and plenty in the prototype stage, too).

I used to try every new model, every hot technology, every funky gizmo. No more. I had too many injuries wearing shoes that weren't right for me. This isn't to suggest that the new shoes won't work for you; my point is, don't try new footwear simply because it's different. When you find a shoe that works for you, don't switch just out of curiosity. New isn't necessarily better.

Of course, once a shoe loses its ability to cushion and control foot movement, it's time to switch to a new pair. But whenever possible, I try to stick with the same model. If that model is discontinued, I'll find one that is technically close to my old favorite (same last, midsole, and control elements).

Here are several more rules: Don't choose a shoe because of its weight, and be careful with racing flats. I never choose a shoe based on its weight. Instead, I choose a shoe based on function, fit, and control. And I never wear racing flats anymore. I don't care how important the race is, racing flats don't provide enough support and cushioning for me. Saving a few ounces of weight isn't worth it. If I want to wear something other than my daily trainer in a race, I'll switch to a lightweight trainer that's an ounce or two lighter and has almost as much stability.

3. Use orthotics for all your shoes. Like many runners, I wear customized orthotics to minimize biomechanical deficiencies. Unlike a lot of runners, I always wear my orthotics. Not just on my daily run, but whenever I'm wearing any kind of shoe, boot, or sneaker. The way I figure it, if they're worth using, they're worth using all the time. I slip my hard plastic orthotics into my tennis shoes, cycling cleats, ski boots, cross-trainers, even my dress shoes (on the biannual occasion when I wear anything but athletic shoes).

As a corollary to the above, it's important for orthotics wearers to select running shoes that function well with orthotics. I stick with relatively straight-lasted, motion-control shoes with a firm midsole, deep heel, and sturdy heel counter.

4. Start and end with walking. By that I mean, I begin and end every run with walking. Whether I'm leaving from my front door or a car, I start every run by walking a few minutes. Usually, it's as short as a 200-meter walk through a parking lot to the beginning of a trail.

The warm-up walk accomplishes several things. It's a brief transition from being sedentary to running. During this time, I check out my various aches and pains (I can shorten the run if any pain is pronounced), warm up with shoulder rotations and leg shakes, adjust my lacelocks or laces, and determine if I need to add or shed any clothes before taking off.

The cooldown walk is different and a little longer, only because it's so enjoyable. I loosen my shoes, wipe my shades, cool off a little, and bask in the endorphin rush. It's a time to celebrate the run, the day, the sweat, the companionship. It's a time to drink and stretch a little—anything—to prolong the moment.

5. Think about where you run. I stay off roads, sidewalks, and tracks. Easier said than done, right? But to me, it's worth the effort (usually a short drive) to run on trails rather than roads. It's not just the hardness of the roads that kills my legs, it's also the camber.

I don't avoid roads just to prevent injuries, though. The bottom line is that running on trails or dirt roads is simply more fun to me. It's less stressful on my body because the surface is much more forgiving. It's also cooler in summer. And because I don't have to deal with traffic, it's much more relaxing—which is what running's all about anyway.

When I travel, I sometimes have to improvise. I'll try to find a football or soccer field, a small park, or any patch of green to run around. If not, I'll run on the roads as a last resort. If I happen to be someplace where the running is truly awful (such as Barcelona during the 1992 Olympics), I'll bag it and just walk, swim, or do something else. I'd rather not run than get injured or even risk getting injured.

6. Be wary of hills. Before anyone accuses me of being a wimp, I plead guilty. But if staying off the hills preserves my body for another run on another day, I accept the verdict. No runner has ever loved hills more than I do. In my previous life (northern California; huge, forested park), I ran a rugged 10-mile hill loop every day. Sometimes twice.

Which may be one reason why I avoid them now. Running hills, especially the downhills, puts too much stress on my back and shins. If I do come across a series of rolling hills on my run, I'll cruise the ups but ease the downs at little more than a brisk trot. Sometimes I'll even walk the downhills.

7. Bring on the ice. My legs have always been tender, and I have suffered from all the major overuse injuries: shinsplints, plantar fasciitis, sciatica, and runner's knee. Fortunately, I learned a valuable lesson a decade ago from a wondrous New Zealand

marathoner, Jack Foster. He finished every run by hosing down his legs with icy water. Foster said that's what trainers do for thoroughbred horses after every workout and race, and he theorized, "If it's good enough for race horses, it's good enough for me."

Foster's method works because a cold compress—ice, ice water, commercial frozen gels, frozen vegetable packages—immediately reduces the muscular inflammation that results from any running effort. Unchecked, this inflammation can worsen. Ice keeps the inflammation under control.

Heeding Foster's advice, I used to soak my legs for 10 minutes after every run in an unheated swimming pool. That soaking was the best therapy that I ever had. I don't have a pool anymore, but I still ice or soak my legs after every run. The ice is so soothing that it has become a part of my routine, whether my legs hurt or not.

8. Pitch the training log. Heresy? So be it. I kept a running log for 10 years, but despite all conventional wisdom, I don't keep one anymore. If you're anything like me, you love to jot down those great workouts—the hill runs, the intervals, the perfect 50-mile weeks—for posterity.

Unfortunately for me, and I suspect others, too, the compulsion to complete those 50-mile weeks was also my ruin. If I missed a day or two with leg soreness, the big, fat zeros in my log drove me nuts. More often than not, I'd go for a run to avoid any more zeros instead of doing the sensible thing and resting.

Now that I don't keep a log, I don't worry about my weekly mileage. A 20-mile week is as good as a 50-mile week—if I'm healthy—but I don't have a clue what my weekly mileage is, nor do I care. I follow the sage advice 1980 Olympic Team member Benji Durden gave me 10 years ago and run by time. A 40-minute run isn't 5½ miles; it's 40 minutes.

By not giving my obsessiveness an outlet in a training log, I have substantially reduced it. These days when a week reaches, say, 37 miles, I'm never tempted to run another 3 miles so that I can round up to 40. My mileage isn't important anymore. The only thing that's important is running healthy.

9. Skip running for at least one day a week. As I said, a zero in my training log used to kill me. Now, I make certain that I take at least one day off every week. Two-time U.S. Olympic marathoner Ed Eyestone never trains on Sunday because of church and family obligations and because his body needs a rest. So does mine.

Sundays are too precious for me to miss a run, but Fridays

aren't. It's the end of the week and the perfect day for me to do something else. Whether that means mountain biking, swimming, tennis, a hike, going to a high school meet, or pigging out with friends at lunch, it's my day to blow off running. This policy also ensures that I go into the weekend fresh for either a race or a long run.

10. Enjoy yourself. This is the easiest one. If it's not fun, what's the point? Sure, I want to stay healthy and fit. But if that's all I wanted, I'd probably ride an indoor exercycle every day. I can't do that because it's too boring and because I'm a runner.

It's true that I don't have any major training aspirations—no mileage goals, no pace goals, no race goals. Still, I run relatively hard once a week and also run long. But the "hard" runs are instinctive, rather than planned, and the "long" runs never last more than an hour.

Although I have had my share of injuries, I consider myself very lucky. I've developed a routine that keeps me healthy and allows me to enjoy my runs for what they are—a time to relax, to visit with friends, to work up a little sweat, to feel better after the run than I did before.

I guess that's where I'm particularly lucky. I'm one of those rare runners who never has a bad run. Some aren't quite as great as others, but if I'm healthy and running on a reasonably nice course, I almost never rate a run as anything less than very good. That's enough to keep me looking forward to the next run. And the one after that.

In 1996, Wish began to violate one of his cardinal principles: Throw out the training log. Wish, like many others, couldn't resist the pull of the 100th Boston Marathon. Without telling anyone, he decided that he'd like to run it.

Of course, you don't just run Boston. You have to qualify. And to qualify, you have to train hard, especially if you have been a "fun runner" like Wish for many years. Frankly, when I began to realize how hard Wish was training—he included 18- to 20-mile runs several times a month—I didn't think he would make it. I had known him too long, and he always broke down.

This time he didn't. He maintained the training and didn't get injured. Not only that, but he ran a strong 3:15 in the Philadelphia Marathon to qualify for Boston. How did he manage? Simple. Even after increasing his training mileage, he stuck to his 10 laws, and they pulled him through.

CHAPTER 14

SELF-TREAT YOUR AILMENTS

Here's a Low-Cost Insurance Plan for Your Running Problems

Many runners are lousy patients. They go to a doctor to get advice and then ignore it. Tell a runner to quit running for two to three weeks to rest an injury, and many will last just two to three days. After that, they figure that they can jog just a little to see how the injury feels. If it's okay, why not run a bit more tomorrow and more still the day after tomorrow?

Runners are too active to take the break they need. But here's a good alternative: Engage runners in their own therapy and recovery. That's an active role. Besides, runners are generally quite smart and quite analytical. They enjoy trying to understand an injury and trying out ways to help it heal.

That's the philosophy of this chapter: Help runners be their own doctors. This can't always work, obviously. A serious injury requires serious medical attention. But many running injuries aren't serious, and they can be cleared up better by the athlete who's finely attuned to his body than by anyone else. Runner, heal thyself.

Injuries happen. And when they do, you can call your doctor, make an appointment for sometime next week, and hope the problem doesn't worsen in the meantime. Or you can treat it yourself at home, immediately, with the help of this guide.

"With a home remedy, you can cure most problems in a week or less," says Warren A. Scott, M.D., chief of sports medicine at Kaiser Permanente Medical Center in Santa Clara, California. "Left untreated, an injury can hang on for several months or up to a year or more."

This guide covers everything from black toenails to exercise-induced asthma. And the remedies come from Dr. Scott and the medical experts who have worked with *Runner's World* magazine for many years.

Now, granted, not all injuries can be handled at home. If your symptoms are severe and your injury is at an advanced stage, or if self-treatment doesn't seem to be working, see a sports-oriented physician.

Of course, the best advice is not to get injured in the first place. You can help prevent injuries by following these smart training principles: Wear good running shoes that fit well and replace them before their midsole cushioning wears out; increase mileage by no more than 10 percent a week; follow hard training days with easy days or days off; stretch and strength-train regularly; and when something starts to hurt, back off or stop running until the pain is gone.

Asthma, exercise-induced: A contraction of the muscles surrounding the air passages, which narrows these passages and causes wheezing, shortness of breath, and heaviness in the chest. Cold temperatures, dry air, and high altitude aggravate the condition, which is suffered by 10 to 15 percent of the population.

Remedies: Before a run or race, warm up for about 10 minutes. Then start running hard, which may cause the asthmatic response, triggering the release of adrenaline, which then dilates the bronchial tubes. When you're able to, run hard for 5 minutes, then slow for 5 minutes; repeat several times, then walk. Stretch and walk a little more. Perform this routine 15 to 30 minutes before you race or run. The intensity of this warm-up results in a refractory period of 60 to 90 minutes during which you should be able to exercise without an asthma attack.

Since cold, dry air can trigger asthma attacks, wear a surgical mask (which you can purchase at a pharmacy or drugstore) or wrap a scarf over your mouth when running in cold weather. If you have allergies and notice more frequent asthma attacks during the spring and late summer, wearing a mask may help then as well. Always inhale through your nose. Also, beware of air pollution and remember that you will have more trouble breathing at high altitudes.

Anxiety can exacerbate an asthma attack. Some experts recommend 30-minute relaxation or meditation sessions several times a week to teach you to relax readily at times of stress.

If you can't run for long without an attack no matter what you do, try running at intervals of 3 to 5 minutes with 2 to 3 minutes' rest between. Eventually, you should build up some endurance and be able to run longer. The bottom line is that exercise is excellent for asthma.

Home remedies may not be enough. Consult a sports-oriented physician about taking one of several safe, effective asthma medications now available.

Athlete's foot: A fungal infection that causes itchy or painful scaling, redness, and blisters between the toes and on the soles of the feet.

Remedies: Apply a fungicide such as Desenex, Tinactin, Lotrimin, or Lamisil (the latter product is fairly new and has received good reviews from doctors for its fast action and effectiveness). Use these products two or three times a day for two to four weeks, and continue to use them for one to two weeks after symptoms are gone. The fungus remains even after the irritation disappears.

To relieve itching, apply an astringent solution, such as Domeboro, or soak your feet in baking soda mixed with water. Remove dead skin with a pumice stone or rub fine sandpaper along the bottoms of your feet and discard the sandpaper.

Athlete's foot fungus is ubiquitous and thrives in dark, moist places. You may get reinfected. If you do, alternate the fungicides you use so that the fungus does not build a tolerance to one brand.

Back pain: Pain or aching in the back, which may have any of several causes.

Remedies: Should you run with back pain? If running doesn't make it worse, go ahead. "Sitting puts more stress on your back than running does," says Dr. Scott. "In fact, exercise rather than rest is recommended for most patients with back problems." If running isn't comfortable, swim, go cycling, or try some other activity. Walking is excellent.

For pain relief, use ice (see "Three Cures" on page 94). But rather than wrap the ice against your back, place it on your bed and lie on it (you may have to bolster your back a bit with pillows if you're too uncomfortable). Some people favor a hot/cold regimen from the start. Alternate 20 minutes of ice with 20 minutes of heat.

Some back problems lie deep in the muscles, where icing won't have an effect. If pushing the site of the injury with your thumb does not cause pain, the injury probably lies too deep.

People with chronic back problems should do stretching and strengthening exercises regularly. Try back extensions, lower-back stretches, pelvic tilts, bent-leg crunches, and trunk twists. Warm up beforehand. When running, stick to soft surfaces and avoid hills, irregular surfaces, and small running tracks with tight turns. When you sleep, put a pillow between your knees when lying on your side; put two pillows under your knees when lying on your back.

If your back pain radiates into your legs or if rest and home treatments don't bring relief, see a sports-oriented physician.

Black toenails: A pooling of blood under the toenail, caused by the toe rubbing or hitting the top of your shoe. Often the toe will throb with the pressure of the blood.

Remedies: To relieve the pressure, you need to make a hole in the nail and drain the blood. Either heat the tip of a small, straightened paper clip and use it to burn through the nail until a drop of blood comes out or sterilize the tip of a ¹⁄₁₆-inch drill bit with heat or alcohol and drill a hole in the nail by spinning the instrument between your finger and thumb. Stick your foot in a pan of water until all the blood comes out. (If you're squeamish about doing this, see a sports-oriented physician.) Apply an antibacterial cream. Relieve inflammation with ice and anti-inflammatories.

If your black toenail isn't painful, you don't have to drain the blood. Lubricate with antifungal cream and cover it with a bandage. But monitor the nail, as it will probably loosen and fall off over the next few months. When it gets loose, carefully pull it off and continue to apply the antifungal cream. In the meantime, buy a pair of running shoes with more room in the toe box.

Blisters: Fluid accumulation between the skin's inner and outer layers because of excess friction.

Remedies: When possible, leave the blister alone for 24 hours to allow it to heal itself. If the fluid isn't reabsorbed, lance the blister as follows: Sterilize a needle by heating it in a flame or boiling water or by soaking it in alcohol. Swab the blister with a disinfectant such as alcohol. Prick two holes on opposite sides of the blister and press it gently with sterile gauze to push out the fluid. Don't remove the loose skin. Smear the blister with 1% hydrocortisone cream, such as Preparation H, and cover it with a sterile gauze pad. If the blister refills, lance again and then soak it in Epsom salts or an astringent solution, such as Domeboro. Before putting on shoes, make a doughnut shape out of molefoam and place it around the blister, then put another layer on top to cover the whole area.

For recurring blisters, eliminate the cause: Wear running shoes that are the right size and shape. Wear synthetic-blend socks. Before you run, apply petroleum jelly or talcum powder to reduce friction.

Calf strain: Pain in the calf, as well as swelling, tenderness, and muscle tightness, resulting from sudden overloading of the muscles during speedwork, hill running, or running on uneven trails.

Remedies: Treat with ice and anti-inflammatories. Wrap your calf with a 4-inch elastic bandage. It should be tight enough to provide relief but not so tight that it cuts off circulation. Wear this all day long and during running for a couple of days.

Stretch your calf 5 to 10 times a day. Try adding ¼-inch cork heel lifts to your shoes and be sure to wear street shoes with a heel height that reduces stress on the muscles; running shoes are often a good choice. Avoid walking barefoot.

People with recurring calf problems should look for shoes that are thicker in the rearfoot and have sturdy heel counters.

Calluses: Areas of thickened skin caused by repetitive friction (such as that of running in ill-fitting shoes) or by abnormalities of the bony structure of the foot. Usually painless, calluses are a natural protective reaction of the skin over pressure sites.

Remedies: When a callus first develops, file it with an emery board, sandpaper, or a pumice stone after bathing and apply petroleum jelly, lanolin, or other moisturizers to the skin. If a thicker callus has formed, use a peeling and softening agent such as Ultra Mide 25 lotion. Don't let calluses get too big; they can crack and become infected.

Very thick, painful calluses should be treated by a sports-oriented physician. To reduce friction when you run, wear thicker socks. Watch for blisters that may occur next to thick calluses and treat them as described earlier.

Flat feet: An inherited condition in which there is little or no arch to the bottom of the foot. (*Note:* Running cannot cause flat feet.)

Remedies: Flat feet in themselves are not a problem. Many runners with flat feet overpronate, however, and overpronation can cause problems in your feet, shins, and knees. If running is giving you aches and pains, first check your shoes—a motion-control shoe with a straight last is best. (The last is the shape the shoe is based upon. You can see this shape by turning a shoe upside down.) Over-the-counter arch supports or orthotics can provide additional support. If none of these help, see a sports-oriented physician for custom-made orthotics.

Hamstring pain: Pain in the muscles at the back of the thigh, occurring during sprinting or speedwork.

Remedies: Treat with ice and anti-inflammatories and stretch the hamstring several times a day. Wrap your thigh with a 6-inch elastic bandage. The muscle should be squeezed but comfortable.

Do leg curls to strengthen the hamstrings. When doing them, lift with one leg at a time so that a strong leg cannot compensate for a weaker one, and make sure that you feel the work just in the hamstring, not the buttocks and calf.

Heat exhaustion and heatstroke: These are similar problems, but they are not the same. Heat exhaustion refers to overheating of the body from excessive loss of water or, in rare cases, salt depletion. Symptoms include thirst, headache, pallor, dizziness, and possibly nausea or vomiting. In severe cases, your heart may race and you may feel disoriented.

Heatstroke occurs when the body's thermoregulatory system

stops working. Many of the symptoms are the same as for heat exhaustion. Cessation of sweating, difficulty walking, disorientation, and fainting or unconsciousness, however, indicate heatstroke. Runners suffering heatstroke will be too disoriented to help themselves. Learn to recognize the symptoms and treat the problem in someone else.

Remedies: For heat exhaustion, stop running and get out of the sun—preferably into an air-conditioned building. Drink water or, better still, a sports beverage, taking it slowly rather than gulping it down. If you don't feel better within 30 minutes, go to a hospital emergency room.

Heat exhaustion is not fatal, but heatstroke can be. The key symptom to look for is disorientation. A person who is functioning well mentally isn't in danger. Someone who's becoming "jelly brained" is in trouble. Pack ice around the runner's neck, armpits, and groin, splash water on the skin, and fan the runner. Elevate the legs. If the person is conscious, give plenty of fluids—1 to 2 quarts— preferably a sports beverage, but water is fine. The person will probably be nauseated and may not want to drink anything, but fluids are essential.

If you get heatstroke once, you may be likely to get it again. All runners should take care to dress appropriately for the heat. Wear synthetics, not cotton. Wear a light cap, sunglasses, and sunscreen (which actually helps cool your skin), and drink, drink, drink. Try to schedule your runs during the cooler hours of the day—morning or early evening.

Hypothermia: Low body temperature—96°F or lower—which can be fatal if left untreated. Symptoms include shivering, slow pulse, lethargy, and a decrease in alertness. In severe cases, muscles become rigid, and the victim can lose consciousness. Dehydration makes you more prone to hypothermia.

Remedies: Keep moving to generate heat. Get to a warm place, wrap yourself in blankets, and drink warm liquids. Snuggle up to the Saint Bernard for his body heat, but refuse the whiskey around his neck—alcoholic beverages do not warm you. In fact, they cause more heat loss and promote fluid loss.

Runners who are most at risk are those who run in rural areas and on trails. Run with a partner and dress appropriately—in layers, all synthetics. Cotton doesn't wick away your sweat, and wet skin loses 25 times more heat than dry skin. Wear a polypropylene hat and gloves. Carry a fanny pack and take along 1 to 2 quarts of a sports beverage.

Leg-length discrepancy: A difference in the length of the legs.

This alters the alignment of the spine and makes it more vulnerable to the shock forces generated by running. A leg-length discrepancy isn't painful in itself, but it can cause other problems and injuries. If you experience regular bouts of iliotibial band syndrome or have sciatica-like pain that radiates from your buttocks down into your legs, you may have a leg-length discrepancy.

Remedies: Here's a home test for determining if you have a leg-length discrepancy: In your underwear, stand with good posture in front of a full-length mirror. Look to see if your shoulders are level (if you have played a lot of throwing sports, your dominant shoulder will hang lower and may not be an indication of leg-length discrepancy). Look at your pelvis, then let your body sag and look again. Put your fingers on the bony areas at the front of the hip and look to see if they are level. If they're not, place magazines under the foot of the shorter leg, building up until both sides are even.

If the difference amounts to more than ½ inch and you have suffered from foot, ankle, knee, thigh, hip, or back pain, see a sports-

Three Cures

Ice, anti-inflammatories, and stretching are common treatments for many running injuries. Here are the best ways to implement them.

How to Ice an Injury

Cover the skin with two layers of plastic wrap. Put ice on top and compress with an elastic bandage or tight-fitting clothing such as spandex or Lycra. Ice for 20 minutes, stop for 10 minutes. Ice again for 20 minutes, stop for 10. Ice for 20, stop for 10. "If you can do this three times a day for three days in a row, you'll get a tremendous anti-inflammatory effect," says Warren A. Scott, M.D., chief of sports medicine at Kaiser Permanente Medical Center in Santa Clara, California. If you don't have the time for this regimen, do what you can. Crushed ice, 1- to 2-pound bags of frozen peas, and gel packs work well.

"Heat does not have the anti-inflammatory effect that ice does," says Dr. Scott, "but hot tubs and heating pads can be very relaxing to your muscles and your mind. Go ahead and use them if you want." Rubs and balms applied to the skin have no healing effect. They create a mild stinging sensation in the skin to trick the brain and distract you from your pain, Dr. Scott adds.

oriented physician. If the difference is about ¼ inch, try a ¼-inch cork heel lift in all your shoes and see if this relieves the problem.

Muscle soreness or delayed-onset muscle soreness: Muscle pain and inflammation following a race, speedwork, downhill running, or other hard workouts.

Remedies: At the end of a hard run, race, or marathon, walk rather than stop completely. Then cool your legs off with cold water poured over the entire leg. Take anti-inflammatories, stretch often, and, if possible, get a massage. After a marathon, take three days off from running and go cycling instead. Pick up running again on the fourth day if you want.

To help prevent muscle soreness, add some downhill running to your training, every two to three weeks, especially when you're preparing for a downhill race. Your quadriceps will thank you.

Overpronation: Excessive inward roll of the foot after landing, such that the foot continues to roll when it should be pushing off. This twists the foot, shin, and knee and can cause pain in all those

How to Use Anti-inflammatory Medicines

Inflammation, common in running injuries, is characterized by pain, swelling, redness, and warmth and is treated with anti-inflammatory medications. Ibuprofen and naproxen sodium are the best, but aspirin is okay, too.

Follow the instructions on the bottle and take these medicines for one to two weeks. Always take them with food.

If you have chronic aches and pains that you can't get rid of, such as those associated with osteoarthritis, and you've been to the doctor to have them checked out, use acetaminophen to relieve pain. It's very safe and works well.

A Few Words on Stretching

When stretching, make sure that you feel the tension in the muscle you are stretching, which isn't necessarily the site of the injury. Do not bounce. Hold the stretch until you feel the muscles relax, usually between 15 and 30 seconds.

It's best to stretch warm muscles, but it's okay to stretch gently when you haven't warmed up. Where stretching is indicated as part of the treatment for an injury, it's a good idea to stretch several times a day.

areas. If you are an overpronator, you'll find excessive wear on the inner side of your running shoes, and they'll tilt inward if you place them on a flat surface. Flat feet contribute to overpronation.

Remedies: Wear shoes with straight or semicurved lasts. Motion-control or stability shoes with firm, multidensity midsoles and external control features that limit pronation are best. Over-the-counter orthotics or arch supports can help, too. You know you are making improvements when the wear pattern on your shoes becomes more normal. Overpronation causes extra stress on and tightness in the muscles, so do a little extra stretching.

Overtraining: Fatigue, stale training, poor race performance, irritability, and loss of enthusiasm for running, caused by excessive mileage or too many hard workouts. Serious overtraining can cause sleep disturbances, hampered immune function, poor appetite, and in women, the cessation of menstrual periods.

Remedies: Cut back on your running for a minimum of two weeks. Experiment with cutting back on mileage, adding rest days, and substituting cross-training to see what works best.

If you suspect serious overtraining, cut your running back to only two or three days a week, 30 to 45 minutes at an easy-to-moderate effort. You can supplement this with more stretching and some cross-training on other days of the week, but no more than an hour at an easy-to-moderate effort.

When you're feeling better and you're ready to increase your running, look at your training over a year and plan periods when you'll train hard and race; follow these with periods of easier running and lower mileage.

Runner's knee: Pain all around and under the kneecap, and stiffness of the knee joint. In severe cases, flexing the knee may produce a painful grinding sensation. Runner's knee results from running too much or too hard, too soon.

Remedies: Poke around the knee. If you find a sore spot, ice it; if you don't, ice won't help. Take anti-inflammatories. If the knee swells, ice it and see a sports-oriented physician. Swelling indicates a major problem, and it may take three to four months for the knee to heal.

Runner's knee can occur when hamstrings are tight, when quadriceps are much stronger than hamstrings, or, in the case of new runners, when quadriceps are weak. All runners should stretch and strengthen their quadriceps and hamstrings regularly.

If you can run through this injury, avoid downhills; flat running and uphills are easier. Wear shoes with adequate sole padding and good motion-control properties. Consider wearing a rubber sleeve with a hole that fits over the kneecap to reduce pain caused by too much flexing.

Sciatica: Sciatica is a pain in the butt, literally. Caused by an irritation of the sciatic nerve, this pain can radiate down the back of the leg and all the way to the foot. It feels like burning, pins and needles, or an electrical sensation. It has many causes, including tight hamstrings, tight buttocks, biomechanical problems, leg-length discrepancy, back sprain, or a herniated disk.

Remedies: Do not ice, but do take anti-inflammatories. Lots of muscles will get tight—stretch the back, buttocks, hamstrings, iliotibial band, gluteal muscles, and calves. Consider cross-training, and when the pain diminishes, try a walk/run. Sitting can aggravate sciatica. Make sure that your sitting posture is good (especially in the car) and use pillows, if needed, to adjust your back and buttocks into a more comfortable position.

Sciatica is secondary to an underlying problem. A leg-length discrepancy is often the culprit. If home treatments don't relieve the pain or if your condition gets worse, see a sports-oriented doctor. (*Note:* Don't ignore sciatica pain. It will follow you to your grave if you don't deal with it.)

Side stitches: A sharp pain usually felt just below the rib cage (though sometimes farther up the torso), caused by a cramp in the

To Run or Not to Run

Should you run with an injury? "It's okay as long as you run at a level below the threshold of pain," says Warren A. Scott, M.D., chief of sports medicine at Kaiser Permanente Medical Center in Santa Clara, California. When an injury occurs, cut back your mileage and intensity until you can run without pain (but don't ever take medications or ice an injury before testing whether or not you can run). If it hurts no matter what, stop running and cross-train. Walking, cycling, swimming, pool running, rowing, stair climbing, and cross-country skiing all work with most running injuries.

If you need to stop running, take a week off and then try a walk/run. If that feels okay, you can begin to return to running. If it doesn't feel good, take another week off and test your legs again. Always reintroduce yourself to running through a walk/run regimen that eventually progresses to regular, steady running.

diaphragm, gas in the intestines, or food in the stomach. Stitches normally come on during hard workouts or races.

Remedies: If you get a stitch on your right side (which is more common), slow down for 30 seconds or so and exhale forcefully each time your left foot hits the ground. If the stitch is on the left, exhale hard when your right foot lands. Continue until the pain recedes. If this doesn't help, try slow, deep "belly breathing" (your abdomen should go in and out with each breath). Or run with your hands on top of your head and your elbows back while you breathe deeply from your belly.

Another remedy is to take your fist and dig it under your rib cage. Push the fist in with your other arm and bend your torso over almost to 90 degrees. Run like this for 10 steps. This stretches the diaphragm (most stitches are caused by a spasm of the diaphragm). If none of these techniques work, stop and walk until the pain subsides.

And here's a no-brainer: To prevent stitches caused by food in the stomach, don't eat before you run.

Supination (or underpronation): Insufficient inward roll of the foot after landing. This places extra stress on the foot and can result in iliotibial band syndrome and Achilles tendinitis.

Runners with high arches and tight Achilles tendons tend to be supinators. Shoes will wear on the entire outside edge, and the side of the shoe becomes overstretched. If you place shoes on a flat surface, they tilt outward.

Remedies: Wear shoes with curved lasts to allow pronation. Lightweight trainers are often best, as they allow more foot motion. Also, check for flexibility on the inner side of the shoe. Supinators should do extra stretching for the calves, hamstrings, quadriceps, and iliotibial band.

The hardest lesson that I had to learn as a runner was the importance of rest—total rest—when recovering from an injury. On more occasions than I'd like to admit, I prolonged my injury problems by failing to let them heal completely before running again.

One year, having developed a stress fracture in my foot, I went to a doctor who said I was fine—I just needed to take six weeks off from running. I took two days off, but then started running again. Just a little at first, and then a little more, and then a little more. After three weeks I was almost back to my usual training program. Until I took a hard run one day and fractured the foot bone all over again.

The result, of course, was that I lost three months of training instead of six weeks. I've made similar, less serious mistakes with injuries, and I have known hundreds of other runners who have done the same. Now I am wiser (I hope), and I see things more clearly.

I know the truth about injuries: Rest cures them. Usually in remarkably little time. When you have a nagging ache or pain, take a couple of days off. If it doesn't get better right away, take a week off, two weeks if you need to. It seems like a lot of time when you're not running, but it's nothing compared to the amount of time you'll lose if you're chronically injured.

So get healthy first. Totally healthy. Then ease your way back into running.

4

WOMEN'S
RUNNING

CHAPTER 15

ADVICE THAT COULD SAVE YOUR LIFE

Being Aware Is Only Part of Running Safely

The safety question is the most troubling issue that women runners face. On the one hand, simply raising it restricts women runners. Instead of thinking of their workouts as a time of freedom and release when they can expand their horizons, they see limitations—the kind of shackles that women have long had to fight against. On the other hand, not to consider the safety question is sheer insanity.

At Runner's World *magazine, we encourage women to run by pointing out all the positive things about running. And we do this often and easily. After all, our women readers are constantly telling us about the many benefits that they have received. We get testimonials in the mail nearly every day.*

But we can't stop there. Women have also been attacked, raped, and murdered while running. Writers and editors can't stop violence against women, but we can tell women how to be vigilant and how to protect themselves. That's the purpose of this chapter: to inform women runners while still liberating them.

Every 17 seconds someone becomes a victim of violent crime. Every minute in America, 1.3 adult women are raped. If you think that your runner's speed and fitness will protect you against assault, you are giving someone out there a huge opportunity to hurt you. To protect yourself, you must first get rid of that it-could-never-happen-to-me attitude, and then take the precautions that are necessary to protect yourself from violent crime.

To find out how you can run safely, J. J. Bittenbinder, formerly with the Chicago Police Department, now an inspector and lecturer assigned to the Cook County Sheriff's Department in Illinois, offers some tips. After more than two decades of working with more than a thousand offenders, witnesses, and victims of violent street crime, Bittenbinder has seen it all. And he has come up with some tough strategies to keep you safe on the streets. Indeed, what he has to say could save your life.

Q: **Do women runners need to be constantly aware that they are potential victims?**

A: I'd hate for women to run scared every step of the way. You have to realize that bad stuff can happen to anybody, anyplace, anytime. But if you have a plan of action, you won't have to concentrate on the fear. Every bad guy is different, but you have to be trained to do certain things and use certain skills if a bad situation comes up. Then your attitude changes—instead of being afraid, you say to yourself, "This stuff can happen, but I know how to prevent it." You'll be more self-assured, and believe me, that comes through in how you look and behave toward potential bad guys.

Q: **Is there anything that a woman can carry with her while she's running that she can use if someone threatens her?**

A: Yes. You can try a self-defense spray, such as pepper spray, or a personal alarm. And not only will these things help you get out of a threatening situation, but just carrying them will make you feel tougher. And if you feel tough, you'll look tough. And the bad guys will be more likely to leave you alone.

Q: **How harmful are they?**

A: Self-defense sprays cause enough pain in an attacker's eyes to stop that person instantly, but they won't cause permanent blindness. I recommend the varieties that contain a mix of ultraviolet dye, tear gas, and pepper juice. They act immediately.

Q: **How do you use a spray, and is there any danger of it going off accidentally while you run?**

A: No, it won't go off accidentally. Carry it in your hand or clip it on your waistband. It weighs only a few ounces, so you won't be bothered by it. I recommend that women carry it so that others can see it. Like an animal baring its teeth, you are displaying your weapon of aggression. To use, pump it like you would any other spray.

But before you go out on your next run with a product like this, I recommend that you test it at home. Spray a small amount on a paper napkin, dab your finger in it, and rub it lightly an inch or so below your eye—don't rub it in your eye. If it's effective, you should feel a slight burning. Then, take the spray out in your backyard to see how far it squirts. If it goes 10 feet, then you know to use it when somebody comes within that distance. And if somebody should come up at you from behind, squirt it over your shoulder.

Q: **Where can you purchase sprays and alarms?**

A: Sporting goods stores should carry them. Many are available through mail order.

Q: **Should runners carry money or identification?**

A: Carry some coins in case you want to run to a phone booth and call for help. And sure, carrying identification is a good idea.

Q: **Running clothing has evolved from heavy, baggy sweatpants and sweatshirts to light, form-fitting tights and tops. Could wearing these clothes invite the wrong kind of attention?**

A: You have the right to wear whatever you want. But if two women are running side by side, with one wearing baggy sweats and the other flashy skin-fitting tights, for example, the woman who is wearing less will not feel as confident because she is revealing more of her body. She may look away when people approach. Or she may look down at her feet—a sign that the bad guys look for when they are evaluating how vulnerable someone is.

If you want to wear sexier clothes, it's up to you to be alert to what's going on around you. You will attract attention—some good and bad—so you have to look tough to discourage the attention that you don't want. By the way, I have a T-shirt with Northside Homicide on the front—I guarantee you, with a T-shirt like that, no one is going to mess with you.

Q: **We tell runners not to wear headphones. Do you agree?**

A: Get rid of them. I don't like those things. They're like wearing sunglasses in the dark. I realize lots of people love them. In fact, I've had women come up to me and say, "But I feel so confident when I'm listening to my own music." Well, that's because you are blocking out reality. You are in never-never land. When you wear those things, you may not have that extra 3- to 4-yard head start to break away, and that could be the difference between making it or not—all because you couldn't hear the bad guy approaching.

Q: **What time of day should women run?**

A: Early-morning hours are the best because the bad guys are still in bed. We get a lot of reports of sexual assaults in the early evening, around 6:00.

Q: **Where should women run? Are country roads safer than city streets?**

A: The boonies are not the place to be. If the bad guy looks both ways on a country road and it's empty, he knows there will be nobody to interrupt him. But a deserted city street doesn't make things as easy—there could always be somebody looking out a window or driving around a corner. Run where there are people and activities around you.

And vary your routes and the exact time you exercise so that someone who notices you won't be able to track your whereabouts by the minute.

Q: **What if a stranger is approaching a woman—should she ignore him or acknowledge him?**

A: When a man and woman approach each other, there comes a point when the woman looks away. And the reason she looks away is because, if she doesn't, she may encourage a comment from this guy that she doesn't especially want to hear. So she looks away—most often down.

But that's like saying, "I'm weak," or "I don't want to be here." I suggest that you wave your eyes across him one time, but don't look down when you are done. Look to the other side or over his head. Remember, it's the one who looks the toughest who won't get picked as a victim. Meeting someone's gaze adds to a strong self-image, which is exactly what you want to project.

Q: **Do you advise that women run with dogs?**

A: Yes. A dog is an unknown thing to a bad guy. He doesn't know what the dog is capable of, and he doesn't know about the intensity of the bond between dog and master. Just don't call your dog Muffin or something like that when a suspicious character is around. I like Fang or Bandit a lot better.

Q: **Is there a profile of a bad guy?**

A: No. Because they look like you and me and your father and uncles and brothers and neighbors. Because that's who they are. Don't assume that a guy dressed like a runner won't pose a threat, either.

Q: **So what do you do if a runner comes up alongside you and begins running with you?**

A: It's all right to talk to him and run with him, if you want. Just don't leave your regular running route. If he suggests going somewhere else, refuse. On the other hand, if you feel scared right away because this guy is staring at your chest or making crude remarks, you say, "Don't talk like that. Leave me alone." If he moves too close, use your spray or personal alarm.

Q: **What if you are being followed—should you confront the person and say, "Are you following me?"**

A: No. Don't ask questions. If you are suspicious, forget your normal route and take off for an area where there is more traffic or people. Never, ever ignore your instincts. When you feel the hair rise on the back of your neck, that's a few million year's worth of evolution at work. Don't ignore it—ever.

Q: **What if somebody is trailing you in a car or stops to ask directions?**

A: If anybody ever stops to ask, "Do you know . . . ?" or "Have you got . . . ?" or "Can you spare . . . ?" just say, "No." Don't enter into a conversation. If he keeps it up, you should yell "No" again and "Leave me alone. Get out of here." And believe me, you will be inspired to run away, even if you are at the end of your workout.

Q: **What if someone grabs you? What can you do?**

A: Flee if you can, but use the spray if you can't get away. If for some reason you have dropped it and he is trying to grab you, you have to use your legs to fight off the attack. Women don't have the upper-body strength necessary to keep a man's body off them. But you—especially runners—have the strength in your legs. If you get knocked down, start kicking hard.

Meanwhile, yell, but don't yell for help. Too many people tune that out. You have to yell, "Fire! Fire! Fire!" And keep on kicking, yelling, and using the spray or the alarm if you're able to. Don't ever get on your knees during this struggle because he could get you in a choke hold, and then it's all over.

Q: **Let's make the scenario more threatening. What if the bad guy is trying to force you into his car, and he has a gun? How should you react?**

A: First of all, remember this: You must never get into a car. When you do, it's over. Ted Bundy picked up his victims in a car; Dahmer used a car; Gacy used a car. They all used cars. And all those women whose bodies were found in forest reserves— they weren't out there hiking in the woods when they were attacked. They were brought there in a car.

You must resist quickly. You must run away. If he gets a hold of your jacket or shirt, you rip it off or pull it over your head and break away. Remember: The first few seconds of contact between a victim and offender are crucial—the offender has the least amount of control at that time because he's not sure how you are going to react. The more time you spend with him, the more he's got control.

Q: **But what about the gun—won't you risk being shot?**

A: So what? It's better than getting in the car. Believe me, if you get in the car, you're dead. Just run. Let's look at the chances of your getting shot and killed. If you break and run, you'll have a 50 percent chance of being hit. And if you're hit, you'll have another 50 percent chance of being seriously wounded and then another 50 percent chance of being killed. Well, that's only a 12.5 percent chance of being killed. Pretty good odds compared to the car. And furthermore, the Department of Justice reports that the real figure is less than 5 percent.

Q: **Have you ever interviewed a runner who was attacked?**

A: No. But recently, a Chicago woman who was running on the lakefront at dusk was attacked. Two young guys slashed her. They weren't trying to rob her because she had no money with her. They wanted to rape her, but she resisted, and they ran away. A cab driver passing by saw her lying on the ground and took her to the hospital. She survived because she fought back.

Q: **Unfortunately, rapes occur. What does the victim need to know about reporting the crime?**

A: The first thing you'll want to do is go to the hospital. And I realize that this may be extremely difficult, but you must not bathe or clean yourself in any way. I know it's the first thing a woman instinctively believes she must do, but the fluids retrieved during the physical exam are what enable police to positively identify the offender through DNA analysis. And he will go to jail.

Q: **How would you describe the woman runner who presents herself as a tough target?**

A: She looks self-assured. Her head is up, and she looks straight ahead instead of down at her feet. She doesn't wear headphones. She carries a spray or alarm in her hand to help her fight off an attack, and she pays attention to everybody and everything, even cars that are traveling around her. If she hears somebody come up from behind, she makes a point of turning around to look at who it is. And if she is the least bit suspicious, she makes sure that the guy sees the spray or alarm in her hand so that he knows she could make things difficult for him.

In addition to following the good advice in the preceding pages, women runners can do one more simple thing: They can run with a group. There's strength in numbers, after all, not to mention it's a lot of fun.

All across the country, small (and sometimes large) groups of women get together for regularly scheduled runs. They meet in the early morning before daybreak and in the evening after the sun has set. They run together because it adds to their motivation (it's hard to skip a workout if others are waiting for you), because it becomes a social time, because it's easier to train hard with teammates and for dozens of other reasons unique to every group. Often, safety is the least of their concerns but an important payoff nonetheless.

If you can't find a women's running group, look to run with a male friend. It only takes one, and many women can run as fast as the guys, so it's no problem keeping up. If you can't keep up with the fast guys, then run with them on their easy days when they run slowly. Check for running partners at work, with your running club, or in the neighborhood. If you have just one or two days a week when you have to run in the dark or in an area where you don't feel secure, you may be able to schedule escorted runs on those days.

A final (and regrettable) word about trail running. As trail running becomes more and more popular, increasing numbers of women find themselves drawn to it. And why not? It's hard to beat a relaxed run in a scenic, natural environment. Unfortunately, trail running raises a number of safety concerns, so don't go it alone. Get together with a friend or friends to enjoy trail running as a group activity.

CHAPTER 16

A WOMAN'S ENCYCLOPEDIA OF RUNNING

You'll Be a Better Runner with This Primer

The Runner's World *editors have spent years discussing and debating the differences between men and women. No, we're not dense. We've simply been trying to figure out the most intelligent way to write about women's running.*

When women first began running in sizable numbers in the mid-1970s, we searched for the obvious topics: pregnancy, menstrual periods, running bras, and so forth. In our rush to provide women-specific stories, we concentrated too much on the physical differences between men and women. We ignored all the ways women runners might be like men runners and focused instead on the ways they were different.

Convinced later that we had stereotyped women in this manner, we plunged headlong in the opposite direction in the 1980s. We even dropped our monthly "Women's Running" column from the magazine. Women didn't need special treatment, we decided. They could learn everything they needed to know about running by reading the same articles as our male readers.

In the 1990s, we changed course again. This time I hope we have things right. While we acknowledge the many similarities between men's and women's running, we also see differences. Differences that are not just physiological but also social and emotional. This chapter examines many of the key issues for women runners.

Knowledge is power—in running as in any other pursuit. The more you know about training, nutrition, and health, the better you'll be at getting the most from your running, whether that means fitness, weight loss, great race performances, or just plain fun. Below, you'll find lots of useful information from experts around the country to help you reach your goals.

Some of these facts and tips apply to all runners, but many address the specific needs of women. You may find things that you already know, but you're bound to discover many new ideas that can help you become the runner you want to be.

1. Running is a state of mind. The only thing that determines your success, or lack of success, is the way you think about your running. If it works for you—if it relieves stress, burns calories, gives you time to yourself, enhances your self-esteem—then it doesn't matter what any other person or any stopwatch says about your running.

2. Exploring your competitive side offers benefits beyond running. Racing helps you tap into your goal-setting, assertive, and self-disciplined side. Channeled correctly, these attributes can boost your success in other parts of your life—such as in the workplace.

3. You don't have to be the competitive type to enter a race every now and then. You'll find that lots of other racers aren't overly competitive, either. They're out there because it's fun and social and it motivates them to keep on running.

4. A woman runner should consider herself an athlete, whether she's fast or slow, tall or short, small or large.

5. In the United States, heart disease kills 10 times more women than breast cancer does each year. One of the best weapons for fighting heart disease is exercise. Exercise lowers your blood pressure and resting heart rate, raises your good high-density lipoprotein (HDL) cholesterol levels, and helps you maintain a healthy weight.

6. A survey of thousands of U.S. women found that while 44 percent of the respondents actually were overweight, fully 73 percent *thought* they were. So, women who run for weight control, like all women, may lose perspective on what is an appropriate body size.

7. Trying to lose fat by eating less and running more and more doesn't work. The more you exercise and the less you eat, the more likely your body is to hibernate. That is, you'll conserve calories and thwart your efforts to lose fat. The better bet is to exercise reasonably and to increase your food intake early in the day to fuel your training. Eat breakfast, lunch, and an afternoon snack. Then eat lightly for dinner and afterward.

8. The two minerals that women runners need to pay the most attention to are calcium and iron. (Iron is especially important

for menstruating women.) Your Daily Value for calcium is 1,000 milligrams; good sources are dairy products, dark green leafy vegetables, broccoli, canned sardines, and salmon. Your Daily Value for iron is 18 milligrams; foods high in iron include liver, fortified dry cereals, beef, and spinach.

Note: Women runners who train intensively, have been pregnant in the past two years, or consume fewer than 2,500 calories a day should get a more comprehensive blood test than the routine one for iron status, since these test only for anemia, the final stage of iron deficiency. Instead, request more revealing tests, including those for serum ferritin, transferrin saturation, and total iron-building capacity.

9. Taking antioxidant supplements may substantially reduce muscle damage and inflammation. A research study that measured levels of malondialdehyde (a barometer of muscle tissue oxidation) in 25 women before and after 30 minutes on the treadmill found that postexercise levels increased by 32 percent in women who did not take antioxidants, but decreased by 28 percent in those who had taken 400 international units of vitamin E daily for three months.

10. For female runners, controlled anaerobic training—intervals, hill repeats—may lead to gains in strength and speed similar to those produced by steroids but without the noxious side effects. Why? High-intensity anaerobic running is one of the most potent stimulators of natural human growth hormones—those that contribute to stronger muscles and, ultimately, enhanced performance.

11. Fast running burns more calories, but slow running burns more calories than just about any other activity. In short, nothing will help you lose weight and keep it off the way running does. Besides, it's inexpensive, it's accessible, and, if necessary, it can be done while pushing a stroller.

12. Speedwork allows you to explore the boundaries of your ability and can add an exciting element to your regular running. Though you may have taken up running just for fitness, after a while it can be fun to see just how fast you can go.

   Start with short "pickups" (bursts of speed) sprinkled throughout a regular run and move up to formal, once-a-week interval sessions on a track (for example, running four to six fast 400s with 200-meter recovery jogs in between). You'll be delighted with the results.

13. One of the smartest things that a woman runner can do is to include strength training in her weekly regimen. Lifting weights can help prevent injuries by correcting the muscle imbalances caused by running. It has also been proven to enhance bone health and elevate moods.

14. We all have our strengths and weaknesses. One important study of running injuries shows that women are much more likely than men to suffer ankle sprains, shinsplints, stress fractures, and hip problems. (Yet women are much less susceptible to Achilles tendinitis, plantar fasciitis, and quadriceps injuries.) To help you avoid injuries, make cross-training—such as pool running, bicycling, and weight lifting—part of your program.

15. Just because you're married and have young children and a job doesn't mean that you don't have time to run. Running is time-efficient and the best stress reducer on the market. You need this time. Taking it for yourself (by, say, letting your husband babysit while you run) will benefit the whole family.

16. Morning is the best time for women to run, for lots of reasons. One, it's the safest time; statistics show that women are more likely to be attacked late in the day. Two, studies have shown that morning exercisers are more likely to stick with it, because what you do first thing in the day gets done—not so with "maybe later on." Three, it saves you a round of dressing, undressing, and showering at lunchtime or later. Four, it gives you a feeling of accomplishment, which is a great mental and physical start for the day.

17. Running with headphones outdoors is a safety hazard in more ways than one. You won't be able to hear cars, cyclists, or someone approaching who intends to do you harm. Attackers will always pick a victim who looks vulnerable. When you have headphones on, that means you.

18. Women who run alone should take precautions: Leave a note at home stating when you left, where you'll be running, and when you expect to return.

Carry a personal alarm or self-defense spray. Stick to well-populated areas and don't always run the same predictable route. Avoid running at night. Don't wear jewelry or headphones. Pay attention to your surroundings. Carry identification but include only your name and an emergency phone number.

19. Running with another woman or with a group of women on a regular basis will help keep you motivated and ensure your safety. Plus, it's a lot more fun than running alone. Women runners become more than training partners; they're confidantes and counselors, too.

20. Like women, men are a good source of many things running, from camaraderie to information to safety to inspiration. Running is the perfect melting-pot sport for the sexes. Of course, if you beat your men friends in a race, they may not want to train with you anymore.

21. Running with a dog provides the best of both worlds—you get to run alone but with a friend. A dog is both a faithful companion who will go anywhere, anytime, and a loyal guardian who will discourage anyone from harming you. The optimal running dog is medium-size with a bloodline bred for endurance. An easy rule of thumb: Hunting breeds make the best runners.

22. It may not be much consolation, but men are sometimes verbally harassed and occasionally threatened on the run, just as women are. Run smart, but don't let insignificant taunting limit your freedom.

23. A run is a wonderful first date. It's relaxed and casual, yet you get a chance to show off your body, your stamina, and your style. It can mean as much or as little as you and your date wish it to mean. Conversation is rarely a problem, thanks to all those mood-lifting endorphins. If things go well, you can move on to a postrun meal. If they don't, you can always say that you have to go home to wash your hair.

24. Statistically, women run approximately 10 percent slower than men at all distances (based on the average difference between men's and women's world records). And although a University of California analysis showed that elite women have been improving twice as fast as elite men over the past three decades (14 meters a minute per decade versus 7 for men), women are not going to catch up with men.

The improvement can be traced to, among other things, dramatic increases in the number of women competing, opportunities to compete, and better coaching. Of course, certain individual women can far outpace most men. Ingrid Kristiansen's marathon world record of 2:21:06 is faster than what 99.9 percent of the world's men are capable of achieving.

25. While no one has ever proven the old theory that women are better marathoners than men (because they have more body fat to burn), you never hear anyone argue the opposite. Men tend to use their strength to push ahead in short races, but this can backfire in the marathon. Women seem perfectly content to find a comfort zone and stay there. This makes them ideally suited for the marathon—the ultimate keep-your-cool and keep-your-pace distance. So set your sights on a marathon.

26. Women sweat less than men. Contrary to popular belief, however, women dissipate heat as well as men. The reason is that women are smaller and have a higher body-surface-to-volume ratio, which means that although their vaporative cooling is less efficient, they need less of it to achieve the same result. Nonetheless, drink plenty of water (until your urine runs clear) to offset the effects of sweating and prevent dehydration.

27. Women generally have narrower feet than men, so when you're buying running shoes, your best bet will probably be a pair designed especially for women. But everybody's different; if your feet are wide, you may actually feel more comfortable in shoes designed for men. The bottom line is to buy the shoe that fits your feet. If there is any question—or if you suffer blisters or injuries because of ill-fitting shoes—consult a podiatrist who specializes in treating runners.

28. No matter what your breast size, it's a good idea to wear a sports bra when you run. By controlling breast motion, a sports bra will make you feel more comfortable. Look for one that stretches horizontally but not vertically. And, most important, try it on before you buy. A sports bra should fit snugly, yet not feel too constrictive. Run or jump in place to see if it gives you the support you need.

29. Running doesn't make your breasts sag or make your uterus collapse. These old myths resurface from time to time. In fact, running tightens and firms all the muscles it uses, so it will help prevent sagging rather than cause it. There are no recorded cases of running resulting in a fallen uterus (or any other organ, for that matter). Where this idea got started is a mystery.

30. A Harvard University study found that running women produce a less potent form of estrogen than their sedentary counterparts. As a result, women runners cut by half their risks of developing breast and uterine cancer and by two-thirds their risk of contracting the form of diabetes that most commonly plagues women.

31. Running can help produce healthy skin. According to dermatologists, running stimulates circulation, transports nutrients, and

flushes out waste products. All of this leads to a reduction in subcutaneous fat, which will make your skin clearer and your facial features more distinct.

Women to Remember

Women runners should know about the history of their sport. Here are the 10 most significant dates in women's distance running. Study them. Quiz your training partners. Quiz the guys. They should know these things, too.

April 19, 1967: Kathrine Switzer runs "men-only" Boston Marathon, and Jock Semple tries to rip her number off. The resulting photo puts women's running on the map.

June 2, 1972: The first women-only road race, the Crazy Legs 10-K, is held in New York City's Central Park. (It later becomes the L'eggs Mini Marathon, now sponsored by Advil.)

October 22, 1978: Grete Waitz wins her first of nine New York City Marathons in a world record 2:32:30.

August 5, 1984: In Los Angeles, Joan Benoit Samuelson wins the first women's Olympic Marathon.

April 21, 1985: Ingrid Kristiansen sets the women's world record in the marathon, running 2:21:06 in London.

November 1, 1987: At age 42, Priscilla Welch wins the women's race at the New York City Marathon.

September 17, 1989: Ann Trason wins outright the USA 24-Hour Championships in Queens, New York. She outdistances the second-place (male) finisher by 3½ miles.

March 21, 1992: Lynn Jennings wins her third-straight World Cross-Country Championships in Boston.

September 8–12, 1993: Chinese women rewrite the distance-running record books, setting world records for 1500 meters, 3000 meters, and 10,000 meters.

July 18, 1994: Yekaterina Podkopayeva, 42, becomes the first masters woman to break 4 minutes for 1500 meters with a 3:59.78 in Nice, France.

32. "That time of the month" (or even the few days preceding it) is not the time when women run their worst. The hardest time for women to run fast is about a week before menstruation begins (a week after ovulation). That's when women's levels of the key hormone progesterone peak, inducing a much-higher-than-normal breathing rate during exercise. The excess ventilation tends to make running feel more difficult than usual.

33. There's no need to pass up a run or a race just because you're having your period. If you're suffering from cramps, running will often alleviate the pain, because of the release during exercise of pain-relieving chemicals called endorphins. Speedwork or a hill session can be especially effective, according to researcher Jody Weitzman of Women's Health and Support Services in Maryland. To guard against leakage, try using two tampons (side by side) for extra protection. Just be sure to remove them after your run.

34. If you run so much that your periods become light or nonexistent, you may be endangering your bones. Amenorrhea (lack of a monthly period) means that little or no estrogen is circulating in your body. Estrogen is essential for the replacement of bone minerals. Amenorrheic women can stop—but not reverse the damage—by taking estrogen and getting plenty of calcium. Any woman with infrequent periods or no periods should consult her gynecologist, preferably one sensitive to the needs of runners.

35. Medical wisdom upholds that moderate exercise during a *normal* pregnancy is completely safe for the baby. The most important precaution: Avoid getting overheated (a core body temperature above 101°F could increase the risk of birth defects). To make sure that you're staying cool enough, early in your pregnancy take your temperature rectally immediately after a run. As long as your temperature is below 101°F, you can maintain that same level of effort throughout your pregnancy. If you increase your intensity or duration, check your temperature again. Also, skip the postrun hot tub.

36. If you were a regular runner before you became pregnant, you might have a bigger baby—good news, since larger infants tend to be stronger and weather physical adversity better. Researchers at Columbia University in New York City found that women who burned up to 1,000 calories a week through exercise gave birth to infants weighing 5 percent more than offspring of inactive moms. Those who burned 2,000 calories per week delivered babies weighing 10 percent more.

37. If you ran early in your pregnancy, you might want to try switching to a lower-impact exercise during the latter stages and after delivery. Because of the release of the hormone relaxin during pregnancy, some ligaments and tendons might soften, making you more vulnerable to injury. Walking, swimming, stationary bicycling, and pool running (you'll be even more buoyant than usual) are good choices.

38. Phooey! If your nursing baby gags and spits your breast milk back at you, it may be because babies dislike the taste of post-exercise breast milk, which is high in lactic acid and imparts a sour flavor. A study at Indiana University in Bloomington found that nursing moms who logged 35 minutes on the treadmill faced off with grimacing, reluctant infants if they nursed soon afterward. Researchers recommend that you either collect milk for later feeding or breast-feed before running.

39. Older female runners can be very positive role models for girls just learning about the sport. Any show of support can be helpful. This might be something as simple as attending a local high school cross-country meet and cheering for the girl down the street.

I have long argued that women are better suited to running than men. The reason? Reread point number one above, and you have it: Running is a state of mind. Or, as I would explain it at greater length: Women are better runners than men because they have fewer state-of-mind obstacles to overcome.

The biggest obstacle men face is their typical notion of competition in sports. Men think that sports are about beating the other guy. That may be true in boxing, but it's not true in running. Runners must learn to compete with themselves and not against anyone else. If they race against others, they will soon give up, because they will find so many others who are faster than they are.

Women seem to find it easier to understand that running is its own reward. It's not a question of your win/loss record, your batting average, your strokes per round, or any other sports statistic. It's not a matter of what you can do to an opponent; it's a matter of what running does for you.

If it makes you feel better, if it helps you control your weight, if it gives you 30 minutes of quiet time every day, then that's enough. Women accept this and learn to run with great success even if they never succeed at beating anyone.

CHAPTER 17

ASK *RUNNER'S WORLD*

Answers to Some Important Questions

Since many women runners don't have a long history of sports participation, every new step they take on the way to becoming a runner and an athlete is filled with questions. Questions about nutrition, technique, and, most important, their changing bodies.

No doubt about it. When you begin running, your body changes, and never in ways you expected. You may gain pounds at first, when you had expected to lose weight. Your muscles will get sore, when you only wanted them to get firmer. You'll need to drink more; you'll have strange, new food cravings, and you may notice differences at the most basic level of your female physiology—your periods, for example.

Because all of this is new and different, it will make you nervous. At one time or another, you'll think that something is surely wrong with you. You'll wonder about the answers to questions that you don't dare ask.

So let me give you two thoughts: It's unlikely that there's anything wrong with you, and ask anyway. Decades of research have shown that running changes people in many ways that are almost all positive. Where not positive, the changes are generally not negative either. They're just different.

But ask your questions anyway. The answers will reassure you. For starters, here's a sampling of questions that women runners often ask.

Most women are a bit sheepish about asking certain health questions. You know the ones. Questions about your period and your breasts and bladder control that are next to impossible to blurt out when you're looking a physician straight in the eye. Too bad that these questions are often easier to leave unspoken. You hope that you'll come across the answers somewhere else.

Welcome to somewhere else. Six ticklish questions below have been answered by the experts. Their answers aren't scary, and you'll learn a lot from them. Hopefully, these answers will encourage you to talk more directly with your physician next time. Remember that there's no such thing as a stupid question.

RUNNING AND YOUR BREASTS

Q: I've been running for years but only recently began experiencing discomfort in my breasts. Should I wear a sports bra when I run? Will running for 15 years without a special bra contribute to sagging breasts as I get older?

—*S. B., Ann Arbor, Michigan*

A: Wearing a sports bra is a good idea. Why? Because sports bras are designed specifically to minimize breast discomfort and stretching that may occur during exercise. But just because you have been running without one doesn't mean that your breasts will automatically sag as you age. Four factors contribute to sagging breasts: breast size, body weight, history of pregnancy, and genetic makeup. In combination, they determine whether your breasts will sag or not.

Many women experience breast discomfort on a monthly basis, often just before their periods. Most discomfort occurs as the breast bounces upward and then drops back down. So a sports bra, which is designed to reduce breast motion, may alleviate some pain.

But one type of bra won't work for every woman. You have to let your body be your guide. Keep in mind that bras are made either to bind and compress or to divide and conquer. Women with small breasts and no unusual tenderness often favor the compression style.

But if you wear a size C cup or larger or experience cyclical changes in your breasts, you may do better with a bra that encapsulates each breast. I recommend wearing a style with seamless cups to prevent nipple burn and a wide nonelastic band under the breasts to help prevent the bra from riding up as you run. The straps and cup support should be nonelastic as well, and the bra should have covered metal attachments that hook in the back. Styles that connect in the front allow more breast motion.

As for sagging, most of it results from pregnancy and lactation, not running. Breasts are composed primarily of glandular tissue and fat. If your breast size increases while you are nursing or as a consequence of a gain in weight, no ligaments exist to support the extra tissue. Stretching and sagging are the unwelcome results.

—*Carol Otis, M.D.*

RUNNING DURING PREGNANCY

Q: **I'm confused about how much exercise a well-conditioned pregnant woman can perform safely. I'd like to continue doing speedwork and long runs, yet many physicians recommend limiting exercise intensity to no more than 140 heartbeats per minute. That's not much of a workout for me. Are there other guidelines to follow?**

—*K. H., Ossining, New York*

A: Many obstetricians use 140 beats per minute as an exercise guideline for pregnant runners, despite the fact that there is no scientific evidence to back it up. Because 140 ends up being too high for sedentary women and too low for women like you, I tell my patients to pay strict attention to their perceived level of exertion and to run more conservatively.

I advise you to continue running at a speed that feels easy to you, slowing or even stopping if you begin cramping, gasping for breath, or feeling dizzy. Skip the speedwork, don't attempt to improve your times or build distance during the next nine months, and limit your workouts to no more than 30 minutes.

Why? Because after 30 minutes, core body temperature begins to rise, and elevated core temperatures can cause birth defects. Besides, no one knows exactly how long the flow of blood can be diverted from the uterus (as happens during exercise) before the fetus is compromised. For this reason, reserve a few minutes at the end of your workout to cool down slowly. Blood won't circulate back to the fetus if you stop abruptly, so end your run with a walk.

Many women runners shoot for the perfect pregnancy and the perfect child. And that's okay. But to achieve that goal, you may have to decrease some very important numbers in your life. For instance, if you're accustomed to training at an 8-minute pace, you may have to slow down a bit. And you may have to decrease your mileage as well.

—*Mona Shangold, M.D.*

WHEN YOU DON'T GET YOUR PERIOD

Q: **I haven't had my period for close to a year now, but I would like to start a family. I assume my amenorrhea is caused by strenuous training, so I'm curious how I should go about decreasing my mileage in order to conceive in four to six months.**

—*V. R., Arlington, Virginia*

A: Menstrual dysfunction isn't always caused by intense training. Perhaps your percentage of body fat is too low to prompt your period. Maybe you have a thyroid problem or even premature

Other Resources

Want more information on women's health issues? Try one or more of the organizations listed below. Many provide publications created especially for women involved in sports and fitness activities.

Melpomene Institute
1010 University Avenue West
St. Paul, MN 55104
(651) 642-1951

Named for the plucky Greek woman who sneaked into the first Olympic Marathon in 1896, Melpomene was founded in 1981 as a unique research and resource center for active women. The institute provides a wide array of publications, including numerous brochures, books, the *Melpomene Journal,* and informational packets on subjects ranging from body image and PMS to breast care, eating disorders, and osteoporosis.

National Women's Health Network
514 10th Street, N.W., Suite 400
Washington, DC 20004
(202) 347-1140

This network answers specific questions on all women's health issues, provides referrals to clinics and organizations in your area, and publishes more than 50 different packets on a wide variety of health subjects including AIDS, infertility, breast cancer, hysterectomy, and menopause.

Women's Sports Foundation
Eisenhower Park
East Meadow, NY 11554
(800) 227-3988

Call the foundation to receive brochures on women's health concerns and sporting activities. The foundation also offers 15 informational packets on topics such as nutrition and weight control, pregnancy and exercise, and the psychology of sport.

menopause. (You don't have to be middle-aged to experience menopause; it's not age but an egg deficit in the ovaries that causes menopause.)

I suggest that you see your family physician or gynecologist for a checkup that includes a pelvic examination, a hormonal evaluation, and a discussion or careful measurement of how much you are eating.

Because I avoid advising runners to alter their running schedules, I generally recommend drug therapy, such as clomiphene (Clomid) or other hormonal stimulants, to induce ovulation. Many women who have an aversion to drugs may opt on their own to cut back on their training. And if diet is a contributing factor, they may also choose to consume more food. Some even do both—run slightly less and eat more.

Although I realize that your first priority is conception, you must keep in mind that when you don't menstruate, your body probably doesn't produce enough estrogen. Low levels of estrogen lead to osteoporosis, which predisposes you to breaking bones now and as you age.

So it's essential that you supply your body with the hormones it has stopped manufacturing. Although running does counteract the effects of low estrogen, it also puts additional stress on your bones. Unless your hormonal balance is restored, you may find yourself nursing a broken bone before an infant.

—Mona Shangold, M.D.

EFFECTS OF BIRTH CONTROL PILLS

Q: **I read somewhere that birth control pills reduce aerobic capacity. Is this true? Will they impair my ability to run competitively?**
—L. P., Fredericksburg, Pennsylvania

A: For contraceptive protection the Pill is your best bet. That much is certain. But even in this day and age, scientists still know very little about the Pill's effect on overall health and athletic performance. Opinions vary, but since you asked for mine, here goes.

If you want to perform at your best, I advise against taking the Pill. As a naturalist, I believe the Pill throws off your body's natural balance. Studies published several years ago indicate that maximal oxygen capacity (max VO_2), which measures the greatest volume of oxygen that can be dispatched to your muscles during exercise, falls significantly in active women who use oral contraceptives. And other studies have demonstrated that women on the Pill lose some endurance and isometric strength.

Furthermore, many women say that they feel tired and sluggish once they start taking oral contraceptives. Although weight gain may be the culprit, I suspect the changes in blood cholesterol and triglycerides (a form of fat in the bloodstream) are more at fault.

Pill users have elevated levels of triglycerides, which are readily available for the body to use as fuel when you run. But the metabolism of 1 gram of triglyceride requires more oxygen than the metabolism of 1 gram of carbohydrate (glucose), so triglycerides are considered a less-efficient fuel. This may be why women on the Pill find running more difficult—their bodies are using triglycerides instead of carbohydrate as fuel. Perhaps this is also why max VO_2 drops in Pill users.

I suggest that you talk to a gynecologist—a sports gynecologist if possible—for more information on oral contraceptives and athletic performance. And then weigh your options. I believe, personally, that the true human model is the best.

—Christine Wells, Ph.D., exercise physiologist

EATING RIGHT

Q: **I eat a low-fat, high-carbohydrate diet, but I'm not sure whether I take in enough protein. As a woman runner, do I need more protein than other people? Are there any signs of protein deficiency that I should be aware of?**

—S. G., Sacramento, California

A: Concern over your protein intake is well-placed. Many women squeeze the protein right out of their diets simply by skimping on calories. If you average only 1,500 to 1,800 calories a day and make a point of eating lots of carbohydrates, it's very difficult to meet your protein, vitamin, and mineral needs.

A breakfast of fruit and a bagel, for instance, is high in carbohydrate and low in fat but doesn't contain the quality protein you need to replace what you use during hard training. Perhaps you fall into the same trap by avoiding meat for health reasons. Vegetarians lower their fat intake and the amount of protein they take in unless they include vegetables such as black beans, kidney beans, and lentils in combination with grain products in their diets.

What happens if you don't get enough protein? You may experience more injuries, fatigue, and mood swings or frequent bouts of illness (such as nagging colds or chronic respiratory infections). You may experience menstrual irregularities or cease having your period altogether. And the quality of your training and racing will suffer for sure.

Because the body uses protein for fuel during endurance exercise, all runners should boost their protein intake to 50 percent more than the Daily Value. For your own personal guideline, multiply your body weight in pounds by 0.54. Say that you weigh 130 pounds: 130 times 0.54 is 70.2. So you would need no fewer than 70 grams of protein a day—and a menu to get you started. Following is a sample diet that supplies 80 grams of quality protein within an 1,800-calorie diet.

Breakfast:
1 cup plain low-fat yogurt topped with fresh peaches and nectarines, whole-wheat bagel with low-sugar jam, herbal tea

Lunch:
2 ounces tuna tossed with fresh greens, olive oil, and vinegar; pita bread; fresh-fruit compote with kiwifruit, oranges, and strawberries

Snacks (to be eaten throughout the day):
Soft pretzel, sports bar, 2 cups air-popped popcorn

Dinner:
Baked potato with ¾ cup low-fat cottage cheese, 1 cup steamed broccoli, two oatmeal cookies

—Liz Applegate, Ph.D.

GAINING CONTROL OF YOUR BLADDER

Q: My running partner is just starting to train again after the birth of her daughter, and she's having a difficult time. She must perform Kegel exercises to strengthen her pelvic muscles, wear a diaphragm to stop urinary leakage, and use a pad to absorb the leaks she does have while running. Is the same fate in store for me when I get pregnant? And what about my bladder? Can it actually drop as a result of running too much?

—M. P., Seattle

A: Your running partner has stress incontinence, a problem most women experience in some form or another after labor. In fact, about 22 percent of all adult women are incontinent. Many report their first episodes after childbirth or pelvic surgery, which sometimes displaces pelvic organs and weakens muscles along the pelvic floor.

In your friend's case, the tube connecting the bladder and urethra (the bladder neck) has dropped out of normal position. So whenever she does anything that creates intro-abdominal pressure or stress, such as coughing, sneezing, laughing, or running, leakage occurs.

Stress incontinence after childbirth usually doesn't last for more than three months. In the meantime, your friend should dispense with her diaphragm (it will not help, although a tampon may), continue her Kegel exercises, and consult a specialist who may prescribe drugs, a biofeedback program, or weighted vaginal cones, which are inserted like tampons and tend to slip out unless the wearer contracts the appropriate muscles. (By contracting the proper muscles, many women can control incontinence.) She should consider surgery, which isn't always successful, only as a last resort.

There's no way to predict whether you, too, will experience stress incontinence after childbirth. Your best defense, however, is a regular training program of correctly executed Kegels. The first step is to identify the muscles involved in the exercise. While you're on the toilet, tighten your muscles to stop the flow of urine. These are the muscles you need to contract during a Kegel. Many women mistakenly isolate abdominal, thigh, or buttock muscles.

To begin, do three sets of Kegels a day. Do 5 contractions in each set, holding each contraction for 3 seconds. Gradually increase the time to 5 and then 10 seconds. Work up to 10 contractions of 10 seconds each, and do them three to five times a day. Be sure to schedule a few sets while you're running.

By the way, running may jiggle your pelvic organs a bit but will not cause your bladder to drop.

—Kristene Whitmore, M.D.

In searching for a health-care provider, women runners face two central issues. First, finding a physician they feel confident in and comfortable with, whether that physician is male or female. Second, finding a doctor who understands sports medicine and the special needs, physical and mental, of women who regularly exercise.

No one but you can decide when you feel right about a primary-care physician—your first line of defense in any health-care situation. You have to talk with the individual, evaluate the way he or she interacts with you and answers your questions, and then make the most intelligent choice you can. With some luck, you'll find a doctor who at least understands that exercise is important to you.

At times, this will be absolutely essential to your care and treatment. A physician who doesn't keep up with exercise physiology may actually miss certain diagnoses among women runners—for example, false anemia, which isn't anemia at all but the increased blood volume common to regular runners. Just as important, a doctor who doesn't understand the psychological benefits of running will often tell you to quit running when in fact you may be able to continue at a more moderate level or at least switch to a cross-training regimen.

So when you're interviewing physicians, don't hesitate to ask questions about their experience with exercise and sports medicine. You need a doctor who can treat you as a whole person, including you, the runner. Don't settle for one who sees only your parts but not the way they fit together.

CHAPTER 18

TO DARE, TO CREATE, TO DREAM

Joan Samuelson Tells How Women Runners Can Excel

Joan Samuelson delivered this address to the graduating class at Colby-Sawyer College in New London, New Hampshire, on May 12, 1990. She graduated from Bowdoin College in 1979.

When I was thinking about what I wanted to say to you this morning, about the challenges facing women these days, I kept remembering a scene from my childhood.

My friends and I were killing some time after a kickball game, sitting on the split-rail fence that (theoretically) kept us off the Episcopal church lawn, and somebody brought up the subject of college. We all assumed that we were going to college—most of our parents had gone, and many of us had older brothers and sisters who were making the rounds of New England schools, looking for the perfect place. It was on our minds.

All-male colleges were just beginning to go coed in those days, and along with all the other upheavals that marked the 1960s, this was proving to be a painful process. Each of us knew someone who was among the first to break the barriers, a woman who went to Yale or Harvard or Princeton and received a less-than-warm welcome from many male students and alumni. Although numerous magazine articles appeared at this time saying that women controlled most of the wealth in the United States, it was still a man's world, and every girl on the playing field that day knew it.

Even so, our ambition was to attend Bowdoin College. We agreed that it was the best college in Maine, and the fact that Bowdoin was still for men only didn't worry us. Somehow—at least when we were 10 years old—we had faith that if we wanted something, we could get it, no matter what the odds.

From this great distance (over 20 years have passed since that kickball game was played), I can pinpoint that attitude as the key to the successes I have had in my life. Yes, it was a man's world. Yes, it was difficult to imagine a career in athletics when there wasn't so

129

much as an organized team for girls below high-school age in my hometown. And yes, even as I got older, I had to operate more on faith than on any evidence that things were going to change for women athletes. Where boys my age could realistically aspire to professional careers in any number of sports, my role models were few, and my opportunities were severely limited.

It is easy to look back now and see that I made the right choice when I decided to stick with distance running and let fate take care of itself. The sport has been good to me, especially in that it has given me the chance to test the limits of my ability and find the strength of my heart. But it wasn't easy for me then—and I know it isn't easy for young women now—to forge goals that were acceptable to parents, teachers, other mentors, friends, and myself. Worthy accomplishments come at the end of a long, lonely road of work and frequent disappointment, and it is difficult, in the absence of any concrete results, to explain the need to see a dream through. If I had a dollar for every time one of my parents asked my why I didn't settle down and find a stable career—well, you know how that goes.

Dreams, by their very nature, are often at odds with the sensible recommendations made by those who love us and who want what is best for us. But so is faith, and so is selflessness, and so are many of the other human attributes we say we admire in this society. And just as it is important to hang on to what you believe in, it is important to identify and follow your dreams. If you don't make your dreams come true, no one else can. No one else knows you as you know yourself. No one else sees your potential the way you do. You are the one who has nurtured the sparks of your character and your commitment this far, and you are the one who can make those sparks burn throughout your life.

For young women, the challenges and the opportunities may never have been greater than they are today. Although there have been some ominous things written and said in the last few years about women who want to have it all, it is now common for women to balance careers and family. Today, the woman who doesn't work outside her home is the exception, and the man who objects to his wife holding an outside job is an anomaly. This social configuration would have been impossible to predict 20 years ago when I was first trying to find my niche, and it would never have come about if women had been willing to squeeze themselves into available roles rather than create new ones.

My achievements as a runner are due, in part, to the hard work done and the chances taken by women who preceded me in the sport. Not very long ago, it was common knowledge that a woman could not run long distances. Conventional wisdom held that women were too frail and delicate to run more than a few thousand meters. Less than 30 years ago, some doctors wrote articles about the alarming things that would happen if women tried to do more. Women would pass out, fall by the roadside, do irreparable harm to their bodies. More recently, a spate of articles appeared saying that women athletes who engaged in normally rigorous training activities were risking their ability to conceive children.

The underlying message, of course, was that running and athletics in general were unfeminine. I heard that loud and clear as a teenager in Maine, and for a short time I chose to do much of my training at an abandoned army post near my home rather than run where people could see me.

But even as I hid out, women such as Bobbi Gibb, Kathrine Switzer, Mary Slaney, and many others were facing down the notion that there were limits to what women, even highly feminine women, could do in sports. The strides women distance runners made in these years—both in lowering times and in cracking previously all-male bastions such as the Boston Marathon—made it possible for runners of my generation to concentrate on training instead of on controversy. My appearance in the 1984 Olympic Marathon would not have been possible without the kind of pressure that was applied by Jacqueline Hansen, who spent more than 10 years—from her glory days in the 1970s (she was the first woman to break 2:40 in the marathon) until the race was sanctioned for the 1984 Games—working to make a far brighter future for women distance runners.

I choose to speak to you about the changes that have come about for runners in the last 15 years because running is—for the moment, at least—what I know best. It is fast being overtaken by *Sesame Street* and the fine art of keeping a play group of two-year-olds occupied, but for the moment, I'm on my most solid ground when I talk about running.

I have no doubt, however, that if you were being addressed by a woman scientist or historian or writer, she would also cite the women who helped pave the way for her. One of the most exciting things about being a professional woman in the latter part of this century is that you can trace your roots, so to speak; you can appreciate the pioneer women in your field because they are close to you in time. They brought you and me here today. They put the world within our reach and asked us to take from it what we need.

What we owe them in return, I believe, is not only excellence in the fields where barriers to women have been knocked down but also an effort of will and imagination that will push the boundaries out even further so that generations of women to come will have choices that you and I have yet to dream of.

My daughter, Abby, will have dreams and goals of her own someday—beyond getting into the china cupboard when I don't want her to and going one whole day without wearing shoes—but their genesis will probably be in your experience. Only if you follow your dreams, despite the risks and against the odds, will she be free to follow hers.

For her sake, I urge you to dare, to create, to dream. The challenge is enormous, and you may not—as I haven't—meet every goal. But the journey is sweet, sweeter today for women than ever before, and the well-imagined destination is always worth the trip.

5

BUILDING STRENGTH, ENDURANCE, AND SPEED

CHAPTER 19

TIME-TESTED ADVICE

A Review of the Top 25 Training Advances

When Runner's World *celebrated its 25th anniversary in the early 1990s, we asked the magazine's first editor, Joe Henderson, to write a special article for us. Even after he left his full-time, day-to-day responsibilities with the magazine, Joe continued his active role in the running community, publishing a newsletter, speaking at many races, and serving as a sort of elder spokesman for the sport. We figured that this made him the perfect person to write about the most important advances in training knowledge and technique that he had observed over the years.*

Joe's article hits them all. You can't find a better big-picture snapshot of training developments in recent decades than this one.

Best of all, many of these guidelines remain as true as when they were discovered, whether that was yesterday or 20 years ago. As you read this chapter, ask yourself this simple question: Does my training program violate one of these principles? If it does, you should seriously consider making a change.

In January 1966 New Zealander Arthur Lydiard's revolutionary training methods had just arrived in the United States, imported chiefly by University of Oregon and U.S. Olympic coach Bill Bowerman. At the same time, Ken Cooper, M.D., was testing his running-as-exercise training plan on Air Force personnel in Texas and preparing to write a revolutionary fitness book called *Aerobics*.

These separate forces of change would soon meet and merge on the roads, where people of all ability levels began running. The number of runners increased steadily through the 1960s, 1970s, 1980s, and 1990s. As the sport grew, so did an interest in finding the best ways to train. Coaches, researchers, and runners tried various methods and techniques in their search to improve performance and to make running an enjoyable, healthful, long-lasting activity. Here are the 25 most important training advances of the past 30 years.

1. Training without straining. Effective training, said famed New Zealand coach Arthur Lydiard, traces a fine line between hard

enough and too hard. This principle grew from the theories of Hans Selye, the endocrinologist credited with describing how stress works on the human body, who found that repeated exposure to a mild stress stimulates adaptation. In other words, through running, which is a stress, the body learns to adapt to the demands of running and eventually performs better. Selye also pointed out, however, that too much stress overwhelms the body's ability to cope. Thus, if you run too hard, your body will not be able to adapt. This philosophy formed the cornerstone of Lydiard's system, which encouraged runners to train hard without straining.

2. Aerobic training. Dr. Cooper, the president and founder of the Cooper Aerobics Center in Dallas, plucked the term *aerobics* from physiology jargon and made it an international phenomenon. His research concluded that prolonged low-intensity exercise improved physical endurance better than brief, explosive workouts. Training aerobically meant choosing a running pace that allowed you to talk and that kept the heart rate at about three-quarters of maximum. The result was an easier, yet still effective, training effort.

3. Specificity of training. This philosophy states that you will reap in races what you sow in training. Long, slow runs prepare you to race slowly, whereas short, fast runs only train you to race short distances. Jeff Galloway applied this rule of adaptation to his now-popular marathon-training program, which requires a long run of 26 miles.

   Similarly, Jack Daniels, Ph.D., assistant professor of physical education and an exercise physiologist at the State University of New York in Cortland, has followed this principle in using tempo runs (runs that start easy, build up to a steady speed, and then finish at an easy pace) at about 10-K race pace to lift slow runners out of their training ruts. The typical distance runner's training schedule now includes some of both: Long runs are used to increase strength; short, fast workouts are used to build speed. The final mix and mileage depend on the type of race you're preparing for.

4. Long runs. The long run was Lydiard's most lasting gift to training. Few runners still do his 100-mile weeks, but almost everyone—from a miler to a marathoner—runs longer than his norm at least once a week. The long run builds endurance, and it provides a great opportunity to spend time with friends.

5. Surviving the marathon. Speaking of long runs, about 15 years ago, a new breed of runner came to dominate marathons—at least numerically. These athletes treated the event not as a race for time or place but as a survival test to be passed just by finishing. In the 1970s Jack Scaff, M.D., of the Honolulu Marathon Clinic, developed a program to prepare runners to reach the marathon starting line in good health and able to complete the distance. His program downplayed high levels of weekly mileage and speedwork and emphasized the long training run.

6. Hill training. Hill work, another staple of the Lydiard system, was overlooked early on in the rush to 100-mile weeks. Lydiard's runners used hills in two ways. Regularly, they would do their long runs on extremely hilly courses. Also, prior to the sharpening phase of their training, which emphasized speedwork, they would do hill repeats. We now know that hills are speedwork in disguise. Uphill running strengthens the upper leg muscles, which produce speed, and downhills force runners to go faster.

7. Speed training. Runners once shunned speedwork because it meant circling the track endlessly in an exhausting race against the stopwatch. It meant enduring boredom and pain. Not anymore. Dr. Daniels provided more humane, but still effective, choices: tempo runs, done at a steady pace but lasting only about 20 minutes; and cruise intervals, run at tempo pace but broken into three to six repeats with brief rest periods between them.

8. Races as training. Four-time Olympian George Young, now a successful college coach in Arizona, pointed out that the most effective speed training occurs where it is most exciting to do: in races. Now, with races on the schedule almost every weekend in most areas, many runners take their speedwork this way, which helps explain why 5-K and 8-K are the fastest-growing race distances. Similarly, runners looking to do a long training run with a group help flesh out the fields for half-marathons and longer races.

9. Recovering from races. As the road-racing schedule grew to fill the year and to crowd each weekend, so, too, did the temptation to overrace. New Zealander Jack Foster, who held the masters marathon record for 16 years, came up with a valuable rule of thumb: He followed his races with a recovery period totaling one day for each mile of racing. He didn't stop running during that recovery period; he simply wouldn't race or train hard again until the appropriate time had passed.

10. Hard and easy days. Coaches and runners learned that recovery from hard training is also important. Long runs, hills, and speed-work all place the runner on training's edge. Bowerman produced as many top runners as any college coach ever has. Tests on his young, strong athletes showed that none thrived on more than three hard training days in a row, and most did best by alternating a hard day with an easy one. One of Bowerman's athletes, Kenny Moore, became a two-time Olympic marathoner. He would train hard one day and easily the next two. The importance of easy days was confirmed by exercise physiologist David L. Costill, Ph.D., director of the Human Performance Laboratory at Ball State University in Muncie, Indiana, whose research showed that most runners need 48 to 72 hours to recover fully from even a moderately hard effort.

11. Recovering from hard days. Long, slow distance (LSD) provided the means to recover from hard workouts. LSD—a product of the 1960s—was originally misunderstood as an invitation to run too long and slowly. A better term would have been *gentle running*. As originally practiced, long, slow distance meant running slower miles between more difficult workouts. It fits perfectly into the hard/easy training plan, and this remains its best use.

12. Days off. LSD goes one step further and becomes rest. In other words, take a day off. The word *rest* was once a dirty word among runners. Real runners ran every day. It took advice from some of the sport's heaviest hitters and most respected physiologists to convince runners that resting could sometimes be as valuable as training—especially for older runners with slower recovery rates. Rest days, of course, mesh with Bowerman's hard/easy plan and Dr. Cooper's five-day schedule for fitness running (see training advance 25 on page 141). Two more converts to this philosophy, the late George Sheehan, M.D., and Galloway, switched to practicing and then preaching every-other-day training.

13. Tapering before races. Gentle running became important prior to racing, too. Runners training for marathons used to take their last long run—and often the longest one—a week before their race. The smart ones now space these efforts three weeks apart to restore full life to their legs. Research done by Dr. Costill indicates that runners need to cut back on their mileage level for three days to three weeks prior to a race, depending on the degree of training that they have been doing and the length and seriousness of the race.

14. Running cycles. If you take Bowerman's hard/easy system and extend it beyond days to seasons or even years, you have peaking. Lydiard maintained that no one could race and train at their highest level year-round. He recommended scheduling alternate seasons of peak training and relaxed training. Lydiard's runners, winners of five Olympic medals, were masters of peaking. The all-time best athlete to use this training principle was four-time Olympic winner Lasse Viren, whom Lydiard influenced.

15. Training by time. Digital watches put an accurate measure of performance on every runner's wrist. They provided race splits and final times instantly. But another important value was more subtle. The digitals also let runners adopt another of Lydiard's recommendations: Train by periods of time instead of distance. This freed runners from measuring road courses and trying to run those courses faster with each workout. Thus, it helped prevent runners from working too hard during an average training run.

16. Preventing overuse injuries. The purpose of training is to improve, to get stronger and faster. So it is easy to get caught in an ever-increasing schedule that has you constantly building on speed, distance, and hills on the theory that more work and a harder effort will continue to improve your performance. But runners soon learned that they were overdoing it. They trained too long, too fast, and too often, and found their breaking points. Podiatrists treated growing numbers of injuries over the years, until runners began to realize that sometimes less is more.

17. Listen to your body. Dr. Sheehan taught this valuable lesson. He told runners that they didn't need to follow complex training formulas, monitor their pulses, or even try to run a certain pace. All that a runner needed to do in distance training, said Dr. Sheehan, was "set the inner dial to 'comfortable,' neither too hard nor too easy. The pace that feels right is right." He endorsed Gunnar Borg's scale of perceived exertion, which measured feelings instead of heartbeats or minutes per mile. Heart-rate monitors arrived later to do the same type of listening electronically.

18. Stretching. Runners needed to learn to listen to their bodies not only to determine what level of training exertion was right for them but also to detect minor problems and correct them before they became injuries. Dr. Sheehan wrote, "Three things happen when you run, and two of them are bad." The good one is that you become a more efficient runner. The first bad one is that runners—especially those who run the same slow pace all the time—lose flexibility. Their muscles grow tighter and more susceptible to injury. To prevent this, runners were encouraged to do slow, gentle, yogalike stretches.

19. Strengthening. The second bad thing that happens to runners, wrote Dr. Sheehan, is that they develop strength imbalances. Muscles at the back of the legs overpower those in front, a setup for injury. In addition, the muscles of the upper body lag in strength behind those of the lower body, which get all the exercise. Dr. Sheehan advised that runners should supplement their miles with exercises that restore strength balances and make fitness more complete.

20. Carbo loading. Beyond taking care of their muscles, runners learned about the important effects of diet. New menus came to the training table as runners began to shun meat in favor of low-fat proteins and high-energy carbohydrates. The technique of carbo loading before races was first tested by Swedish physiologists, and British marathoner Ron Hill proved its value. Dr. Costill found that carbo reloading after races and hard training was equally valuable.

21. Hydration. Dr. Costill pointed out the folly of not drinking enough water before, during, and after long runs. He showed that as the dehydrating body's temperature rose, performance declined, and the risk of heat injury increased. Runners started to drink more water, and then more than water. They began downing sweetened and electrolyte-laden solutions. Florida researchers invented Gatorade, and soon many other replacement fluids flooded the market.

22. Cross-training. Many runners are finding that they can benefit from sports outside running. Also known as alternative or supplemental training, cross-training received its greatest push from the triathlon boom that began in the mid-1980s. Triathletes sent runners the message that total fitness requires more than running and gave them the okay to switch activities on days when extra miles seemed unwise or unappealing. Many paths lead to the same destination of aerobic fitness. Swimming and bicycling are but two among dozens of activities that runners can mix and match for a complete fitness program.

23. Water training. Running in a pool while wearing a flotation vest or belt may be the single most valuable variation on land running. Injured runners can continue normal training efforts and stay running-fit without aggravating the problem that put them in deep water. Oft-injured Mary Slaney gave water work cre-

dence when she trained this way for six weeks following a mishap at the 1984 Olympic Trials. A few days after returning to the track, she broke the world record for 2000 meters.

24. Walking. The word *walk* used to make runners turn away in disgust. They wouldn't think of stopping to walk during a run and certainly not in a race. Tom Osler, who successfully mixed walking breaks into his own ultramarathons, started changing this thinking. He wrote that runners could greatly increase the length of their longest run by inserting brief walks at regular intervals. Marathoners whose only goals are to finish will purposely take walking breaks. Galloway even found that some marathoners could improve their times by taking a 1-minute walking break every mile. Also, runners coming back from injuries or illness, and new runners building their endurance, can mix walking with running in an effort to increase distances.

25. Fitness training. Dr. Cooper once ran for sport, but he came to see a wider role for the activity. He took his running-for-fitness message to nonathletes who would never have thought of training to enter a race. That's fine, said Dr. Cooper. It's not necessary. Instead, he proposed a running program of 2 to 3 miles, three to five times a week. As health studies in the mid-1990s showed more and more Americans becoming overweight, Dr. Cooper's philosophy encouraged many of these formerly sedentary people to begin running for weight control and health improvement.

> *Our knowledge of training changes—but slowly. The process is far more evolutionary than revolutionary. If I were coaching a would-be Olympian today, I would tell him to review the principles above carefully and to make them the foundation of any training program. Because these are the basics, and no runner can advance very far without observing them.*
>
> *Strengthening, hill training, and cross-training are still very popular. Runners, and in particular runners past age 40, have come to recognize the importance of strength training; one important component of strength training is hill work. The growth of cross-training is everywhere, and even though the physiologists continue to make the "specificity" argument—that the only thing that makes you a better runner is running—thousands of runners have found that cross-training makes them stronger, healthier, and more injury-resistant. And these three combined will certainly make anyone a better runner.*

CHAPTER 20

IDEAL PACES

How to Know When Your Training Is Right

Every runner, from the newest beginner to the Olympic gold medalist, has one basic question about his training: How fast should I run? How fast should I run when I jog up the road and back, how fast should I run when I cover longer distances, and how fast should I run when I go to the track to do speedwork?

Thirty years ago, coaches didn't have any good answers to these questions. Runners were encouraged in the manner of whoever was the current star: Jim Ryun or Frank Shorter or Bill Rodgers or Joan Benoit Samuelson. This worked fine for the 0.1 percent of runners who were nearly as talented as their role models, but it destroyed the other 99.9 percent.

Fortunately, we have since learned how to scale training paces to make them appropriate for runners at all levels. This chapter will help you find the training paces that will work best for you, and then it will tell you how often to run at these paces. It's a simple, handy guide that produces results.

For too many years runners have been told to train as they feel. The problem is that no one tells you how you're supposed to feel when you're training right. Lacking this, many runners unconsciously fall into the no-pain, no-gain trap. They train too hard. You know what comes next: burnout, fatigue, injury.

Some runners make the opposite mistake: They don't train hard enough. Their specialty is junk mileage—running so slowly that they receive little or no training effect.

Unfortunately, neither the too-fast nor the too-slow runners realize that their training is off the mark. Both are running as they feel, just the way they have always been told. Without any other guidelines, they'll no doubt continue training the same way.

This may or may not end up hurting them, but it certainly does not amount to efficient, scientific training. Yet such training is within your grasp even if your spouse isn't an exercise physiologist and your basement doesn't contain a human performance laboratory.

Ask yourself the following question: At what pace or paces should I be training to maximize my fitness and my running performances? If you can answer this question, you have the key to a successful training program.

Over the past 15 years a number of researchers have begun to apply the results of certain studies to the training of runners and other endurance athletes. Most of this work has been done piecemeal in far-flung locations around the United States and the globe. Yet the scientists and coaches involved in the programs, and their early successes, are so impressive that their remarkably similar systems seem certain to catch on.

While the researchers have read the same journals and, indeed, have reached nearly identical conclusions, each interprets and applies the information in a slightly different manner. In the sections that follow, the material on the various training systems has been mixed together in such a way that it will prove useful to the greatest number of runners.

Exercise physiologists and coaches generally agree that there are three ways to improve running performance: You can increase your maximum oxygen uptake, or max VO_2, which measures the greatest volume of oxygen that can be dispatched to your muscles during exercise; you can extend the point at which your muscle efficiency falls off significantly (your lactate threshold, or LT); and you can improve your endurance, or running economy (RE).

It follows that the most effective training takes direct aim at one or more of these three factors. Training that isn't specific will still produce results, but it won't produce the best, most efficient results. In other words, you can go out and jog around town for 30 to 40 minutes a day, and your condition will definitely improve. There's no denying that haphazard training works, and a lot of runners aren't willing to tamper with a method that's already producing results.

At some point, however, you're bound to start wondering if there isn't a better way. It's not a matter of seeking shortcuts, it's simply a desire to train smarter.

And that desire leads straight to max VO_2, lactate threshold, and running economy.

QUICKER ON THE UPTAKE

Your maximum oxygen uptake is the greatest amount of oxygen that your muscles can use while you're exercising as hard as you can. Note that max VO_2 is not just the amount of oxygen that your heart and lungs can provide. As you train, your leg muscles become more efficient at burning the available oxygen. This is specificity of training, which helps explain why a fit swimmer might not run very fast, and a fit runner might not swim very well. Both have great cardiovascular systems, but an athlete has to train the muscles specific to a particular event.

Many famous runners have their max VO_2s measured in laboratories. You may have seen the results listed in magazines and books, but the figures probably didn't mean much to you, because the usual unit of measurement is milliliters per kilogram of body weight per minute. Anyway, famed runner Steve Prefontaine had a max VO_2 of 84.4, and 1984 Olympic Marathon gold medalist Joan Benoit Samuelson's is reputed to be around 78. This is all very exciting, but it doesn't tell you how to train come Monday morning.

What's needed is a simpler method of understanding max VO_2. "Running Your Paces" should help. Using this table, you can locate your own max VO_2 pace. Research indicates that regular training at this pace will increase your max VO_2. That is, it will make you fitter and faster.

Let's note a few more things about this max VO_2 pace. First, it's not the same as your all-out sprint speed. It's a pace that you could hold for an 11-minute race. If you chose to sprint for just 30 seconds, say, you could run much faster than pace. Faster isn't better, however. The best pace for improving your max VO_2 is your max VO_2 pace.

Running a daily 11-minute race time trial isn't the answer, either. It would quickly lead to chronic fatigue. Except when racing, don't try to run continually for more than 5 minutes at your max VO_2 pace. Nor should you use the table to pick out some illusory or goal max VO_2 pace. You must train at the pace appropriate to your current racing performance. Only after your race performances improve should you drop down to faster training paces.

While training for an upcoming competition, run a max VO_2 workout about once a week. (During off-season or maintenance periods, you don't need to do max VO_2 workouts.) Run an interval session on a track, where you can closely monitor distance and pace. A good workout would be 800 meters, 3 to 6 repeats, at your max VO_2 pace, or 400 meters, 8 to 12 repeats, at the same pace. Take a 2- to 3-minute recovery jog between repeats.

The idea behind this kind of interval training is that you can safely go up to or beyond your maximum capacity of 11 minutes of max VO_2 running, because the recovery jogging gives you regular rests. Adaptation without exhaustion is the foundation of all training programs. Once you've become accustomed to the effort level of max VO_2 training, you can take it off the track to the roads or another location of your choice.

We can't overemphasize the importance of running at your max

Running Your Paces

Find your 10-K time in the left-hand column and then trace across to the right to locate your max VO$_2$, lactate threshold, and running economy training paces. If your 10-K time is between the whole numbers, you can easily adjust your training paces by adding or subtracting several seconds.

Your 10-K Time (minutes)	Your Max VO$_2$ Pace (min./mile)	Your Lactate Threshold Pace (min./mile)	Your Running Economy Pace (min./mile)
27	4:08	4:41	5:50
28	4:16	4:51	6:03
29	4:25	5:02	6:15
30	4:33	5:12	6:27
31	4:42	5:22	6:40
32	4:50	5:31	6:52
33	4:58	5:41	7:04
34	5:07	5:51	7:17
35	5:16	6:01	7:29
36	5:25	6:11	7:41
37	5:33	6:21	7:53
38	5:41	6:31	8:05
39	5:50	6:40	8:17
40	5:59	6:50	8:29
41	6:08	7:00	8:41
42	6:16	7:10	8:53
43	6:25	7:19	9:04
44	6:33	7:29	9:16
45	6:42	7:38	9:28
46	6:50	7:48	9:39
47	6:58	7:58	9:51
48	7:07	8:07	10:02
49	7:15	8:16	10:14
50	7:24	8:26	10:25
51	7:32	8:35	10:36
52	7:41	8:45	10:48
53	7:49	8:54	10:59
54	7:57	9:04	11:10
55	8:06	9:13	11:21
56	8:14	9:22	11:32
57	8:22	9:32	11:43
58	8:31	9:41	11:54
59	8:39	9:50	12:05
60	8:47	10:00	12:06

VO_2 pace. Far too many runners think interval training means speed-work. No doubt you can and have run 400-meter repeats faster than your max VO_2 pace. Well, stop it! If you stand by your former habits, then you're still following the old hit-or-miss school of training, and you just might miss. Running too fast leads to fatigue and break-down. Running at your max VO_2 pace—it's not slow running, but rather controlled speed—raises your maximum oxygen uptake, which improves performance potential.

EXTENDING YOUR THRESHOLD

Lactate threshold is one of the more confusing and hotly debat-ed topics in exercise physiology and training. It's also one of the most important. Scientists always knew that runners with high max VO_2s tended to produce the fastest running times. More recent research has elevated lactate threshold to a position of equal importance.

Shorter, the 1972 Olympic Marathon champion, and Derek Clayton, the first man to break 2:09 in the marathon, provide two of the best examples of the importance of lactate threshold. Both had relatively low max VO_2s for elite athletes. Yet their lactate thresholds were so high that they could run marathons at 85 percent of their max VO_2s, while other athletes could only maintain levels of 75 to 80 percent.

Lactate threshold is not just important to marathoners. No mat-ter what your distance, the higher your lactate threshold, the faster you can go before your muscles stage a walkout.

The way to improve your lactate threshold is to train at your LT pace, shown in column three of "Running Your Paces" on page 145. These LT paces are calculated at 85 percent of your max VO_2, or just a little bit faster than your marathon pace.

Your weekly schedule should include one LT workout in which you cover 3 to 6 miles at your LT pace. There are any number of ways to do this. For instance, you could go to the track and run repeats of 1½ to 2 miles at LT pace. Do two or three of these with a short recovery jog between efforts.

It's also easy to do LT training as part of your regular roadwork if you have a measured course. A short road workout might consist of a 1-mile warm-up, 3 to 4 miles at LT pace, and a 1-mile cooldown. If you're training for a marathon, you could do 3 to 4 miles of LT running in the middle of a long run.

REAL RECOVERY

This is in some ways the most perplexing of the three training paces. RE training doesn't improve any single factor the way that max VO_2 and LT training do. Rather, it works on all aspects of your running endurance—the cardiovascular, the biomechanical, the biochemical, and the psychological—in a generalized way.

The other two training paces are much more efficient and effective. But you can't do them every day. In fact, you shouldn't do either more than once a week. That leaves you guessing about the rest of the week.

You could always decide to do nothing on the other five days, but then your condition wouldn't improve. It might even deteriorate. You could run 100 miles during the other five days, but that isn't very prudent for most people.

So what you probably end up doing, like almost everyone else, is going out for a lot of easy runs. That's fine, except for one thing: Too many runners, when they head out the door for "just an easy run," run too fast. As a result, they don't get the recovery they need after their harder training days.

The secret to easy running is to find the slowest pace that will still provide all the generalized aerobic benefits you want. Here, slower is better—up to a point. If you run too slowly, you get almost no training effect, and your workout time is essentially wasted. So, the big question becomes, How slowly can you run and still be training?

Research indicates that the dividing line is at about 65 percent of your max VO_2 (see column four in "Running Your Paces" on page 145). If this pace seems ridiculously slow, don't worry about it. So long as your everyday training pace is truly comfortable and recuperative, you can run at 70 to 80 percent of your max VO_2 without excessive strain. On the other hand, if you often feel tired before workouts and force yourself to run at an arbitrary (and perhaps too stressful) pace, you might enjoy knowing that you could run a lot slower and still make deposits into you training account. RE pace is also the right pace for your long runs, the purpose of which is to accustom your body, in a generalized way, to spending several hours on the road.

One important effect of RE training that shouldn't be overlooked or underestimated is calorie burning. On days when it's RE or nothing, RE training will help keep your weight in check. Otherwise, you're likely to start gaining weight, which will have a negative impact on your running, not to mention your overall health.

FINE-TUNING YOUR TRAINING

Simplicity is one of the great virtues of this system. But if you want to go beyond the basics, here are a few additional points to ponder.

Pace training. Many athletes and coaches believe in training at hoped-for racing pace. Particularly if you're preparing for a race that will take less than 11 minutes, you should add race-pace repeats to your training diet.

Racing. Any race of 5-K or more counts as a max VO_2 run. In most situations you shouldn't do another max VO_2 workout during a week in which you race.

Pulse rate. If you're not training on a measured course, you can use your pulse rate to determine when you're running at the correct percentage of your max VO_2. First, approximate your maximum pulse by subtracting your age from 220. If you are 30, for example, your max pulse is about 190. When you're running at max VO_2 pace, your pulse should reach its max, 190. When you're running at LT pace, 85 percent of your max VO_2, your pulse should reach 90 percent of its max ($.90 \times 190 = 171$). Since it is possible to run anaerobically, that is, without oxygen, max VO_2 can exceed 100 percent. Since pulse tops out at 100 percent and max VO_2 goes to 120 or so, pulse percentages are always relatively higher than max VO_2 percentages. For RE training, 65 percent of your max VO_2, you must raise your pulse to 75 percent of its max ($.75 \times 190 = 143$).

To check your heart rate on the run, stop in the middle of a workout, take your pulse for 10 seconds, and multiply by 6.

Alternative training. If you're looking to substitute some bicycling or other aerobic exercises for certain running workouts, the best substitution days are your RE training days. Because of the law of specificity of training, you can't expect a hard bike ride to have the same beneficial effects as a max VO_2 running workout.

Overtraining. Anytime you experience extreme difficulty completing one of your workouts, plan a rest period. Sometimes a day or two of easy running will suffice; sometimes you will need several weeks. Don't return to max VO_2 or LT training until your RE runs are going as comfortably as they should.

The discovery of lactate-threshold training had more impact on my running than any other training development that I can think of. Before lactate-threshold training became widely understood, I believed, like far too many other runners, that a workout couldn't be doing that much for you if it didn't hurt. The old no-pain, no-gain philosophy.

I have learned a lot over the years from being injured, and it was an injury that taught me about the wonders of lactate-threshold training. I couldn't prepare for my favorite fall race with the usual blood-and-guts workouts, so I substituted lactate-

threshold workouts instead. I wasn't happy about this—it's hard to get excited about an injury that forces you to train slower than usual—but I didn't have any alternative.

Come race day, I expected the competition to blow me away. In my head, I wasn't nearly as fit as I had been in earlier years. As it turned out, my head was wrong. Once the race got underway, I felt strong and smooth, and I won the race in a time equal to what I had run the previous two or three years when I had trained much harder and faster.

The inevitable conclusion: Lactate-threshold training worked. Since then, I have always made it a focus of my training, and I have heard from countless other coaches and runners who have also had success with it.

CHAPTER 21

STRETCH YOUR LIMITS

Develop a Program That Will
Double Your Endurance

Runners almost always want to go farther and faster. Even when we reach the point where we're running as far as we want, we hope to make it feel easier, which is one of the hallmarks of increased endurance.

Fortunately, no other activity teaches endurance as readily as running. We start, beginners all, barely able to make it to the end of the block. But with dedication and persistence, we soon learn that our bodies can do more. They adapt, get stronger, run farther.

By following more advanced techniques, we can do even more to increase endurance. Tens of thousands of runners who never thought that they'd complete a mile have gone on to finish marathons—often dozens of them. Other runners have never done a marathon and never want to, but they are excited to run 3 to 5 miles at a time because it represents such a quantum improvement and a genuine commitment to optimal health and fitness.

To endure. It is the essence of running. To withstand the fatigue and continue running for miles and more miles of road or track—this is our goal. We begin with a certain level of endurance and hope to improve it.

Endurance is the ability to continue activity of a set intensity for a prolonged period. It depends upon three physiological factors: oxygen uptake, lactate threshold, and efficiency.

Oxygen uptake means exactly that—how much oxygen your body takes in and sends to your muscles, where it is used to create energy. *Max VO$_2$* is the technical term for the maximum volume of oxygen that your body can transport to your muscles. The higher your max, the more oxygen your muscles receive, the greater your endurance.

No matter what your max VO$_2$, lactic acid accumulation eventually causes muscle seizure. "An untrained person may accumulate lactic acid at levels as low as 30 to 40 percent of his max VO$_2$," says

Russell Pate, Ph.D., director of the Human Performance Laboratory at the University of South Carolina in Columbia and a former 2:15 marathoner. "More highly trained endurance athletes will be able to work at 80 percent or more without accumulating lactic acid."

The final factor that affects endurance is your efficiency. This is defined by biomechanics and economy of motion. The smoother your running style, the less oxygen you consume at a particular speed, and the longer you can run.

"To increase endurance, you need to improve these three factors," says Dr. Pate. "The optimum would be to have a high max VO_2, a high lactate threshold, and an economical running style."

RUNNING FARTHER

We all begin with a certain natural capacity for endurance determined by our genes. Nevertheless, "anybody can improve endurance with training," says exercise physiologist David L. Costill, Ph.D., director of the Human Performance Laboratory at Ball State University in Muncie, Indiana.

The key to endurance training is to "systematically expose your system to gradually increasing amounts of exercise stress," says Dr. Pate. "Your muscles will adapt to the increased stress, and your endurance will improve.

"In order to induce an adaptation, you must force your system to do something that it is not currently used to doing," continues Dr. Pate. "This is the reason that elite runners show smaller gains in endurance than beginners. Their muscles are already used to a high level of stress.

"Give me an untrained person, and doubling that person's endurance is a piece of cake," claims Dr. Pate. "The trick is to apply a stress sufficient to adapt the system without the undesirable side effects—injuries—that come with doing too much."

By mixing workouts that stress your body with gentler ones, you can teach your muscles to adapt to faster, harder, longer running while avoiding injury. The best endurance-training program will include workouts from the following four components.

1. High-intensity runs. "For decades exercise physiologists have studied changes in max VO_2, and it is modifiable," says Dr. Pate. "I think it's debatable whether or not we know the best way to modify max VO_2, but high-intensity activity is key. Exercising at intensities that take you beyond your current max VO_2 is important for improving your endurance."

What type of training does that? Long repeats at a speed faster than your typical 10-K pace. A typical high-intensity workout would be repeat miles: 3 x 1 mile with a 5-minute-or-more break of walking or jogging between miles. A person capable of a 45-minute 10-K (about a 7:15 pace) should run repeats at that pace or slightly faster. One of the benefits of workouts at this speed is that it gets you used to training at or near race pace.

2. Medium-intensity runs. "Recent training studies have looked specifically at how to increase endurance performance," says Dr. Pate. "Some evidence suggests that prolonged activity at intensities close to your current lactate threshold will help raise that threshold."

Dr. Pate prescribes runs of 20 to 60 minutes that are "not as fast as an interval workout but faster than the pace used on a long run." In other words, a pace that's 15 to 30 seconds slower per mile than your 10-K time. The runner capable of a 7:15 pace in a 10-K race, would do lactate threshold runs at around a 7:45 pace.

3. Low-intensity runs. Another piece of the puzzle: longer runs at a slow pace. This is what many runners typically do on a weekend morning. You should run at a comfortable pace—slow enough that you can carry on a normal conversation with your training partner. The runner capable of a 7:15 pace in a 10-K would run at an 8:45 to 9:15 pace on long runs.

"Long runs are valuable," says Dr. Pate, "particularly when your goal is marathon performance." They teach your body how to run through the kind of energy depletion encountered in races that last 2 hours or more. Psychologically, too, you learn that you can stay on your feet and in motion for that length of time.

4. Rest. Equally important to training success is regular rest, either a short, slow run or a day off. "For most runners, rest-day activity should be minimal," says Dr. Pate. "If you do too much, you risk getting injured or so tired that you have to back off on your hard days, which defeats the main purpose of the training plan."

TIPS FROM THE EXPERTS

With these four principles in mind as the basis of your training, you can now create your own individualized workouts to improve endurance. Following is some specific advice on endurance training collected from running coaches around the country.

First, take three to five months to build a broad base of endurance during the off-season. The more experienced the runner, the less time it takes.

Second, run overdistance workouts, defined by the distance you race. Typically, my runners train 1½ times their longest race distance. For example, someone who normally races at the 10-K distance does long runs of 9 miles. They do this long run every 7 to 14 days. Ten days would be perfect, but that's tough to fit into a work schedule. My runners do these long runs at 10-K race pace plus 90 seconds (if your 10-K race pace is 6 minutes per mile, you would run these long runs at a pace of 7:30 per mile).

Third, late in base training, we add short recovery intervals on the roads: 3 minutes at 10-K pace followed by a 1-minute recovery. At this point, I'm not concerned with distances; I'm more concerned with intensity.

—Joe Friel, Fort Collins, Colorado

There's no magic to improving endurance; you just increase volume. I ran 110 miles a week 10 years in a row. For many people, half of that or even less is plenty. To reach your goal level, you have to move through a gradual progression in increments of 10 percent a week. Then every third or fourth week, unload: Drop back close to the starting point to recover.

If you build constantly week after week, you get stronger for a while, but then you reach your breaking point. You get injured, you get a cold, or your body rebels in some other way. To avoid this, build your training in steps. Go up two or three steps, then drop back one, then climb back to where you were and start increasing again.

—Lee Fidler, Atlanta

I still love those long runs on Sundays. They're the mainstay of any training program. You don't get results immediately. It's like saving pennies. Put them in a jar, and at first it doesn't seem as though you have much. But after a few months, the volume begins to look impressive.

I like to see 10-K runners do 14 to 16 miles. My marathoners go 20 to 22 miles. You can't do these runs every week if you run them hard. I recommend that you do them several minutes slower than your 10-K race pace. It's great to run with a group because it can be lonely out there by yourself.

—Robert Wallace, Dallas

I have my runners do their long workouts on hilly courses. The combination of hills and distance builds the muscles and aerobic power that increase endurance. Many people shy away from hills, especially when they go long. They make it easy on themselves, but that limits their improvement.

It's a matter of strength: The more you repeat something, the stronger you get. We run long every week for best results (but not back-to-back hard, long runs). Wait longer than a week, and you fail to improve. I start novice runners on courses of 3 to 6 miles. Gradually we build: 8, 10, 12, 14, 16, then level off. We'll start on a series of small hills spaced apart. As the runners get stronger, we seek steeper hills that are closer together.

—Joe Catalano, Walpole, Massachusetts

You have to learn to push through your fatigue when you're tired. Not all the time, but often enough so that you realize you can do it. My high school runners do piggyback workouts. They run on the track at my pace, rest for a lap when they get tired, but then get right back into it on the next lap. My philosophy is that anyone can run until it hurts, then quit. I teach them to push beyond those initial feelings of being tired.

With triathletes, I work with them one-on-one because they need to learn to run when their legs are tired. Anybody can move from the water to the bike. But when you come off the bike, it's hard to start running. When they run with me and have trouble keeping up, I say, "This is the part of the race where you get tired. Now is when you push."

—John E. Tolbert, New Haven, Connecticut

When you get older (and I'm over 40), you have to learn to mix your sports training together. I participate in a lot of sports. In addition to running, I bicycle during the summer and ski in the winter. To build endurance, I increase my long runs to 20 to 22 miles, but I find that I have to vary them with cross-training, too.

During the summer when I'm not teaching, I may run 15 miles in the morning, wait several hours, then do 30 to 40 miles of steep hills on the bike. I'll do that three days a week to get ready for a fall marathon.

—Hector Leyba, Raton, New Mexico

I often tell runners that the human body is a biological machine that's been programmed to get fitter and gain endurance. Just as a seed with the proper soil, sun, and moisture can't fail to sprout and grow, runners can't fail to improve their endurance if they stick to a regular, progressive training program.

Of course, those are two crucial words: regular and progressive. Regular means that you have to do the activity at least three or four times per week. Progressive means that the workouts should get gradually longer, with the emphasis on gradually. Most running experts believe that you should increase your training by as little as a mile or two per week.

Because of this gradual progression, the successful runner must learn patience. Runners who expect too much, too soon, get injured. They rush, they try to beat a deadline, they get overly competitive with a co-worker. The result is inevitable: an injury that forces you to take time off and lose, rather than gain, endurance. Speeding doesn't pay. Take your time. Marvel at the gradual improvements you do make. Relax. Eventually, you'll get exactly where you want to be.

CHAPTER 22

THE EXPERTS' TRAINING SECRETS

Top Coaches Share Their Best Strategies

In the two decades since the running boom of the late 1970s, running has become a local and regional, as well as a national, phenomenon. As a result, you can find excellent coaches everywhere. Some have developed at high schools and colleges, some have taken their own running successes and turned them into coaching successes, and some have come from more scientific backgrounds.

Most tend to mix the basic tools of training with their own particular expertise. The result is hundreds of different training "recipes"—just like the hundreds of different recipes for apple pie. And all the recipes work; the best is simply the one that has the most appeal for you.

Remember that as you read the following sections. Don't look for the perfect recipe. Look for the one—or ones—that will fit best into your life and training program.

Every runner needs a coach—at least some of the time. A coach can tell you when you're overstriding at the end of a workout or that you need to do more speedwork or that you should begin a routine of upper-body strength training. The best coaches know all these things because they combine personal knowledge, an understanding of basic physiology, and years of practical experience coaching runners. Of course, needing a coach like this is much easier than actually finding one.

In this chapter, many of the country's best distance-running coaches reveal their favorite techniques—the coaching secrets that they have had the most success with. Hopefully, some of these following secrets will work for you or give you new insights that can improve both your performance and your enjoyment of running.

BETTER PLANNING

The coach: Rich Sands

The goal: Organize your training into fully planned cycles that lead you to maximum performance in your most important races.

How to do it: Many runners fail to achieve their goals because their training is too haphazard. They train hard for a couple of weeks only to lose their focus and miss key workouts. In a panic, they devise a new crash training program that lasts for several weeks more before they fall off it again. This pattern repeats itself over and over again.

To break free, you have to organize your entire year in a manner that is structured, yet flexible. First determine your goals: Are you primarily interested in running a fast 10-K? A marathon? Getting ready for a masters track meet?

Next, divide your training and racing year into two six-month macrocycles. Each of these cycles consist of 12 weeks of preparation (base building and strength training), followed by 12 weeks of focused training, and then 2 weeks of rest. And finally, subdivide the focused-training cycle into six 14-day microcycles.

That's the big picture. Of course, you still have to select the actual workouts that you'll run during each cycle. I suggest doing this with both a general and a specific approach. First, gradually increase your weekly mileage during the 12-week base-building period. For the first 6 weeks, keep your running loose and relaxed and do two leg-strengthening workouts per week. For the next 6 weeks, drop the strength training but run hills twice a week. All other runs should remain slow and easy.

Then, organize your 12-week focused-training cycle by deciding what days, in general, work best for you in terms of long runs, speedwork, rest, and so on.

Finally, use the 14-day microcycles to plan your specific workouts, such as 600s on the track, a slow 10-mile run, a day of cross-training, and so on. This gives you a precise road map for each two-week microcycle. It keeps you on schedule to achieve your goal.

All parts of your yearly plan must be subject to change. Let's face it, people do get sick and change jobs and have children and get injured. A training program that isn't flexible is a program that won't work.

When you need to change yours, look at all parts of it—the macrocycle, the 12 weeks of focused training, and the microcycles—and make the best adjustments you can. If necessary, re-evaluate your goal. As long as you know exactly where you're going, it's relatively easy to decide how to get there.

MORE MOTIVATION

The coach: David Virtue, Ph.D.

The goal: Make running easy, interesting, and motivational, especially for beginners.

How to do it: Research has shown that runners who want to run fast must associate with what they are doing. This means that they must focus on their form, breathing, and feelings while they run. They monitor signals from all parts of their bodies that allow them to run their hardest.

This often isn't the best strategy, however, for beginning and intermediate runners. When beginning runners associate, they usually hear a voice that says, "Stop running. This hurts. You can't do it. This isn't fun." If they associate too much while running, they notice their labored breathing, for instance, or feelings of awkwardness or the pain in their calves.

To succeed at running and gain more experience, beginning runners need to dissociate—to override these feelings and let their minds go blank or drift away to different thoughts.

San Diego State University psychologist John Martin, Ph.D., has found that dissociation is the most effective strategy for keeping beginning runners motivated. Dr. Martin conducted an experiment in which one group of beginning runners paid attention to how their bodies felt, while another paid attention to external stimuli. His results showed that the second group had better attendance at weekly training sessions and continued training longer after the sessions ended.

Given the evidence, I teach the runners that I coach a "notice game" that allows them to open their minds to their surroundings. It also works for veteran runners who want to slow down and run longer and more relaxed.

The game works like this: As you run, pretend that everything you see and hear is like a videotape that you're watching at home. Look for particularly appealing sights—a birdhouse, pretty flowers, leaves that have been raked, an unusual car—and latch onto them with your mind. If you're in a race, you can even lock onto the other runners around you—the ones with unusual clothes or shoes or running styles.

At first, it sometimes helps to say aloud what you have just noticed. Soon, however, you'll find that your mind takes over and continually feeds you fascinating scenes from the environment. You won't have to play the game anymore; it will happen automatically.

And these dissociative thoughts will help you recognize and appreciate all the beauties of running.

FASTER RUNNING

The coach: Roy Benson

The goal: Improve your form and increase your speed.

How to do it: Most runners get scared when they hear the word *speedwork,* but this important form of training doesn't have to be too fast or too hard. That is, it shouldn't be anything that scares you. Particularly for adult runners, I recommend what I call short sprints, or aerobic intervals.

These are short pickups of no more than 20 seconds that you can easily incorporate into your training program. Short sprints can help you balance strength and flexibility and improve leg coordination. Even if most of your training is slow, easy distance—particularly during your base-training phase—you should include aerobic intervals to avoid loss of biomechanical efficiency.

Do short sprints with a fast, but easy, effort. Think legs, not lungs. The idea is to use as big a range of motion and as rapid a turnover as possible but for a short enough distance so that you never huff and puff.

Twenty seconds seems the perfect amount of time. Research suggests that lactic acid buildup in the muscles is insignificant up to 20 seconds of fast running but almost quadruples between 20 and 30 seconds. That causes eccentric contractions to begin and forces your muscles to extend while still tight. When this happens, you'll tie up.

You can do this workout at the track—sprint the straightaways and jog the turns. Or on the road, you can run hard for 20 seconds and then jog for 40 seconds.

You can even throw speed bursts into the middle of your long runs. About two-thirds of the way through your run, start doing 15- to 20-second pickups. Cover 1 to 1½ miles this way. But keep the effort easy. Don't force yourself, or you'll defeat the purpose of the workout.

RESTING FOR BETTER TRAINING

The coach: Bill Wenmark

The goal: Use extended rest periods to achieve the right balance between undertraining and overtraining.

How to do it: Many runners take a day or two off when they feel fatigued or hit a plateau. This is fine, but I also recommend including low-mileage weeks as a regular part of your training. Too many runners push harder week after week as they progress toward their goals. The result is an almost inevitable breakdown.

I call my plan the 3–1 Plan. Many veteran marathoners that I have coached, including Dick Beardsley, have trained this way.

My runners train hard for three weeks, then back off during the fourth week to gather strength for the next three-week cycle. They generally do a mileage "step-up" each week. For example, they might do weeks of 40 miles, 50 miles, and 60 miles. These weeks will include a variety of long tempo runs (a run that starts off easy, builds to a steady speed in the middle, and then finishes at an easy pace), hills, mile repeats (running a set of 1-mile distances with rest periods in between), and cross-training. I emphasize high intensity but also recommend single rest days.

During week four, my runners cut back to 30 miles of nothing but easy running. They do these easy weeks as much for the mind as for the body. All the running that they do for that week is fun running. Your mind and body need these breaks to take full advantage of your training program.

I emphasize consistency. You don't have to train hard day after day to achieve your goals. The 3–1 Plan is an effective way to relieve both physical and psychological pressures and to prevent injuries. Best of all, my athletes enjoy it, which means they'll stick with the program and keep improving.

CONCENTRATING ON BETTER FORM

The coach: Mike Manley

The goal: Increase concentration while you're running.

How to do it: Running is a mental effort as well as a physical one. If you want to learn to run better, you need to learn how to concentrate on your running while you're running.

I recommend a workout that I call rhythm strides. These are short, controlled sprints on the track. You run 100 meters up the track at a pace somewhat faster than your 5-K race pace, then do a 30-meter jog-around and run 100 meters back down the track.

While you're running these rhythm strides, concentrate on your biomechanics—your relaxation and stride frequency. You should maintain an upright body carriage and run as efficiently as possible. The whole idea is to run from the inside out, rather than from the outside in. What I mean by this is that you should concentrate on how you want to run and then run that way.

If you can learn to run more efficiently over short distances, it may translate to greater efficiency over longer distances. The beauty of rhythm strides is that they are so short. I could tell runners to do all the same things while running a 400 or even a 5-K, but they wouldn't be able to keep their minds centered for that long. When it's just 100 meters at a time, however, anyone can stay focused.

A workout that includes 10 to 40 rhythm strides is a fairly good workout all by itself. But you can also insert rhythm strides at the end of a long run. Finish your road workout, walk a few minutes to catch your breath, and then do four to five rhythm strides. You'll find that the strides will make you feel 100 percent better, no matter how much you were dragging before doing them.

Veteran runners should know all about concentration, but they're often the ones who forget. Sometimes, after you have been running for many years, you get so comfortable with your routine that you let yourself drift along while you're training. And you keep getting slower. But if you regain your concentration, you may be able to regain some of your lost speed.

MODERATING YOUR WORKOUTS

The coach: Jack Daniels, Ph.D.

The goal: Combine training and racing without burning out.

How to do it: The three most important factors for improvement in running are consistency, moderation, and patience. Doing unbelievably hard workouts in hopes of reaching your goal fast simply doesn't work. Two or three hard workouts a week are all you need, and most of those don't even have to be that hard. The key is to continue training at a steady level throughout the year. The biggest challenge is to limit the amount of time you lose either because of injury or mental fatigue.

Many runners find it difficult to accept, but you can succeed and improve by training at relatively modest levels. Most hard workouts shouldn't get harder and harder. They should continue to feel about the same as you get in better shape. The only things that should change are the numbers—the speed and the distance. But your perception of the difficulty of these workouts should remain the same.

Anytime you look forward to getting a workout over with, you should ask yourself if you're running too hard. Anytime you finish a workout exhausted, you probably have run too hard. You should finish each workout with a feeling of excitement about the next workout.

If you're training for a 10-K, you should do most of your speed training at a slightly faster pace (about 5-K pace). For example, you might do repeats of 800 meters to a mile at your 5-K race pace. For longer tempo runs lasting anywhere from 15 to 20 minutes, run a pace slightly slower than your 10-K race pace.

Always save your best effort for races. Except during a non-racing period of your training program, workouts should never approach race-level effort. You can expect to run an all-out race only once every two weeks. If you work out at peak effort in training, you won't be able to perform at your best in competition.

ACHIEVING A MENTAL EDGE

The coach: Brad Jaeger

The goal: Perform at your best on race day.

How to do it: I'm a big believer in the importance of attitude. You can get a lot more out of most runners by working with their heads than by working with their bodies. Masters runners may not be able to run 100 miles a week, but they can train an hour a day and use their mental strength to achieve success.

I teach a highly effective mental technique that I call anchoring. It means focusing on something at which you achieved success. You recall this achievement when you're striving for a new goal.

I ask my runners to "anchor" as they're peaking for an important competition. These runners aren't world-class athletes, so they aren't going to recall an Olympic victory. But they have probably had a business triumph, a personal relationship, or some memory that makes them feel very positive.

When you find this memory, anchor to it. Relive the sights, the smells, the season, the time of day . . . anything about the previous success that makes you feel good. And remind yourself: If everything clicked for me once, it can happen again.

You can't use this technique too often or you'll blunt its effectiveness. I ask my runners to select a maximum of five goal races during the year. Before each of those races, we try to re-create the circumstances of their previous successes. I constantly remind them about that event and the upcoming race. We use cards, phone calls, and conversations with friends, spouses, and children. We try to focus all our energy on creating a positive attitude about the race.

Everybody is different. You can't use the same techniques for every runner. But every runner can come closer to his goal performance by creating a positive mental environment on race day.

> *We tend to think that running success is built totally on the success of a training program—the speedwork, the hill repeats, the long runs. It isn't.*
>
> *Several parts of this chapter remind us that the mental approach is just as—if not more—important. The mental or attitudinal secrets had the biggest impact on me.*
>
> *Anyone can train . . . for a while. Anyone can get faster . . . for a while. But the runners who succeed, both in competitions and in the race for greater health and fitness, are those who make haste slowly. That is, the winners are those who keep fit and keep running for many, many years.*
>
> *And you can't do this with any number of magic workouts. You can only do it with a mental approach that allows you to stay committed to your running program. That's why I particularly like Dr. Virtue's comments on dissociation and Jaeger's on anchoring. These techniques, and others similar to them, can help you get the most mental and emotional rewards from your training. And that's what will keep you going.*

THE NEED FOR SPEED

Spice Up Your Speedwork with Variety

As a young runner, I was lucky. My coach, a runner himself, believed that the sport was meant to be enjoyed for many intrinsic reasons: the beauty of movement, the beauty of nature, the beauty of an activity that combined the two. He thought that running should be fun and taught us to enjoy its varied splendors. We prospered.

But we never learned how to do speedwork. I think—in fact, I'm quite sure—this was because my coach himself had had an unpleasant experience with a college coach bent on subjecting him to torturous track workouts. He resolved that, as a coach, he would never do the same to his young charges.

On the whole, I'm glad he didn't. He taught us the aesthetics of running—far more important than the mechanics. Still, I think I could have run faster and gained a deeper appreciation of the sport if we had done more speedwork of the type Olympian Jeff Galloway describes here. And, as Galloway is quick to point out, this kind of running can and should be fun. You only have to approach it correctly.

Most runners burn out on speedwork because they don't allow themselves to have fun—the workouts are too hard and repetitious. Most of us perform our speedwork according to that worn-out adage, "No pain, no gain." The result? Often, it's little or no gain.

But if you start doing workouts that are fun, you'll want to do more of them. And that alone will help you improve, to race better.

Yes, I said fun, even when it comes to speedwork, the type of training many runners dread most. Speedwork can and should be fun. It simply has to be tailored to your particular ability and needs.

Speedwork helps you run faster and stronger in three ways: It improves running form, eases your adaptation to oxygen debt, and helps you push through the mental barriers of discomfort and doubt. Hard work, of course. But it doesn't have to be those dreadful interval repeats on the track with short rests.

In fact, the best—and fastest—way to build strength and speed is by combining hill, fartlek, and interval sessions. If you approach the following workouts with a little imagination and inspiration, you can enjoy some moments of real joy and satisfaction.

THE UPSIDE OF HILL RUNNING

Running hills increases strength and drive from the legs and also helps prepare you for taxing interval workouts. It may be the best type of speedwork.

The Speed Doctor

Speedwork is great for improving your form, your ability to handle oxygen debt, and your skill at overcoming mental barriers, but it can also fix specific problems with your running. Here are some common problems and how speedwork can cure them.

You lose steam at the end of races. Try longer speed workouts. Instead of 10 repeats of 440s as your longest workout before a 10-K race, increase the number of repetitions over eight weekly workouts to 20 repeats of 440s, running each 5 to 7 seconds faster than your goal race pace. Try to run the last 4 of each workout 2 to 3 seconds faster than the other 440s (but never run all out).

Just past midrace, you gradually slow down. For the 10-K, build your speedwork gradually until the hard repetitions equal 14 to 16 repeats of 440s (at 7 to 8 seconds faster than goal pace). Run each of the middle 4 to 5 repeats of 440s at 2 seconds faster than the others.

You always run a slow first mile. For the 10-K, run a maximum of 12 repeats of 440s at 8 to 10 seconds faster than goal pace, then hang on through the rest of the workout, running 6 to 8 seconds faster than goal pace.

Hills wipe you out. Study the course that you plan to run. Run a hill workout once a week, gradually increasing to three to four more hills of the same size and grade as those on the course. You may also run the same number of hills, but make each one longer and/or steeper than those on the race course. Be sure to work on efficient downhill running to balance your skills.

Oxygen debt prevents you from running your best. Cut down the rest between repetitions during your interval workouts. For the 10-K, gradually build to 20 repeats of 440s at 3 to 5 seconds faster than race pace. Take the shortest rest interval (jogging) that you can tolerate and finish the workout in the time assigned.

A few years ago, I was concerned that a talented high school sophomore would burn out by running too much track work. So, during track season, he and I ran four to nine 400-meter hills (on a moderate 5 percent grade). With no other speedwork, and after just eight of these weekly sessions, he lowered his mile personal record from 4:32 to 4:18.

Many coaches and strength experts believe that hills provide better leg strength for running than weights or machines. Pushing up the incline builds the lower leg muscles.

Weight lifting strengthens those same muscles but won't train them for the demands of running. The large and small muscles in the legs must work together perfectly to produce a smooth stride. Hill running does that by building strength and coordination at the same time.

That added leg strength also improves running posture. An efficiently moving body saves energy. Additionally, good running posture reduces wear and tear on easily injured parts of the body.

What's more, hill training forces you to develop quick push-off and faster leg turnover. Unlike the explosive strength that high jumpers and long jumpers rely on, distance-running strength is measured in quick little pushes. Given the number of steps you take per mile, even a small increase in efficiency will pay off in a 10-K, and even more so in a marathon.

You only need to do hill work once a week. Pick a hill with a moderate grade, 5 to 8 percent. Start with 3 to 4 repetitions and gradually increase to a maximum of 8 to 12. Your goal is to build strength, not oxygen debt, so take plenty of rest between each hill. Remember: Short, steep hills develop quick, dynamic strength, while long, sustained hills build stamina.

Maintaining the correct running form is an important part of hill training. Keep a short stride with your feet directly underneath you. Once you find the perfect stride, you'll feel lighter and smoother. If you overstride during hill work, you'll miss out on some of the possible form improvements, and your recovery will slow.

FEEL GOOD ABOUT FARTLEKS

You have probably run fartlek workouts—even if you were too embarrassed to pronounce the word in public. It's the simplest form of speedwork: You just accelerate when you feel good, then jog easily until you recover.

Popularized in Europe, *fartlek* (the Swedish word for "speed play") prepares you for the turbulence of racing. Many runners feel that they get a better workout when they do fartlek than when they do track work because the random nature of the running helps them push beyond artificial physiological and psychological barriers.

Let's assume that you tell yourself that you'll end an acceleration at a street corner. Even though you're tired and in need of a rest, you push past the corner. You have entered the "worry zone" of races when most runners question themselves and then slow down. By pushing through fatigue, you'll learn to run past your doubts and keep moving toward your goal.

Fartlek can help improve your running in many ways. For example, if you have trouble surging or staying with someone who surges, then work on this in fartlek sessions. When tired, push the pace for 50 to 60 yards, then come back to your basic pace instead of just jogging to recover.

If you slow down in the middle of races, then work extra hard in the middle of each fartlek workout. You can train yourself to perform at top capacity at the end of races by saving the roughest part of your workout for last and trying to overcome fatigue.

Fartlek is easier and more fun with a partner. By sharing the hard running, both of you get a better workout, reduce stress, and simulate race situations. Remember to increase the distance of your fartlek workouts according to the distance of your goal race. To prepare for a 10-K, try running the hard parts slightly faster than race pace for a total workout of 3 to 4 miles. If you're training for a marathon, you can increase the length of your fartlek bursts, run them slower, and log 4 to 6 miles of fartlek running in the middle of an 8- to 10-mile workout.

THE IMPORTANCE OF INTERVAL TRAINING

Interval training does two things better than other types of speed training: It improves your running mechanics and provides direct feedback on pace. While repetitions may be boring, they allow you to develop a fast running rhythm in a controlled environment, which helps improve running form. Your time for each lap tells you exactly how you're performing and teaches pace judgment.

Scientifically designed interval workouts can gradually help you tolerate oxygen debt. When muscles are overloaded, they cannot process enough oxygen to burn fuel efficiently, hence the term *oxygen debt*. As you add one or two repetitions to a workout each week, you can increase your body's capacity to handle this oxygen debt.

Interval sessions also help you peak for races. By reducing the rest interval between the hard repetitions, you'll find that your body gets more prepared for the intensity of a hard race.

Safe Speed

According to some studies, speedwork ranks among the leading causes of running injuries. Fortunately, you can reduce your chance of injury by being prepared for speed, inserting strategic rest before you need it, and running under control. Here are some basic tips.

Start slowly. To prepare for speed, pick up your pace gradually. Instead of jumping into track work after months of slow running, begin with a series of four to eight weeks of once-a-week hill workouts. These will give you a strength-building transition zone. Run the first two hill workouts conservatively, then gradually increase the intensity of subsequent hill sessions.

Warm up well. To get your leg muscles ready for speedwork, warm up with 10 to 20 minutes of slow running and walking. Speedwork demands top performance from the body, and so it's also important to take four to eight light accelerations (100 to 200 yards). Starting at a slow pace, gradually pick up speed until you are running about the pace you'll run in the workout, then decelerate. Jog slowly or walk between accelerations. Afterward, walk or jog for 3 to 5 minutes.

Don't forget about rest. When you add speedwork to your program, you put extra stress on the muscles. This produces more microtears in the muscles and tendons. Unless you build some quality rest into your program, the microtears will accumulate and result in an injury.

Most six- to seven-days-a-week runners can improve performance by dropping to five days a week (three running days, one day off, two running days, one day off). Keep the same mileage per week, but add swimming or biking on the easy days.

Schedule your hard days before an easy day and after a day off. Never run two hard days back-to-back.

Stick to it. Start a year-round program of light acceleration work—a few repetitions with maximum rest between. You can use them as warm-ups (as above) or to keep sharp during easy days or the off-season. After an easy 5- to 10-minute warm-up, pick up the pace for 100 yards or so at random places around the track. Or choose specific parts of the track where you'll start and finish. Run on trails or roads if you like, but, wherever you run, stay relaxed throughout each repetition. Don't time them, don't run all-out, and don't feel too tired during this workout. Run hard enough to feel invigorated, not fatigued.

To compensate for individual problems, such as midrace let-down, run interval workouts like fartlek sessions. Try surging in the midst of hard repetitions or going out fast and hanging on. This psychological war with yourself will push you into and past the worry zone.

How to Make It Fun

You can reach a high level of conditioning by properly mixing your speedwork components—hills for strength, fartlek for mental toughness, and intervals for peaking. In addition, light accelerations will keep you in good form throughout the year. Each stage develops strengths and capabilities that you'll need during the next phase of training.

But what about the fun? It's the little things that make you feel good about your workout and that make it easier. To add a little spice to running hills, for example, break them up mentally: Relax for the first third, run the second third hard, and hold the pace over the top.

The most powerful motivator may be the chemistry of your running partners. Of course, everyone needs to have a cooperative attitude and to avoid goading each other to be "the workout winner." With the right group, you'll establish respect and gain irreplaceable friendships.

Alone or with others, play games. Imagine that a fierce competitor is just ahead of you. As you near the end of the hill or repetition, visualize yourself gaining and then cruising by at the finish. Many runners prefer world-class fantasies.

Billy Mills did. On practically every run for three years, this mediocre college runner imagined that the world-record holder (Ron Clarke of Australia at that time) was just ahead. Finishing each run in a blaze of glory, Mills would visualize himself lunging for the tape in quest of the gold medal.

Mill's fantasy became reality. This almost unknown runner rounded the final straightaway of the 1964 Olympic 10,000-meter final a distant third. When he saw the finish tape, he didn't have to think. His mind and body were exhausted, but they did what they had been doing for the last 1,000 days. He didn't even have to lunge for the tape to take home the gold medal.

> *The loneliness of the long-distance runner. The camaraderie of the long-distance runner. Which one will it be?*
>
> *Both, no doubt. Each in its proper place. And the place for camaraderie, in my mind, is when doing speedwork. As long as*

I have been running, I have always performed my best and had the most fun when I was part of a regular speedwork training group in college with a tight group of buddies in my late twenties, or with my colleagues at work now.

Running hard and fast at least once a week in the company of friends has long been among my greatest running pleasures. As Galloway says, there's a chemistry that develops among training partners.

The chemistry changes depending upon the runners, of course, but two things remain constant: Running hard and fast with a group is fun, and this kind of speedwork makes you faster. You would be hard-pressed to find a better training combination than this.

6

THE
MENTAL
SIDE
OF RUNNING

CHAPTER 24

SEVEN STRATEGIES TO BE YOUR BEST

How to Think Like a Champion

The more years I run, the more I'm impressed by the mental side of running. In my earlier days I used to think that success in running was purely a matter of finding the right training combination. If you did the right long runs, if you did the right speed workouts, if you worked all the numbers, well, you would be ready to run great.

Of course, I still believe in the importance of training. But now I believe that attitude is even more crucial. Because running will always humble you, as Bill Rodgers put it many times, and you need something to keep you going when the going gets tough.

Now, in many regards, humility is a good thing. It teaches respect, which is where learning begins, and we can all stand to learn something new every day. But too much humility is like too much apple pie—it begins to weigh you down. And runners need to be light, positive-thinking people to overcome the inevitable obstacles they face. This chapter explains how positive thinking can lead to powerful running.

Roger Bannister's historic first sub-4-minute mile, recorded on May 6, 1954, ranks as one of the greatest and most widely known moments in the history of sports. What's less well-known is the intriguing fact that in the next 12 months, four other runners also broke through the previously impossible barrier. Why? Had the human species suddenly evolved into a higher organism, capable of running with greater speed and endurance?

Of course not. The only explanation for the post-Bannister rush of sub-4 milers is that 4 minutes had represented more of a mental barrier than a physical barrier. Knowing that Bannister had run a 3:59, the rest of the world's milers could no longer believe such a time was beyond their reach. They had little choice but to redouble their efforts to run as fast as Bannister and faster.

The Bannister story is perhaps the best example in running of this basic concept: Negative thinking limits performance. Turn the thinking around, and suddenly the impossible becomes possible. This doesn't apply just to breakthrough performers, world records, and gold medals. It applies to every one of us, to every race we run, and, indeed, to every situation we face in our lives.

If you can train your mind—and you can—your body will follow. In the rest of this chapter, I'll describe a number of techniques that you can use to improve your performances and increase your enjoyment of running.

BELIEVING YOU CAN

By 1954 more than 50 medical journals had carried articles saying it was humanly impossible to break 4 minutes in the mile, but Bannister didn't buy their arguments. He refused to limit his own potential. His success proved that we are capable of those things that we are capable of believing. Or, to put it another way, as an athlete, you should always act as if you can. With this positive attitude, you can then find out the truth of your athletic potential by living out the experience.

Far too many of us do the opposite: We decide ahead of time that we can't. We think we're too old, too heavy, not well enough trained, not tough enough, not blessed with the right muscle fibers. The list goes on and on, developing into a litany of negative, limiting language and beliefs. And the outcome is always the same: If you think you can't, you can't.

Henry Ford described both sides as well as anyone when he said, "If you think you can do it, you're right. If you think you can't do it, you're still right." When you believe and think "I can," you activate your motivation, commitment, confidence, concentration, and excitement, all of which relate directly to achievement. If you think "I can't," on the other hand, you sabotage your chances of achieving your goals.

Over the years, I have worked with a wide range of athletes— from Olympians to midpackers—and during those years I've noticed one clear and consistent pattern: The most successful runners think like champions. The "I can" belief forms the foundation of their approach to all things in life. They refuse to accept "I can't" unless they have collected objective data showing that a goal is beyond their grasp. Even then, they don't say, "I can't." They simply reformulate their goals to move them within reach.

The same approach will work for you. It won't necessarily turn you into an Olympic champion, but it will help you to run better and enjoy it more. The "I can" attitude will also allow you to adopt the following mind-sets, all of which are designed to help you unlock the extraordinary potential that each of us possesses as a runner.

BOUNCING BACK FROM FAILURE

To succeed, every runner must learn to deal with mistakes and failures. All champions realize that the path to personal excellence is cluttered with obstacles. Arriving at the top is a process that involves many setbacks. Champions accept this process, under-

---

The Makeup of a Champion

Champions share many characteristics, none of which are determined by their running speeds. How many of these statements describe your running and your life?

- A champion has the courage to risk failure, knowing that setbacks are lessons to learn from.

- A champion uses a race to gain greater self-knowledge as well as feedback on physical improvement.

- A champion trains thought processes as well as the body to produce a total approach to performance.

- A champion understands his athletic weaknesses and trains to strengthen them.

- A champion actively creates a life of balance, moderation, and simplicity—values that help improve running and life.

- A champion views competitors as partners who provide challenge and the chance to improve.

- A champion understands that running performances are like a roller coaster, with many ups and downs, and that you have to accept both the good and the bad.

- A champion enjoys running for the simple pleasures it provides.

- A champion has vision. A champion dreams of things that haven't been and believes they are possible. A champion says, "I can."

standing that you can't stretch your limits without encountering some rough moments along the way.

I recall the attitude of Herb Lindsay after one of his few losses in 1980, a year when he was the country's top-ranked road racer. When I asked Lindsay how it felt to finally lose one, he said that he would bounce back at the next race and that he considered every loss a lesson in how to become an even better champion. Lindsay didn't get down on himself. He created a personal environment in which failure and losses were acceptable learning experiences that could help him improve.

We have all learned everything we know physically—from walking to running a marathon—by trial and error, so there's no reason to become our own worst enemies when we suffer a setback. From time to time everyone falls short of their goals. It's an illusion to believe that champions succeed because they do everything perfectly. You can be certain that every archer who hits the bull's-eye has also missed the bull's-eye a thousand times while learning the skill.

When you create a mental environment that accepts mistakes, you free yourself to keep trying, to keep extending yourself, to keep taking risks. Sure, you'll have some bad days, but if you accept them as opportunities for growth, you can learn much from the experiences. An accepting attitude helps you perform with greater relaxation, which, as all champions know, is one of the key building blocks of success.

A New Definition of Winning

To bring out your best, you also need to adopt the champion's true attitude toward winning. No matter who you are, there has to be more to running than taking home a medal or age-group award. Philosopher Alan Watts once said, "You don't sing to get to the end of the song." The same applies to running: You don't run to finish or to get it over with.

Of course, we all like to do our best, to succeed, to set new personal records. Our performances provide a handy gauge of self-improvement, and the recognition we receive is rewarding. But too many runners suffocate their enjoyment of running by overemphasizing the importance of fast times.

About all this does is build up your tension and anxiety, which can't help you run better. In fact, these responses actually interfere with your natural fluidity and speed, thus creating an obstacle to the goal, to say nothing of how such attitudes diminish the fun of running and racing.

In his classic work *The Zen of Running,* Fred Rohé states: "There are no standards and no possible victories except the joy you are living while dancing your run . . . you are not running for some future reward—the real reward is *now!*"

That's quite similar to the motto of the modern Olympic Games: "The important thing in the Games is not winning but taking part. The essential thing in life is not conquering but fighting well."

If you run with this attitude, the results will take care of themselves. While running, focus on the internal battle. Concentrate on overcoming fear, self-doubt, and other limiting beliefs. Forget about external issues, like your time. Such outward concerns will only deplete your energy, create tension, and slow you down.

APPRECIATING YOUR OPPONENTS

Thinking like a champion also means adopting a new attitude toward your opponents. Traditionally, being a good competitor meant being a good predator. You succeeded most when you attacked and thrashed the opposition. But it doesn't have to be this way.

In the movie *Running Brave,* Billy Mills slows down near the finish of one race, even as a coach stands on the sidelines screaming, "Crush your opponent! Take him for everything! Own him!" But Mills is well ahead of the other runners and understands that he will gain nothing by destroying them. That the real Mills made this choice doesn't mean that he wasn't a fierce runner. In 1964, he won the Olympic 10,000 meters in Tokyo, considered by many to be one of the biggest upsets in Olympic history.

Obviously, the killer instinct isn't a requirement for optimal performance. It's much healthier and more beneficial to view opponents as partners who, because of their great efforts, afford you the opportunity to raise the level of your own performance. You depend on them to extend your limits. Think about it: How often do you run as fast in training as you do in races?

When I race, I often recite an affirmation that reminds me of how my opponents help me reach my potential. The affirmation goes like this: "My opponents are very important to me. Because they are here, I experience greater depth as an athlete."

When we come together to try to reach our potential, such as in a road race, others can only help us. With such a view, you will enter a race more relaxed, focused, and energized. You can't help but perform better as a result of cooperation rather than antagonism.

SIMPLICITY IN ALL THINGS

The true champion recognizes that excellence often flows most smoothly from simplicity, a fact that can get lost in these high-tech days. I used to train with a world-class female runner who was constantly hooking herself up to pulse meters and pace keepers. She spent hours collecting data that she thought would help her improve. In fact, a good 25 percent of her athletic time was devoted to externals other than working out. Sports became so complex for her that she forgot how to enjoy herself.

Contrast her approach with that of the late Abebe Bikila, the Ethiopian who won the 1960 Olympic Marathon running barefoot. Fancy clothing and digital watches were not part of his world. He simply ran. Many times in running, and in other areas of life, less is more.

Bill Rodgers won his first Boston Marathon in 2:09:55 while wearing a plain white T-shirt on which he had hand-lettered the initials of his track club. When you learn to run simply, you find that you can concentrate on simply running.

Another proponent of such thinking is Mark Nenow, the American record holder for 10,000 meters on the road. Nenow has never been concerned with weight, muscle biopsies, heart rates, or sports science. He's had no grand expectations and therefore has never been devastated by setbacks. He just keeps running.

Bikila, Rodgers, and Nenow stand as perfect examples of a philosophy that Joe Henderson, *Runner's World* magazine's first editor, has expressed on many occasions: "Don't let the planning and analyzing get in the way of the doing and enjoying." It's an approach that would benefit many runners.

BALANCE IN YOUR LIFE

Runners who think like champions know when they have done enough. Doing too much, especially in training, is one of the greatest misfortunes that a runner can encounter because it can wipe out all your hard-earned conditioning.

More isn't better. Moderation is better. Olympian Jeff Galloway has used this approach with various marathon training groups around the country. Many of these groups, following a program of training every other day, have achieved marathon-completion rates of 98 percent and higher.

Balance is another side of moderation, and something runners occasionally have trouble keeping in perspective. A few years ago, a national-class client of mine was experiencing the classic signs of burnout and fatigue. He was so obsessed with running that he kept getting injured. I asked him to visit my office to discuss his situation. The following dialogue sums up our conversation.

Me: "How much do you need to train?"

Marty: "I'd train 12 hours a day if I could."

Me: "Marty, you really need to consider having more balance in your life."

Marty: "I would be balanced. I'd do 12 hours of working out and 12 hours of sleep. That would be a perfect balance."

Marty may be an extreme case, but many other runners suffer from overtraining. They believe that they won't excel unless they devote everything to the effort. But there are many examples of the opposite.

Ingrid Kristiansen set her marathon record two years after the birth of her first child. Her interests in family and hobbies other than running provided balance in her life and may have enabled her to compete with less tension and anxiety.

When Changes Are Needed

When you're feeling stale and burned out, it could be because you're overtraining. But it could also be because your mental program needs an overhaul. Do any of the following statements describe you? If so, you should consider ways you can change your thought patterns.

- You struggle constantly for external recognition rather than internal satisfaction.

- You measure your self-worth as a runner solely on the basis of each performance.

- You focus on perfection, an unrealistic goal, rather than pursuing a journey of excellence.

- You condemn yourself for failures, setbacks, and mistakes rather than realizing that not only are they inevitable, but they offer good opportunities for learning.

- You blame others or your circumstances when things go wrong. This leaves you feeling out of control.

- You see running as something to conquer.

- You have unrealistic goals that result in frustration, disappointment, and distraction.

Many other women runners have improved after the birth of their children, despite the obvious fact that children demand incredible amounts of energy and attention. This doesn't have to be a negative factor. Indeed, it's a positive when it means that the runner has added more balance to his or her life. Yes, his. Keith Brantly finally made the U.S. Olympic Team in 1996, after finishing fourth in 1988 and 1992, when he brought his seven-month-old son with him to the Olympic Trials.

Avoiding extremes will help you run farther, wiser, and longer in life. Adding balance to your running means decreasing injury and burnout. At the same time, you'll find yourself enjoying your running more, feeling more motivated, and looking forward to many more years of productive, fun-filled participation.

THE ZEN-TAO APPROACH

After his superb victory at the 1990 New York City Marathon, Douglas Wakiihuri, born in Kenya and trained in Japan, stated that his marathoning could not be separated from his search for life's truths. Wakiihuri is right. Winning at racing, as in life, is an inner journey without a destination.

In searching for both athletic and personal growth at the same time, Wakiihuri represents a new breed of champions I call sacred warriors. These runners realize that they will have the most success in their external lives only after they have won the inner battle over self-doubt.

When you adopt a similar attitude, it doesn't mean that you'll run world records or even personal records. You will, however, decrease the pressure and stress you may feel when running. And this can only help you improve your performances and your appreciation of running. By focusing on running as an exciting and fulfilling journey without a destination, you will see that your running can't be anything but successful and rewarding.

You have within you, right now, all that you need to achieve your realistic goals in running. Thinking like a champion will allow you to reach that potential. Remember that all your accomplishments are the direct result of your thoughts. When you choose the right kind of thoughts, you can create the running destiny you have always wanted.

All of the mental strategies in this chapter can work for runners, as shown through a number of telling anecdotes, but the one I find most compelling from my own experience is the power of simplicity. It rings so true to me, because I have seen it in action so often.

We westerners have a tendency to look outside ourselves for secrets and shortcuts. We place great faith, for example, in the secrets of science. We believe it can teach us how to train and race faster. Maybe it can, and we would certainly be foolish to ignore truths that are revealed to us.

But running is such a basic, nontechnical activity that the greatest truths may be the simplest. You have to train hard. You have to take rest breaks. You have to eat well but not too much. You have to expect some bad days and bad races; all life, after all, follows certain cyclical patterns. Excessive worry and hair-pulling won't do much good. The best way to race well another day is to put today behind you.

You can't change it, so you might as well accept it and move onward. Face tomorrow with a fresh, open, confident attitude. If you believe tomorrow could be the day when everything works out perfectly for you, then that may in fact be the case.

DIGGING DEEP

*Discover How You Can Get
the Most out of Yourself*

> *All of us have the feeling that we have more ability than we exhibit, that we could get more out of ourselves if only we knew how to tap our full potential. We see others perform amazing feats, and they don't seem any different or more talented than we are. How do they do it? How can we do the same?*
>
> *In running, this line of thought can be self-defeating. The truth is that some runners do have more talent than others, and no amount of training or concentration is going to bridge the gap. Because races are based on such hard-edged mathematics—someone finishes in 2 hours, someone in 3 hours, and someone in more than 4 hours—we can't escape the reality of our performances. And it's more important to accept ourselves as we are and to practice the sport for its myriad benefits than to get hung up on changing a 4-hour performance to a 3-hour finish.*
>
> *Still, we would like to run as fast as we can—to bring out our best—and we know that the mind holds the key to being better. This chapter by Ken McAlpine explores how different athletes have succeeded in digging deep to reach their maximum running potential.*

Sport hurts. When you challenge yourself in a race, whether it's the muscle-busting seconds of a sprint or the muscle-wasting hours of a marathon, you encounter moments when your heart rocks your ribs, your muscles sear, and your mind strains to recall why you're doing this at all. How you handle these painful, pivotal moments during a race often determines success or failure. Some athletes and coaches suggest that the ability to dig deep and persevere is all that stands between you and your potential.

"To do well, you have to push yourself," says two-time Olympic 3000-meter runner PattiSue Plumer, who has made a career of gutsy performances. "You have to keep going. You have to go beyond what you think you're capable of doing."

Athletes have been pushing the edges of their performance

envelopes since the days of the first Olympics in Greece. Through trial and error, the best runners have developed a retinue of physical and mental techniques for coping with, and occasionally stepping through, the difficult moments that beat the rest of us to a smudge.

There are no universal, surefire methods. Pushing through tough times involves performance intangibles—intelligence, desire, sheer pigheadedness—that don't plug neatly into a formula. But the ability to dig deep and persevere can, to some extent, be cultivated, bringing you a step closer to racing and training at your full potential.

Ration your reserves. Start by recognizing that you can't tap reserves that aren't there. Physiology dictated that you have a finite amount of energy. This energy must be rationed carefully. This may seem like something any dolt would know, but if it were, you wouldn't see a third of every race field burst off the starting line like commuters late for a bus. Experienced athletes parcel out their energy reserves in miserly fashion, knowing full well what will come later.

"As you tire, it takes more effort—physically and emotionally—to pull through the last part of the race," says three-time Western States 100 winner Tom Johnson. "You need to save half of your energy for the last third of the race."

How to measure your energy dispersal? Pay close attention to how you feel.

"If it's early in a race and you start feeling the lactic acid build up, and your heart rate's going sky high, those are pretty clear signs that you're using too much energy too soon," says three-time Olympic cyclist John Howard. "It's okay to feel the lactic acid building up late in a race, but early on you should feel loose and comfortable."

Easing back on the throttle early on can sometimes pay stunning dividends. At the 1990 Canadian Ironman, triathlete Erin Baker pared back her effort during the 112-mile bike ride and uncorked a 2:49 marathon run. "If you just take a deep breath, calm yourself down, and bring your heart rate down 10 to 15 beats per minute, you can actually save quite a bit of energy," says Baker. "A little bit saved adds up to much more than you'd think."

Practice hard. "If you want to learn to run through pain, you have to experience the pain first," states Plumer. "I think the fastest way for most people to improve their performance is by experiencing this pain and learning how to handle it. But most people avoid this."

Plumer recommends at least one intense, race-stimulating interval workout a week. Fine, you say, I do intervals. But do your interval workouts really force you to push back your limits? Perhaps your interval sessions have become rote? Local tracks are brimmimg with runners who can pop off quarters like slot machines. But is that the point?

Traditionally lauded for their physical benefits, intervals offer a crucial psychological boon. Familiarity with discomfort fosters comfort.

"You must experience hurt during training," says 1972 Olympic Marathon gold medalist Frank Shorter. "Then when things get difficult in a race, you just think, 'I've been here before. I know what happens. If I keep up the pressure and the mental intensity, eventually I'll come out of this.' "

Back off from pain. When you do run face-first into pain, know that it is okay to step back a bit. While many athletes see backing off as an overt admission of spineless wormdom, elite runners don't hesitate. When they start to struggle, they ease off the pace, regroup physically, then push on again. No one—at least no one who hopes to finish—grinds on without reprieve.

Shorter points out that races typically take place in surges— hard efforts alternating with bouts of recovery. The winners aren't necessarily the fastest runners, says Shorter; they're the ones who can recover from the surges the fastest.

"The less well-trained you are, the longer it takes for you to recover," Shorter adds. "But if you're trained to any degree, and you slow down enough, you will recover."

So, when your heart feels as though it might burst, and your legs are threatening to turn to cement, the best thing you can do is precisely what you want to do—ease back.

Pushing through difficult moments is largely a matter of maintaining composure. It goes back to relaxation. Experienced runners understand this, which is why they say things like "You fight pain by relaxing and gaining control" and "As the pain intensifies, the response is to become more relaxed." Advice like this may sound silly, especially when your heart is ricocheting about your chest. And, true, relaxing won't make the pain go away, but it will keep you from crumbling.

Take a deep breath. The best way to relax, focus your effort, and maintain your form is through controlled, rhythmic breathing. "Controlling your breathing is crucial," says Howard, echoing a belief voiced by most athletes. "It allows you to focus and concentrate almost entirely on your form. Not a lot of athletes do this. They lose control of their breathing, and they lose contact with their bodies. Their form falls apart. When you lose your form, you're lost."

When the going gets difficult, Howard focuses on inhaling and exhaling long and steadily. Deep, steady breathing triggers the

---

The Second Wind Mystery

Ask exercise physiologists about second wind, and you'll get much head-nodding that, yes, this is an intriguing subject indeed. But no one knows precisely why second wind occurs.

"All we can do is speculate," says Robert Murray, Ph.D., director of the Gatorade Sports Science Institute's exercise physiology laboratory in Barrington, Illinois. "Theories can take you from the top of the body—the brain and the central nervous system—all the way down to the bottom, to the biochemistry of the muscle cells. If you talk to 100 physiologists, you'll probably get 100 different answers."

The most common theory goes something like this: When you start exercising, your muscles burn glycogen as fuel. This requires oxygen. Your body has a limited amount of stored oxygen, and it burns it quickly. After that, if your body can't supply enough oxygen to your muscles, the muscles break down glycogen without oxygen, or anaerobically. This produces lactic acid. You're in oxygen debt, and you feel lousy—your muscles burn, your heart beats quickly. Second wind, that welcome flush of relief, occurs when the body finally begins to supply enough oxygen to your muscles.

"The term *catch up* is important when we talk about second wind," says Glenn Town, Ph.D., an Illinois exercise physiologist who once finished 24th at the Hawaii Ironman. "When you go from total inactivity to heading out on a run, you create an oxygen debt. The payback in an unconditioned individual can be uncomfortable."

Because their more efficient systems can supply their muscles with a steady stream of oxygen, fit athletes avoid oxygen debt, says Dr. Town, and never experience second wind. Beginners can fend off oxygen debt by easing gradually into a run. Start with a brisk walk, move to a slow jog, and gradually increase your speed from there. This may sound pedestrian, but even fit runners often do the same thing, starting their runs at little more than a shuffle.

parasympathetic nervous system, the body's relaxation mode. By contrast, huffing and puffing provokes the energy-burning sympathetic nervous system, the same neurological response elicited when you back over your neighbor's cat.

"You respond either in a controlled, systematic, powerful way, or in a panicked manner, where your body is out of control," says Howard. "Athletes need to learn to use the mind to control the body. That's really what it comes down to. Most of us do just the opposite. We let the body control the mind."

THE POWER OF YOUR MIND

Ultimately, the ability to cope mentally with tough times may be what separates the best from the rest. Unfortunately, sports psychology and its terminology—such as *thought stopping, trigger words,* and *alternative scripts*—tend to turn people off. Before you look away, realize that science has documented a mind-body link. Using sophisticated tools and techniques, researchers have shown that athletes can induce profound changes in their brains during competition, changes that can greatly enhance their performances. Elite archers, for example, can damp down distracting impulses in the left, or analytical, side of the brain, allowing the reflexive, free-form right hemisphere to send arrows flying true. The biology can be complex. Just understand this: It's the foolish athlete who ignores the mind.

"I don't think the average person realizes what sort of impact the mind has on performance," says Leonard Zaichkowsky, a Boston University sport psychologist who has worked with everyone from Little Leaguers to Olympians. "They know it impacts, but at most they might think, 'Well, I read about it once, but it doesn't affect me that much.' Rest assured, it does."

The psychological tactics for pushing on are as varied as the athletes who use them. Many are simply ploys, often outright chicanery, designed to convince the body that it isn't on the verge of meltdown.

Break the run into chunks. Breaking your run down into mentally manageable chunks is one example. Steve Scott, who has run more than 100 sub-4-minute miles, tackles races lap by lap. On the third lap, when things really start to hurt, his goal might be just to stay with the leaders through that lap. Instead of focusing on the pain, and that it won't be ending anytime soon, he concentrates on the competition and the moment—poof, that lap is gone, and there's only one left.

Ultrarunner Johnson, whose mental hurdles are a bit more

daunting, uses the same trick. Seventy miles into a run, there's no positive way to think of the last 30 miles. So Johnson focuses on how quickly he can run the next 5.

"You need something that you can mentally grasp," says Johnson. "After you've done that 5 miles, then you reach out and grab another 5 miles and pull yourself through that."

Pay attention to form. Another simple and effective ploy: concentrate on technique. Focus on keeping your stride long and your arms moving straight forward and back. This helps maintain form,

---

Turn the Wall into Rubble

Much has been made of the wall, and anyone who has ever crashed into it knows why. Your body crumbles, your will turns to mush. At best, your pace falls off to a stagger. At worst, you fall on your face.

Ugly? Yes. Inevitable? No.

"I don't believe that there's a wall out there," states six-time Ironman winner Dave Scott. "It's a bunch of baloney. You can control your glycogen stores so that you never hit the wall."

When you exercise, you tap two fuel sources—glycogen and fat. Glycogen is high-octane stuff. It fuels hard effort; as a rule, effort greater than 60 percent of our aerobic capacity demands glycogen. Fat drives us at slower speeds, and it is an almost inexhaustible energy source. Your body's total glycogen stores amount to 2,000 calories; a single pound of fat contains 3,500 calories, and your body is probably more than 10 percent fat.

"Competing successfully in any kind of endurance event boils down to being able to burn fat and spare glycogen," explains Riverside, California, nutritionist Ellen Coleman. "Making your glycogen last as long as it can, that's the secret to endurance."

The best way to conserve glycogen and tap fat? Carefully monitor your body's signals and keep a keen eye on your pace. High-intensity, anaerobic effort gobbles your precious glycogen reserves.

"Treading that fine line between aerobic and anaerobic, that's the way you go fast over the long haul," claims three-time Olympic cyclist John Howard. "You want to keep the anaerobic efforts to a minimum, conserve your glycogen supply, and then, when the end's in sight, really throw the coals on and cross the finish with nothing left."

and it occupies your mind at a time when pain, fear, and whining pessimism are probing for chinks.

During tough times, sports psychologist Joel Kirsch encourages athletes to focus on their "center"—a spot several inches down and in from the navel that he calls the physical center of gravity. Six-time Ironman winner Dave Scott concentrates on relaxing. Fellow triathlete Scott Molina repeats a mantra: "I can win, I can win, I can win." Whatever the object of focus, the premise is the same. Concentrating wholeheartedly on one thing doesn't leave much room for anything else.

Feel the pain. Confronted with pain, athletes have employed some odd psychological gambits. Runners are particularly creative. In a seminal study of marathon runners, psychologist William P. Morgan noted some innovative attempts to blot out pain: One woman visualized the faces of two co-workers that she detested, then proceeded to squish them, one face and then the other, every step of the race.

Though it may be therapeutic, Morgan concluded that this sort of practiced disregard—which psychologists term *dissociation*—doesn't help performance in the long run. He observed that world-class distance runners actually associated with the pain. Paying close attention to their bodies' feedback kept them in touch and allowed them to make the right adjustments during the race.

Not that dissociation doesn't have its place. Morgan interviewed a Boston Marathon runner who thwarted the pain of Heartbreak Hill by imagining that he was a powerful steam engine—his breath coming in puffs of steam, his legs, driving pistons. Dissociation, concluded Morgan, has powerful advantages, but it should be used sparingly. Ignorance may be bliss, but we shouldn't lose contact with the machine.

Concentration on every step of a marathon—or, for that matter, a 5-K—will turn your brain to mush. Your mental approach should be the same as your physical effort—bouts of focus separated by periods of mental meandering. But when things get ugly, best to look in.

"So many people try to get through events by externalizing," says Howard. "They think about tomorrow's dinner or how great it's going to feel to finish. The real athletes are able to perform better by going in, by focusing very closely on what the body is doing. When you don't pay attention to the body, you lose touch. When you lose touch, you lose control."

None of these mind games will help unless you can bring them into play. Unfortunately, most people view psychological skills, if they think of them at all, in the same light as onion dip—something they can whip up in a moment's notice. Not so.

"These are things that you need to practice before you get into a race," says Plumer. "You can't just expect to call them up and have them work. They're skills. Like any other skill, they need to be practiced."

With practice, you can learn to tap your deepest reserves of strength and energy. You can push yourself beyond what you think you're capable of doing.

"So often you'll hear people say, 'I hit the wall. I ran out of gas. I just couldn't do anything else,' " muses Dave Scott. "I bet you, psychologically, they could have mustered a little bit more energy. I think that a lot of athletes are physically capable of pushing through tough times. Maybe they don't succeed because they don't have the ability to provide the mental push."

Perhaps we need to change our outlook—to embrace the pain and hard effort of our sport. It's impossible to paint a pretty picture of running's demands, and Johnson doesn't as he reels off the list of ultrarunning's hurts: "Dehydration, hunger, blisters, aching muscles, pounding joints, swelling body parts . . . "

Plumer, too, gives testimony to the pain of running when she leans into the final lap of a race, temples tingling, face flushed hot, pain sweeping her frame. Yet, she positively bubbles at the thought.

"That's what's so important, so exciting, about sport," she says. "It teaches us to challenge ourselves. It teaches us to push beyond where we thought we could go. It helps us find out what we're made of. This is what we do. This is what it's all about."

What we dread, we should relish.

I've always been one of those slow-but-steady runners. If I won a lot of races in my day, my success didn't come from any excess of athletic brilliance. It came from discipline and determination, from the fact that I stuck to my programs and goals no matter how slow and sometimes frustrating the progress.

I believed in what I was doing, particularly that the whole was greater than the sum of the parts. Take running the marathon, for example. My goal was always to run a marathon at a 5-minute-per-mile pace. Now, when I considered this goal in its entirety, I was overwhelmed by the impossibility of it. Anyway or anytime you look at a marathon, it tends to seem impossible.

Yet, every week I ran lots of miles—far more than the 26 in the marathon. And every week I ran a few of those miles faster than a 5-minute pace. Not many, but a few. I broke the marathon down into small parts, which seemed much more manageable than the full distance, and I practiced on the parts rather than the entirety. A little mental trick—that's all it was.

And it worked. In the best marathon of my life, I ran the first 18 miles at exactly a 5-minute pace. I slowed a little in the last 8 miles, but still averaged a 5:08 pace for the full distance, finishing in 2:14. On the one hand, I couldn't believe what I had accomplished. On the other, I realized that I had only succeeded to this degree because I had found a way to believe.

CHAPTER 26

SMOOTH SAILING

How Running Relaxed Can
Improve Your Performance

*Running coaches don't agree about much—they tend to dis-
agree, for example, about training programs, nutrition, stretching, and weight training—but on one crucial subject I have
never heard any disagreement. When it comes to good running
form, everyone concurs, the name of the game is relaxation.*

*Coaches tell their sprinters to relax, their hurdlers to relax,
their distance runners to relax, and, I'm sure, their hammer
throwers to relax. The advice is universal—it seems that all
coaches give it to all their athletes.*

*And I have never heard a single athlete fight his coach on
this subject. Who, after all, is going to argue for tightness and
tension? So we have a perfect world here: total agreement.*

*Now if only someone would tell us how to relax while we're
running. Most coaches stand at trackside, red-faced and straining, and yell, "Relax! Relax! Don't tighten up!" Somehow I don't
think this is ever going to do the trick.*

*Fortunately, sports psychologist Jerry Lynch, Ph.D., author
of* Thinking Body, Dancing Mind, *has more to say on the subject than most coaches. And, even better, he has more specific
advice on how you can achieve the universal goal.*

From the time we were young, many of us were taught that if
we tried hard and gave 100 percent, we'd always get results. And
often that's the case. But in many sports, running included, nothing
could be further from the truth. Running often follows the principles
of the Japanese art of aikido: Taking the line of least resistance will
create a smoother, more efficient, and more effective action.

The implication for runners is powerful: Relax, and perform
better. Australian marathoning marvel Rob de Castella credited his
ability to relax as one of his greatest strengths. Indeed, this seems to
be a common denominator among many of the great runners of the
last 50 years—athletes like Edwin Moses, Peter Snell, Abebe Bikila,
Billy Mills, and Toshihiko Seko. They learned to consistently perform at their best by letting go of physical and mental tension.

In the mid-1960s Bud Winter, coach of 1968 Olympic sprinters Ray Norton, Tommie Smith, John Carlos, and Lee Evans, developed the "90 percent rule." By this, he meant that running at 90 percent effort stimulates relaxation and results in faster speed. In his book *Relax and Win: Championship Performance in Whatever You Do,* Winter explains how runners become tense and anxious when they try to run at 100 percent. He encouraged his runners to "let the meat hang on the bones," an image of relaxation that he claims led to smooth, effortless results.

Working with many U.S. Olympic marathoners has reinforced my belief in the importance of relaxed running—the most widely ignored aspect of training. To run smoother and faster, you must concentrate on relaxing rather than pushing for more power. That kind of strained running causes the muscles to tighten and decreases the balance between the hamstrings and quadriceps. And as anyone who has ever raced can attest, in the latter stages of any distance event, it's the runners who remain loose and relaxed who prevail.

WHY RELAXATION WORKS

By definition, optimal performance occurs only when the physical, mental, and emotional selves work harmoniously together. Your ability to relax prior to and during a performance will have a tremendous impact on bringing the "big three" together.

Relaxing can improve your physical self by:

• Making muscles become more fluid, which improves coordination and endurance. Relaxed muscles permit blood to flow more easily and lessen cramping.

• Decreasing blood lactate. Although it is unclear how this happens, research shows that relaxation helps diminish the accumulation of lactic acid.

• Reducing chance of injury. Tension causes the muscles to be in a constant state of contraction, which inhibits blood flow to those muscles. Using relaxation, you can reverse this process and reduce your chance of injury.

Relaxing can improve your mental self by:

• Sharpening mental focus and improving concentration.

• Creating vivid images. When the mind is clear and relaxed, you can visualize success and reduce fear and panic. This skill becomes particularly important as you begin to tire.

Relaxing can improve your emotional self by:

• Lowering stress. Relaxation creates optimal levels of arousal and helps keep inappropriate and harmful stress at bay.

• Boosting confidence. As your running stride becomes smooth and strong, you'll feel more self-assured.

How to Do It

You can create the actual state of relaxation in a variety of ways. Perhaps you've tried meditation, biofeedback, yoga, self-hypnosis, soothing music, or exercise itself. If you're satisfied with one of these methods, don't replace it. Use it in conjunction with others to maximize your relaxation response.

Breathe In, Breathe Out

Try deep abdominal breathing to reach a quick, easy state of relaxation. Here's how to do it.

• Breathe only through your nostrils, since breathing through the mouth is not relaxing.

• Inhale very slowly. As you do, push the abdomen out as if it were a balloon expanding. As a result, your diaphragm will move downward, allowing full extension of your lower lungs.

• When the abdomen reaches full extension, smoothly draw your shoulders back, raising your head, and continue to fill the upper part of your lungs.

• After you've entirely filled your lungs, hold your breath for 5 seconds.

• Release, exhaling slowly through the nostrils. Draw in the abdomen. When the process is complete, hold it for 2 seconds before resuming your next deep breath.

• Repeat this exercise for five breaths (more if needed), and as you do, count down 5–4–3–2–1, saying one number on each exhalation.

• To end the exercise, count slowly 1–2–3–4–5. At 5, say, "I am relaxed, alert, and in fine health." Avoid abrupt transitions if possible. As you improve, try using just three deep breaths.

To improve performance through relaxation, I prefer deep abdominal breathing. I have used this technique with thousands of people, ranging from elite athletes to corporate executives to the average runner interested in better performance. All have reported tremendous success with this tool. You can learn it easily and use it quickly.

Your mind won't get into shape if you disregard your mental workouts, so make deep abdominal breathing a regular part of your daily exercise routine. For at least 10 minutes a day, breathe yourself into a relaxed state. Once you feel calm and loose, visualize your running experience.

When you have learned how to relax, you can incorporate your relaxation techniques into your training and racing. Before a workout, get into a relaxed mode to help regenerate energy that has been drained away by stress. Lethargy will vanish as you relax away accumulated tension, and many of those down days will turn into high-energy workouts.

When you're ready to race, use relaxation to regulate stress right up to the start of the event, particularly if the course is tough or you lack experience at the distance, as in a first marathon. After the race, you can use relaxation to restore the body's equilibrium and hasten recovery.

What about relaxing during the run or race? Practicing deep abdominal breathing on a regular basis before and after your run will produce a carryover effect while you run. You will develop a habit of performing in a relaxed state and creating reference points to focus on as you run. When you simply think "r-e-l-a-x," your body will respond in a positive way. Toward the middle or end of a distance event, you can use the deep-breathing technique.

While racing or working out, try the following techniques to help you run more smoothly, efficiently, and calmly.

- Relax your face and drop your jaw. Facial muscles control much of the tension in the body, so if you loosen up your face, the rest of the body will follow.

- Keep your upper body perpendicular to the ground or to an imaginary perpendicular line if you're running hills. Pull your shoulders back slightly and push your hips forward.

- Keep your hands softly closed as if you were holding a delicate paper sculpture.

- Focus on smooth striding. Avoid overstriding or understriding, because these bad habits waste energy.

Set the Stage

Once you have achieved a relaxed state, use your imagination to see, feel, and hear an event or circumstance before it occurs. Think of it as a rehearsal. Research shows that the way you imagine an event may shape the direction that event will follow.

Use the following exercises to create your own scenes in explicit detail.

Before You Run

- Imagine that all tension has flowed out of your legs and that they feel relaxed and loose.

- Imagine your body as a finely tuned machine, running smoothly and efficiently, with all parts moving in harmony.

- Picture yourself running light on your feet. Say, "This is the best I've ever felt . . . wonderful."

- Imagine various landmarks along the way and see yourself feeling great at each checkpoint. Say, "I'm so relaxed and strong, I could go forever."

- See yourself taking a shower after the run. Feel the warm water and focus on how satisfying it feels to have run so well.

During the Run

- As you run up a tough hill, picture yourself suspended by helium balloons or being gently guided and pushed by a giant hand on the small of your back.

- If you're running into the wind, imagine that you are shaped like a wedge and that you can cut effortlessly through the breeze.

- Imagine that you're a stallion or deer running tirelessly with grace, style, and strength.

- During a track workout, see yourself floating by a cheering crowd at a track meet. They came to see you set a new world record in the mile.

• Relax your shoulders, carrying your arms low. Your shoulders should remain loose yet stable, elbows firm but not locked.

• Move faster by focusing your mind on "r-e-l-a-x-a-t-i-o-n," rather than on power. Applying force creates tension and muscular stress, which interfere with the fluidity of your stride.

One more point that shouldn't be overlooked: humor. Laughter has been shown to exercise the lungs, relax the diaphragm, and raise the oxygen levels in the body. Many of us take ourselves and our running so seriously that we produce too much anxiety and tension. So we need to laugh at ourselves more often.

Harry Groves, head track and cross-country coach at Pennsylvania State University in University Park, has a good handle on humor. It's relaxing just being around him because he sees the light side of everything. He seems to be able to pass it on to his squad to create an ideal, relaxed environment for performance. At a Penn Relays Championship, a team member approached Groves concerned about how his father would feel if the runner didn't race well. Groves quietly replied, "Look, if you run the race of your life, your father will definitely love you. If you don't run well, however, your father will . . . still love you. So go out there and have a great time."

The young man did just that and, in the process, brought home a wonderful victory. With the pressure off, he ran the race of his life.

Humor and anxiety cannot coexist. To succeed like the Penn State runners, start by telling someone something funny about yourself and enjoying a good laugh. Then, fully relaxed, go out and run the best race of your life.

Over three decades of running, I've tried all the relaxation tricks in the book and found two that work particularly well for me. The first is a pre-run routine. The second is something I do while running.

To relax during a run, I have learned, I need to be relaxed before the run. When I'm racing, I've always found this relatively easy to do because I make sure that I arrive early and set aside plenty of time for a warm-up. As part of this warm-up, I set aside about 10 minutes to stretch out in a warm, comfortable place and practice slow, deep breathing. This always brings me a tremendous sense of relaxation—a sort of calm before the storm of racing.

During most days of the week, however, I'm not so good to

myself. I don't give myself the time to relax before a workout. Rush, rush, rush—too often that seems to be the rule of my life and of most other people I know. So I have had to learn a shorter version of my prerace routine. I've found that I feel much better during a typical midweek run if I give myself as little as 3 minutes of slow, relaxed walking before getting ready for a workout (sometimes I do this by walking around the block before heading to the locker room to change).

Once on the road, I have one simple, almost ludicrous trick. If I smile, I feel better and more relaxed. It always works. You feel a little silly doing it at first, and you might have to force it, but I have found that no matter what I'm doing, I feel better doing it with a smile. Even running.

CHAPTER 27

THE MYSTERIOUS BREAKTHROUGH

You Can Achieve This Elusive Triumph

For as long as I have been running, I have been intrigued by the whys and wherefores of improvement in running performances. You'd think the subject would yield to fairly simple analysis and follow certain, almost quantifiable, laws like the laws of physics. For example, the more you train, the more you improve.

Of course, it never happens this way, which is why I have always found the subject so fascinating. In running, the biggest improvements often come when we least expect them. We look back, we try to figure out why, we are driven by the hope that we'll be able to repeat our past successes at future moments when we most need a great race. We too rarely succeed.

So we continue to study the phenomenon of break-throughs—those major leaps forward in running performance. The history of running is rich with anecdotes about athletes who sprang out of the pack one day to become champions. Or runners who were unbeatable in one major race but couldn't duplicate their winning effort the next time out.

This chapter explores the subject of breakthroughs and even suggests ways that you might be able to achieve one of your own.

I headed out on my 20-mile run just before dawn. A few miles down the road, something happened. Suddenly, I found myself running on some higher, transcendent plane. With euphoric detachment, I coasted effortlessly past runners who seemed strangely suspended in slow motion. I felt no pain, thirst, or fatigue as mile after mile went by. Energized by black storm clouds gathering, captivated by the sunrise—a raw red slash on the horizon—I ran and ran, mystically self-sustained, inspired to higher, more surreal speeds. I ran those 20 miles more easily, more quickly, more happily than I had ever run before.

Later that day, I pondered my experience. I wondered if it could simply be explained as an incredible runner's high, but it seemed more potent than a 20-mile endorphin rush. Had I chanced upon a secret set of circumstances that brought on this feeling? If so, could I ever rediscover and replicate those circumstances? Or was this to be a once-in-a-lifetime running experience? Was I now fated to return to a slow, earthly plod, brooding over the same old bodily sensations?

The answer to the last question was no. I continued to run at a pace significantly faster than my previous level. I ran longer and easier, passing people who used to pass me. On hot and humid days, I expected to wither and crawl as I always had done, but now I cruised unhindered by heat and humidity. But I've never totally recaptured the mood and metaphysics of that predawn experience. The running I do now is similar to my previous running—a strenuous effort that can hurt and may turn grim at times. But I am running better than ever.

In races, I've placed higher at every distance from 5-K to half-marathon, and over the last nine months, I've accumulated a string of 12 consecutive personal records. I'm 54, and I've begun to edge up to places not far behind the local superjocks of my age group, even winning a prize on occasion. I'm running faster than ever before in my life and getting faster still.

In short, I have achieved a breakthrough. While breakthroughs have not been documented or explained by the scientific community, few coaches or runners doubt that they exist. Yes, breakthroughs are difficult to describe and define, but that doesn't mean that you can't achieve one. In fact, with considerable attention to details, and a little luck, you can.

RISING TO A NEW LEVEL

Bill Rodgers may have achieved one of the most far-reaching breakthroughs of any runner when he won the 1975 Boston Marathon in 2:09:55—9½ minutes under his previous best. It elevated him to world-class stature and set him on a fast track toward unparalleled road-racing dominance. Over the next nine years, he would run 28 sub-2:15 marathons.

"Actually, I'm not sure if the breakthrough happened in the marathon or in the World Cross-Country Championships a month before," says Rodgers. "In the cross-country meet, I beat a lot of people I wasn't supposed to. In fact, I crushed some who had been beating me handily up until then. But I only won the bronze medal. Still, I was suddenly a better runner. I'd either had a breakthrough, or I was on the verge of it. After I won the marathon, there was no doubt that I'd broken through.

"What brought it on? I trained hard all winter prior to those races," Rodgers recalls. "I increased speedwork, I increased mileage to 130 to 200 miles a week. I was racing on the indoor track circuit, getting outkicked by milers and 2-milers who were doing 80 miles a week and were fresher. But I was building up strength, and once I moved to the longer distances, all that strength came through.

"It was great fun suddenly to be at the top," he adds, "to go from being one of the top guys in New England to being right up with the best in the world. I didn't always do well, but once you make a breakthrough, it really is a turning point."

Getting to that turning point is the hard part, largely because it's so unpredictable. "Breakthroughs happen to different people at different times," says Tom Fleming, who has won the New York City Marathon twice and frequently finished second to Rodgers at Boston and other races.

"My first breakthrough came in 1972, in the San Juan 450, a 20-mile race," Fleming continues. "I was 20 years old, and I was on my first national team. I had been rated the fastest junior in the world and had run a 2:20 marathon at 18, but it was in the San Juan race that I made a real breakthrough, physically and mentally.

"The day was terribly hot and humid," Fleming says. "I didn't have any reason to think I would run so well. But all of a sudden, I clicked with the pace and with the extreme conditions. I ran 1:41, a little over a 5-minute-per-mile pace and 3 minutes faster than I'd ever run that distance. Afterward, I felt elated.

"It's not uncommon to hit a down cycle within just a few weeks. You're tired, both physically and mentally, and you struggle like you've lost it all. That's your body saying it needs to have some pressure lifted. If that means taking a break from running, don't worry—you'll come right around in a week or two. Mentally, you'll need four weeks of light training, maybe six. Then you'll be back up to speed again. That's just how the human body is.

"I had another breakthrough a year later, when I ran a 2:17 Boston Marathon," Fleming concludes. "But that one didn't surprise me. I knew I was going to be good, so the excitement wasn't the same. Right after that, I returned to San Juan and set the course record."

Some breakthroughs come, thank goodness, just when they are most needed. "I don't think there's an athlete I've been involved with who hasn't had a huge breakthrough," says Bob Sevene, who coached Joan Samuelson through her best races. "Joan was in the Oregon Track Club Marathon in the fall of 1982. This was less than a year after she'd had surgery for Achilles problems. She had trained too hard before the surgery and not hard enough after. She had been hanging at the door, trying to run under 2:30, and she couldn't get through. She was close to wanting to retire. But before the marathon she told me, 'I'm just going for it. I don't care about splits. I don't care about anything.'

"In that race, she transcended her training," says Sevene. "She ran beyond her fitness level. She stepped on the line and asked her body to do it, and she ended up running 2:26:11, which then was almost the world record.

"That race put her on a whole different level psychologically," adds Sevene. "She went to Boston the following year, knowing she could break the world record and fully intending to. Her goal was a 2:23 marathon, and she ran 2:22:43. Oregon was a surprise. Boston wasn't. Nor was it a surprise when she won the gold medal in the 1984 Olympics, which she later said was the easiest race she ever ran. Joan had been transformed from a good marathoner to the best in the world. If I could bottle what brought that about, I would be the greatest coach who ever lived."

MANY PATHS TO THE SAME POINT

No one fully understands how and why breakthroughs happen, yet everyone has a theory about them. The only thing that seems certain is that each runner comes to a breakthrough via different circumstances.

"The breakthrough is both mental and physical," says Greg Meyer, who was almost unbeatable for a time, winning the 1983 Boston Marathon in 2:09:00 as well as several other major races, "but it's hard to know whether the attitude or the training is more important.

"Sometimes you know it's coming," Meyer adds. "Other times you don't. Sometimes it looks to be a natural result of good training; other times a breakthrough doesn't even seem plausible when it happens. You can't make it happen, and you can't tell somebody else how to make it happen. It happens for very complicated reasons."

And though one would think that the force behind a breakthrough comes from a love of running and an intense desire to excel, this may not always be the case. "There's a dark side to this, and it has to do with what motivates runners," says Benji Durden, who now coaches and had his big breakthrough with a 2:10:40 marathon that put him on the 1980 Olympic Team. "I've seen people driven to peak performances by stress and anger. I know of a Boston Marathon in which the top three finishers were in the midst of marriage breakups. I know of a marathoner who ran best when her bank balance was low. I myself went through six months of anger when I was an outlaw athlete, at odds with the federation over fiscal procedures. And as I got angrier, my performance level would rise another notch.

"You have to have some sort of demon driving you far harder than everybody in the normal world is driven," says Durden. "If people are content, I don't think they can achieve the big breakthroughs that make world-class runners."

Fleming disagrees, "I don't believe people are motivated to run by horror in their lives," he says. "I firmly believe that you are a better runner if you are happy. I definitely run better when I'm happy."

"I didn't say that you can't be happy and run fast," counters Durden. "I said you can't be content and run world-class."

YOUR MOMENT OF TRUTH

All this is not to say that less-than-elite runners can't achieve breakthroughs. They can, and they do. And by all accounts, their breakthroughs are more unexpected and thus more dramatic than those of world-class runners.

"It can happen to anybody," says Sevene. "As a matter of fact, I think recreational runners have even better chances of making big breakthroughs. They get into running to lose weight or simply to get out of a chair. And all of a sudden, just with burning calories and getting fit, they make huge improvements in performance.

"I suggest runners join a running club and get guidance," he says. "I could recommend speedwork and other specific types of training, but if people do that without direction, they get hurt. Track clubs exist in every city. And runners can learn a lot from running magazines. Running with a friend helps, too."

"The breakthrough comes when you train over a period of time," says Ron Warhurst, who coaches distance runners at the University of Michigan in Ann Arbor. "If you're an 8-minute miler running 40 miles a week, you should maintain that pace and mileage until your body feels comfortable with it. You might need three to four months—or six to eight. Then add 15 to 20 miles a week, and you might break through to a 7:30 pace.

"You have to train harder, but don't think that if 40 miles a week has you running 8-minute miles, then 60 miles will get you to 6:30s and 120 miles will get you 5:00s," Warhurst adds. "It doesn't work that way. With increasing mileage, you eventually come to a point of diminishing returns."

"I don't think anybody knows what happens physiologically to cause a breakthrough," says Bill Squires, who coached the Greater Boston Track Club when Rodgers, Meyer and others there made the most momentous breakthroughs of the 1970s and 1980s. "But I think it happens to anyone who runs enough. You keep increasing your speed training each week and adding 2 to 3 percent more distance to your longer runs, and there will come a day when you feel as though you're in cruise control. It seems as if you can run forever. I think it all has to do with endorphins in the brain."

MY BREAKTHROUGH

So it goes. Every runner's breakthrough is a unique event, subject to as many divergent theories as there are serious believers to postulate and synthesize. As for my own breakthrough, it confounded me.

Elements of a Breakthrough

The phenomenon of breakthroughs falls outside the realm of scientific understanding or control. No one really knows what brings about a breakthrough, but the following factors seem to be common to runners' reported experiences.

1. Breakthroughs do not happen arbitrarily or effortlessly, though they often seem to. They result from hard work and months, maybe years, of training.

2. Although hard training is required to achieve a breakthrough, too much training is worse than not enough.

3. The breakthrough requires a well-balanced program of distance running, speedwork, rest, and diet—though even the most inspired and enterprising training can't guarantee a breakthrough.

4. Breakthroughs don't happen to everyone, and no two runners get there through the same set of variables.

5. A runner could come to a breakthrough alone, but you are more likely to reach one in the company of other runners providing competition, spirit, and resolve.

6. After the first breakthrough, others follow, although subsequent breakthroughs are not nearly as exhilarating or inspiring.

7. Ultimately, there comes a final breakthrough—with advancing age or declining interest. Thereafter, runners must cope with the reality of slowing down—which is another story.

I wondered what theory could explain it. I had jogged alone for a dozen years, had run unremarkably in some short races, and finally set about training for a marathon. I pushed myself to more than 50 miles a week too quickly, and on a 22-mile trek, something came undone in my left hip. It turned out to be tendinitis, and it prevented me from running the marathon. I healed slowly for six weeks, resumed running very cautiously for two weeks, and then experienced my breakthrough on that 20-mile run.

Bill Leach, who coaches the DePaul University track team in Chicago, gave me his thoughts. "You'd been doing a fairly high volume at a fairly slow pace, which has limitations," he said. "But you overtrained, which caused the injury. You probably also were in a period of stagnancy, which comes with too much of the same training. You had to be very tired and needed the rest. But the hard training had made you stronger, and you must have retained a good part of that strength through the six weeks when you were injured and didn't train at all.

"Taking time off was an effective thing for you to do," continued Leach. "It probably brought you out of the stagnant spell. The post-staleness stage is when a breakthrough most commonly occurs. The intense training got you perhaps 90 percent there, but the period of not training was the other 10 percent. When you're really ready, a change like this can precipitate a breakthrough, whether it's a change in training or some psychological experience."

In the end, the reasons don't really matter. On one hand, it would be nice to come up with a definitive and detailed training program that can bring any runner to a breakthrough. On the other hand, perhaps the mystery of the breakthrough is simply one of the many little mysteries of running that make it so special.

What's important in all of this is that I had a breakthrough—that anyone can have a breakthrough. That through some combination of training, persistence, and love of running one can be magically lifted to new heights of performance and pleasure.

Yes, I've had personal experience with the breakthrough phenomenon. In fact, I can recall two times in my life when my performances suddenly leaped forward. Both happened many years ago, but I remember them with great clarity and emotion. Breakthroughs are like that. They have a miracle quality to them, and you don't soon forget what you have encountered.

Both of my breakthroughs followed injuries. That should tell you something; it certainly told me something, though I wasn't as quick to accept the message as I should have been.

In my best running years, I had a tendency to overtrain. I was driven to log huge mileage amounts every week. Indeed, it was as if I was training for the end-of-the-week thrill of adding up my total miles rather than for a specific upcoming race. This overtraining led to a foot bone stress fracture during my sophomore year in college and a pulled leg muscle just after I graduated from college.

I was fortunate that these were my only two serious injuries, and even more fortunate that I ran faster shortly after recovering from the injuries than I had before incurring them. The obvious lesson: I needed to vary my training more, with easy days as well as hard days, and easy weeks sandwiched between the hard weeks.

Ever since, I've been a major proponent of training in cycles that include planned easy weeks. The body needs to work hard and then have time to recover. If you can find the cycle that works best for you, I believe you might achieve a breakthrough of your own.

7
CROSS-TRAINING

CHAPTER 28

THE MANY ROADS TO FITNESS

Cross-Train Your Way to Better Running

Cross-training can be a tough concept for many runners to grasp. It's not that we don't believe that a variety of workouts is good for us. It's just that we can't figure out where the training time is going to come from. Making time for a 30- to 40-minute run is often difficult enough. How are you going to swim and bike and row and all that stuff?

We probably feel this way about cross-training because of all the attention the Hawaii Ironman Triathlon has received in the last two decades. The amazing Ironman athletes swim 2½ miles, bike 110 miles, and then finish off with a jaunty little marathon. And to prepare for the Ironman, which takes 9 to 10 hours (or much more for the middle- and back-of-the-pack racers), some triathletes train almost that many hours per day. Who needs it?

Fortunately, no one but an Ironman athlete needs it. The rest of us can benefit from much more realistic doses of cross-training. Still, it's hard to figure out how to begin and how much and what kinds of cross-training to do. These are the questions that are answered in this chapter.

Life used to be simple. Runners ran, and swimmers swam. Bicyclists pedaled, weight lifters grunted, and Ed Sullivan was on TV every Sunday night. Then everything got mixed up. Runners started cycling, swimmers lifted weights, cyclists starting running. . . .

The weirdness probably started with the first Hawaii Ironman Triathlon in 1978. Things have gotten even weirder since. Now, it's not unusual to see athletes climbing stairs that go nowhere or cross-country skiing over a gym floor. What next? Some futurist will probably figure out a way to ice-skate without ice.

Strangest of all, while these varied activities may look a bit wacky, they're actually very good for you. They stretch certain muscles, strengthen others, and burn plenty of calories.

But what exactly is cross-training supposed to do for runners, you wonder? And, given all the cross-training choices, which are the best ones for you?

This subject has been examined by some of the nation's leading exercise physiologists, debated by numerous elite runners, and discussed in scores of sports-medicine journals. And there's a raging debate on the topic. The controversy involves three major points of view.

1. **The do-more, get-fitter theory.** Proponents of this position believe that runners should cross-train with exercises and activities that are as close to running as possible. The logic: The stronger you can make your running muscles, the better you'll run.

2. **The rest theory.** According to this approach, runners should cross-train with sports that are as different from running as possible. The logic: You can burn calories and get a good workout. At the same time, you'll be resting your running muscles and won't be creating the one-sport muscle imbalances that often lead to injury.

3. **The specificity theory.** Specificity advocates believe that runners shouldn't cross-train—period. It's a waste of time and will only tire you for your next run. When you need a day off from running, take a day off from everything. The logic: Training is sport specific, so the best way to train for running is to run.

No wonder so many runners are confused about cross-training. Who are they supposed to believe, and which theory should they follow? "All of the approaches make sense and could work," says Mike Flynn, Ph.D., an exercise physiologist and one of the nation's leading researchers in cross-training. The trick to optimizing your training program, he explains, is to pick the approach that best fits your current running and fitness goals.

To make your decision easier, we've designed cross-training programs for five different types of runners. Simply find the category that best describes you and follow the suggested advice.

BEGINNING RUNNERS

This is for runners who log 5 to 15 miles per week.

The basics: If you're running to get into shape, the first thing you need to do is build your cardiovascular system. A strong heart and lungs will supply more fuel to your working leg muscles, which will allow you to run without constantly feeling out of breath.

If you're switching to running from another sport, you're probably fit enough to run a few miles without much problem, but don't try to do too much too soon. Running involves more pounding than most other sports, and it takes a while for the muscles, tendons, and ligaments to adapt.

The program: The best cross-training program for beginners is one that mixes running and cross-training in equal amounts. If you're running twice a week, then try cross-training twice a week as well. This will allow you to build your cardiovascular system and muscle strength simultaneously, without undue risk of injury. Another good idea: Since your body may not be prepared to handle more than one hard run a week, split your hard workouts between running and cross-training.

The exercises: As a beginning runner, almost any aerobic activity will help increase your cardiovascular strength. The best exercises are those that also strengthen as many of your running muscles as possible. These exercises will improve the coordination of your running muscles and teach them to process and store fuel more effectively.

The best cross-training exercises for beginning runners are in-line skating, cross-country skiing, and stair climbing. Although circuit weight training won't do much for your aerobic endurance, a twice-a-week program is a good idea. It can help build your body's protection against running-related injuries.

INTERMEDIATE RUNNERS

This is for runners who log 15 to 40 miles per week.

The basics: You have developed a strong cardiovascular system through your running. Hence, easy cross-training workouts won't improve your running performance. You need to choose cross-training activities that either provide a very high intensity cardiovascular workout or specifically target your running muscles.

The program: You should be running two to three times as much as you are cross-training. Run for two or three days, and then do a cross-training workout. If you are doing two hard runs a week, select cross-training workouts that allow you to exercise at a moderate pace. You should be using these workouts just to give your running muscles some extra training without extra pounding. If your body can handle only one hard run a week, then one of your cross-training workouts should be an interval or tempo workout (a run that starts off easy, builds to a steady speed in the middle, and then finishes at an easy pace).

The exercises: Cross-training exercises that provide high-intensity, cardiovascular workouts are cross-country skiing, stair climbing, and high-cadence stationary cycling. "Grinding away in a high gear on a bike will slow your turnover, but using a high cadence (over 90 rpms) will keep you quick and allow you to get your heart rate up," says Tim Moore, Ph.D. For muscle-specific workouts, stick with cross-country skiing, in-line skating, and stair climbing.

ADVANCED RUNNERS

This is for runners who log more than 40 miles per week.

The basics: You have probably maximized your cardiovascular conditioning, as well as the strength, efficiency, and coordination of your leg muscles, so cross-training won't directly do you much good. To improve your running performance, you need more quality in your runs. Running coaches and exercise physiologists generally recommend at least two hard runs per week—a shorter interval session on the track and a longer tempo run on the road or trails.

The program: Since both hard running and high mileage can increase your injury risk, your best bet may be complete rest. This will allow your muscles to recover completely for your next run. If you don't want to take days off, you can consider low-intensity cross-training with a sport that doesn't tax your running muscles. This will burn calories, and the variety will keep you mentally fresh. Some researchers have even found that very light activity may help you recover more quickly than complete rest.

If you choose to cross-train, replace one or two of your easy runs—preferably the ones that come a day after a hard run—with a cross-training activity.

The exercises: Cycling, swimming, pool running, and rowing will all give your running muscles a break and let them recover for your next hard run. A twice-a-week circuit weight-training program will also strengthen your leg muscles so that they can withstand the pounding of high-mileage, high-intensity running.

INJURY-PRONE RUNNERS

This is for runners who experience two or more running-related injuries per year.

The basics: Surveys show that two out of every three runners will experience a running injury in the course of a year. "With two to three times your body weight coming down on your legs with every stride, each step you run brings you closer to injury," says Dr. Flynn. "And if you have even the slightest biomechanical problem, the risk is even greater."

But this doesn't mean that you can't run. Cross-training can

Cross-Training Guide

The chart below provides an outline for your running and cross-training (x-training) workouts. For almost all runners, several circuit weight-training workouts per week will strengthen the upper body and certain leg muscles. Don't mix circuit weight training with a hard running schedule, however.

Beginning Runner

Running Days	Running Days, Hard	X-Training Days	X-Training Days, Hard	Best X-Training Activities
2	1	2	1	In-line skating, cross-country skiing, stair climbing

Intermediate Runner

Running Days	Running Days, Hard	X-Training Days	X-Training Days, Hard	Best X-Training Activities
3–5	1–2	2	1	Bicycling, in-line skating, cross-country skiing

Advanced Runner

Running Days	Running Days, Hard	X-Training Days	X-Training Days, Hard	Best X-Training Activities
5–6	2	0–2	0	Bicycling, swimming, pool running, rowing

Injury-Prone Runner

Running Days	Running Days, Hard	X-Training Days	X-Training Days, Hard	Best X-Training Activities
2–4	0–1	2–3	1–2	In-line skating, cross-country skiing, stair climbing, swimming, pool running, rowing

General-Fitness Runner

Running Days	Running Days, Hard	X-Training Days	X-Training Days, Hard	Best X-Training Activities
2	0	2	1	Swimming, rowing, cross-country skiing, bicycling with arm resistance

help in two ways. First, it can keep you healthy by allowing you to stay fit without the constant pounding of running. Second, cross-training can help forestall the performance losses that come when an injury keeps you from running. Studies have shown that runners can maintain their running times for up to six weeks by cross-training alone if it is done at the proper intensity.

The program: The best cross-training program for injury-prone runners includes two to four runs per week (depending on how much your body can tolerate) and two cross-training workouts. Both cross-training workouts should target running-specific muscles in order to increase their strength and efficiency without subjecting them to pounding.

The extra training of these muscles through cross-training rarely produces injuries since pounding is the primary injury culprit. But if you're unsure about an exercise, ask your doctor. Also, since many running injuries are induced by high-intensity workouts, don't run more than one of these per week. Looking for more burn? Get it from your cross-training, not from your running.

The exercises: As stated above, injury-prone runners should keep their cross-training workouts as specific to running as possible. In-line skating, stair climbing, rowing, and cross-country skiing are good choices. Unfortunately, some injuries—stress fractures in particular—don't afford you many cross-training options. In these cases, cross-training in the pool by swimming or deep-water running is the best alternative. These are non-weight-bearing activities that don't stress the legs.

Twice-a-week circuit weight training is also very important for injury-prone athletes as it helps strengthen muscles, tendons, and ligaments. As a result, the stresses of running are distributed more evenly.

GENERAL-FITNESS RUNNERS

This is for low- to mid-mileage runners who are more concerned with overall fitness than racing performance.

The basics: Look at any elite runner, and you'll notice that running doesn't do much for the upper body. It also neglects the quadriceps in favor of the calves, hamstrings, and buttocks. Furthermore, after the age of 30, all the muscles in our bodies begin to lose some of their strength and energy-producing abilities. Fortunately, exercise can cut the rate of these losses almost in half.

The program: The best cross-training program for general-fitness runners targets the muscles that running neglects. "Running is great for the cardiovascular system, but if you're concerned about your overall well-being, you need to cross-train with a range of activities," says exercise physiologist David L. Costill, Ph.D., director of the Human Performance Laboratory at Ball State University in Muncie, Indiana.

For total-body fitness, run twice a week and do a complementary exercise on one or two other days of the week. In addition, 20 minutes of circuit weight training twice a week will help you condition any muscles that you may have missed.

The exercises: General-fitness runners need exercises that target the upper body and quadriceps. The best choices are rowing, swimming, cross-country skiing, and cycling on a stationary bike that has attachments to work your upper body.

As a fanatic, high-mileage runner in the 1960s and 1970s, I was not a quick convert to cross-training. I admired the Ironman triathletes, to be sure, particularly their ability to run a marathon in the 2:40s at the end of a long, exhausting day. But I wasn't about to do any cross-training myself because I couldn't find any evidence that it would make me a better runner.

I still can't. The exercise physiologists, in particular, claim that the only way to become a better runner is by running. Forget all that stair climbing and stationary cycling.

Yet today, I'm an avid cross-trainer, and not because I think that it will make me a faster runner. I cross-train because I think that it increases my total-body fitness and also because I can do a high-quality workout without pounding my legs the way a hard road run does. End result: fewer injuries. A result that any runner, fast or slow, would be happy to achieve.

Fewer injuries may even make you faster because it will allow you to put together a more consistent, uninterrupted training plan. A cross-training program that develops your leg muscles could make you faster by increasing your stride length. And there are now lots of elite runners who claim that cross-training, especially running in a pool, has made them even more successful competitors.

All of which sounds great to me. But the thing I like the most is that by mixing cross-training with my running, I'm able to continue running pain-free. As far as I'm concerned, that's even more important than running fast.

CHAPTER 29

THE GREAT INDOORS

Look Inside for Training Opportunities

Believe it or not, many running experts believe that the marathon would be better placed in the Winter Olympics than the Summer Games, where they have always been. The reason is simply that heat is far harder for runners to deal with than cold. As I often tell people, you can always get warmer by putting on more clothes, but once you've stripped down to shorts and a singlet during the summer months, there's nothing more you can do to get cooler.

This isn't to say that winter is the best time of year for runners. It's not. But the problem with winter isn't usually the cold; it's the darkness and dangerous road conditions. The early-morning and early-evening hours that many runners find most convenient for their workouts are suddenly dark. Parks and trails, the best places to run during the rest of the year, may now be inaccessible, while many roads are snowy and icy.

So we run outdoors in the sunlight and good weather when we get the chance, or move indoors when we don't. And there, whether in the basement gym or a glitzy health club, we face many confusing options. Should we just run on a treadmill? Or should we try a different kind of exercise that complements our running? This chapter explores several of the best options.

Whether you're a top-level runner whose career depends on training consistently year-round or a runner who simply wants to keep fit without risking injury on snow or ice or from the heat, moving your training indoors is the best answer to your needs. Indoor exercise allows you to train all year long—as much as you want, when you want, in safety and comfort. You may even find, as many elite runners have, that indoor training is enjoyable and enhances your outdoor running workouts.

Some top runners talked about three alternative types of indoor training that they use: stationary cycling, weight lifting, and cross-country skiing. Here's what everyone had to say.

STATIONARY BIKE: MARC CURP

Stationary cycling has been a staple of Marc Curp's training program ever since he received a stationary bicycle as a gift in the late 1980s. "I use the bike a great deal when I'm injured, but I also use it when I'm healthy for recovery workouts," says Curp, who has run a 2:11 marathon.

Typically, Curp cycles for 30 to 45 minutes, two or three times a week during the spring, summer, and fall and five or six times a week during winter.

"I just pedal for the same length of time that I would spend running, at the same intensity," he says. "I use a heart monitor, and although the conversion may not be exact, it's a simple formula, and it works for me." Curp figures that his typical stationary-cycle session of 30 to 45 minutes equals 5 to 7 miles of running. Since he usually does his long runs and speed workouts in the morning, he cycles in the afternoon or evening.

Curp relies on the stationary bike most heavily during the winter, when running conditions where he lives (in the Kansas City area) "can get really nasty," he says. "We don't necessarily get a lot of snow, but it's often really slick, and I have trouble running out on the roads."

Although he also has a treadmill for such occasions, Curp believes that cycling has an important and specific role in his training. "Those second workouts of the day are meant for recovery," he stresses, "and in several ways, I've found that it's better to do them on the bike a few times a week than as runs. For one thing, you spare yourself the pounding, and for another, you strengthen other muscles, like your quads. Also, it's something different."

In addition to recovery runs, Curp has been able to adapt his speed workouts to the bike when he can't do them on the track or roads.

"If I have 400- or 800-meter repeats scheduled, I'll do them by time and heart rate on the bike," he says. "For example, I might do 12 times 1 to 3 minutes hard with 1 to 3 minutes recovery, along with a warm-up and cooldown."

Or he might do mile repeats by cycling hard for 5 minutes, using the heart monitor to gauge intensity, followed by 2 to 3 minutes of rest. Curp has found that he can use these workouts to maintain his speed when he is injured as well. (If you have an injury and are considering doing speedwork on a bike, or on any piece of equipment, check with your doctor first. Some injuries may be aggravated by these alternative activities.)

WEIGHT TRAINING: MARY LEVEL-MENTON

Living in Florida, Mary Level-Menton isn't forced indoors by harsh winter weather. She chooses to work out in a gym, lifting weights, because it benefits her running and because she enjoys it. "Training with weights makes me stronger as a runner," says Level-Menton. "It's the perfect balance to all the running I do. I don't love it quite as much as I love running, but I really miss it when I have to skip a workout."

That doesn't happen often. Level-Menton has been lifting regularly since 1988—twice a week when she's racing, three times a week during her off-season when she's building up mileage and strength. Over these same years, she has improved steadily at every distance from 5-K to the marathon, where she now holds a 2:37 best. Most importantly, she reports, she hasn't suffered a single major injury.

"Regular weight lifting not only strengthens my muscles," she says, "but I also believe it strengthens my joints and bones. It lets me target parts of my body that running doesn't, like the abdominals, my upper body, and certain leg muscles. I find that when I'm strong all over from lifting, I'm less likely to break down.

"And my running form is better," she adds. "I don't have the best upper-body form, and I've improved it by getting stronger, which makes me more efficient. Also, knowing that I've worked hard to get strong all over gives me a mental strength that makes me tougher in races."

Level-Menton has experimented with a variety of weight-lifting regimens, equipment, schedules, and strategies over the years. Her current routine is a 1-hour series of upper-body and lower-body exercises that includes free weights and machines. She stretches carefully for about 10 minutes beforehand, then starts the weight workout with a series of lower-body moves: squats, leg lifts, hamstring curls, and weight-machine exercises for her inner thighs, outer thighs, buttocks, and hip-flexor muscles.

Then come push-ups and sit-ups, followed by a series of exercises, mostly with free weights, for the upper body: biceps curls, lateral pull-downs, triceps extensions, pectoral flies, shoulder presses, and bench presses. She finishes with more stretching.

Level-Menton is surprised that more runners don't lift weights. "So many people say that they just don't need it, that they get strong enough from speedwork, hill repeats, and racing," she comments. "But I think weight lifting prevents injury."

Benji Durden, Level-Menton's coach, heartily supports her weight-training program. "Weight lifting is very important, especially for women, who have proportionally less muscle than men," he says. "I've found that a runner who doesn't strengthen the areas that running can't target is simply waiting for an injury."

He adds that the type of equipment you use and where you work out—at home or a gym—are less important than lifting weights consistently. "Whatever you have access to and enjoy doing is what's best for you," he says. "Dumbbells, leg weights, and calisthenics aren't glamorous, but they get the job done."

CROSS-COUNTRY SKI MACHINE: BOB KEMPAINEN

In 1992, while training for the U.S. Olympic Marathon Trials, Bob Kempainen suffered a stress fracture of the kneecap and tendinitis in the other knee. Unable to run, he turned to a familiar activity, cross-country skiing. A native of Minnesota who graduated from Dartmouth College in New Hampshire, Kempainen had competed for his high school and college cross-country ski teams.

This time, however, rather than risk aggravating his injuries in the unpredictable world of snow, ice, and rugged outdoor terrain, Kempainen headed indoors—to the steady precision of a cross-country ski machine. He trained through December, January, February, and into March on a ski machine, along with some deep-water running in a pool. Kempainen went on to qualify for the Olympic Marathon team and place 17th in Barcelona.

Since then, Kempainen has continued training on a ski machine but for a different reason: He knows that a Minnesota winter can wreak havoc on outdoor runs. "Typically, we'll get several long stretches where the temperature stays around zero," he says. "It's hard to get in quality training when you have to bundle up so much. Other times it snows a lot, and if you run any significant distance, you put yourself at an increased risk for an injury because of the tendency to slip around in the snow. I'll feel the strain in my plantar fascia and in my Achilles tendon from not being able to get a firm grip."

So on days when the risk of injury outweighs the benefit of venturing outside, Kempainen will hop on his ski machine. Just as with the outdoor version of cross-country skiing, virtually every major muscle in the body gets a workout.

Last year, while his knees healed, Kempainen used the ski machine four or five days a week, sometimes twice a day. "My coach and I just adapted everything I'd do in my running program to the ski machine and the pool. I did most of my interval workouts on the ski machine," he says.

A typical interval workout for Kempainen is mile repeats,

which he normally runs on the track at a sub-5-minute pace. To translate this to the ski machine, he would ski hard for 5 minutes, using a heart monitor to match his effort on the machine with the effort he would exert running on the track. A full workout would include five or six of these 5-minute surges with 2-minute recoveries between each.

Kempainen also did some of his easy workouts on the ski machine (and the remainder in the pool). In a typical session, he would ski for 30 to 45 minutes at a moderate training pace—again, gauging the effort with a heart monitor.

Kempainen found the ski machine to be a valuable training tool. "The first week I was a bit down because I missed running so much," he recalls. "But I was highly motivated to train for the Trials, and I didn't have any alternative."

His dedication to his routine was fueled by the knowledge that the machine was doing an excellent job of maintaining his fitness. "It gets the heart rate up and really works both the arms and legs," he says. Because he had been lifting weights to maintain his upper-body strength, Kempainen had no trouble adjusting to the vigorous arm motions used on the ski machine. He suggests, however, that a runner who has not developed upper-body strength gradually ease into using a ski machine. "Even with the lifting I'd been doing, I added bulk in the arms, chest, and shoulders with the ski machine," he notes.

Kempainen also recommends a gradual return to running after extensive use of a ski machine. "You use somewhat different muscles in your legs, and if you try to come back to running too quickly, you may experience a lot of soreness and can become injured," he says.

> *It's pretty obvious from this chapter that the three runners found indoor routines that worked for them. That's probably the most important lesson of the story—there's no perfect indoor workout or program. Find the one that suits you best—whether it's another sport you know well or it fills a gap that your running doesn't—and you'll have a successful routine.*
>
> *When I was young, I was pretty good at all the mainstream sports—football, basketball, and especially baseball—because my father was a YMCA director who schooled me in all the necessary skills. I didn't get any experience, however, in the kinds of activities that now make up the big indoor routines—weight*

lifting, bicycling, rowing, and skiing. I began these in adult-hood as a total rookie.

Twenty years later, I haven't advanced much. I do a full range of indoor exercises and haven't gotten very good at any. The reason? Because I don't truly care to. Running is my main exercise. Always has been, always will be. And I don't feel like putting much effort into anything else. I just want to keep running.

I cross-train indoors simply because I know it's the best way to stay injury-free for running. I also like the variety. So I dabble in other exercises without expecting much from myself. My cross-training isn't about mastery or excellence. I'm not trying to achieve anything or beat anyone. I simply want to stay healthy enough to keep on running. And I do.

CHAPTER 30

RUNNING IN PLACE

A Treadmill Is the Perfect Training Tool

Treadmills didn't come easily to their present-day status. A little more than a decade ago, they were considered tinny, cheap, noisy contraptions that cluttered up a basement and didn't serve much purpose. I didn't know any serious runners who owned one.

And if you did, you didn't admit it. The ethic of distance running virtually demanded that you run outdoors, no matter what the conditions. It was supposed to, among other things, put us in touch with our roots. No roofs overhead for the dedicated runner.

Fortunately, that attitude has largely changed. Just as cross-training doesn't make us less of a runner, neither does treadmill running. The advantages of working out on a treadmill, especially from a safety perspective (the day before writing these lines, I heard of a well-known Canadian runner seriously injured when he was hit by a snowplow while running), are too obvious to list.

Of course, once you buy a treadmill or decide to use one at a health club, you still have to figure out what workouts are best suited to the treadmill. This chapter should help.

Back in 1980 Benji Durden had a secret. The soon-to-be Olympic marathoner was sneaking over to the exercise physiology lab at Georgia Tech University in Atlanta to do workouts on a treadmill. "I didn't tell other runners I was using a treadmill," recalls Durden. "They would have thought that I was strange. Heck, even the lab guys thought that I was a little nuts."

Today, however, thousands of runners are doing their hills and speedwork on treadmills, instead of on the roads or track. Still two basic questions keep popping up, mostly from first-time users. Why should I use a treadmill and how do I use a treadmill? Some coaches, fitness directors, and some of the world's fastest treadmill trainers provided answers.

WHY YOU SHOULD TRAIN ON A TREADMILL

Are you one of those runners who thinks treadmills are only good for rainy days? Well, running on a treadmill offers other training benefits you may not be able to get on the roads. There are many reasons to consider using a treadmill.

Cold. It's January in Michigan, and the scenery looks like outtakes from *Ice Station Zebra.* So you head to the rec room, pop a *National Geographic* special about the Fiji Islands into the VCR, then step on your treadmill for a 6-mile run.

This is the most obvious reason to use a treadmill. Severe winter weather not only can make it tough to train outside, but it can also be dangerous. You probably know someone who prided himself on running every winter day, no matter how miserable the weather was—that is, until he hit an ice patch and ended up on the injured list for two months. "I don't mind the cold too much," says Minnesota's Bob Kempainen, a 1992 Olympic marathoner. "But if it's slippery, I'll get my 10-mile run in on a treadmill. Why risk it?"

Heat. Severe heat is another reason to hightail it to the health club or wherever there's a treadmill inside. Masters runner Carol McLatchie, who lives in Houston, where you can melt your outsoles during the summer, has her treadmill on the back porch next to an air conditioner. She does several summer workouts a week there. "The air conditioner is just a small window unit," she says. "It gets the temperature down to 80°F. But that's a lot better than the 95°F outside."

Job. Job restraints present other reasons why many train on a treadmill. Sometimes a quick 30-minute run on the company treadmill at lunch is the only way to fit in a workout between meetings.

Durden, who coaches several runners by fax and phone, remembers a particularly busy month when he lived on the treadmill in his office. "I did 23 days in a row on a treadmill," he says. "I was afraid that if I went out on a long run and returned in a couple of hours, I'd miss a lot of calls. It was either that or take a cellular phone with me. And I didn't know how well the cellular phone would work when it got all hot and sweaty."

Family. Budd Coates, health promotions manager at Rodale Press in Emmaus, Pennsylvania, and four-time Olympic Marathon Trials qualifier, recalls an evening workout done on a treadmill while watching his baby daughter. "I didn't get a chance to run during the day because of work," says Coates, a 2:13 marathoner. "So I brought my daughter in and sat her down next to the treadmill. And the rhythmic sound of me pounding on the treadmill put her to sleep."

(Coates, however, cautions parents: "The belt of a treadmill is like a spoke on a wheel. It's a temptation for kids to put their fingers and hands in there, so be careful.")

Injury recovery and prevention. World-class masters miler Ken Sparks recommends treadmill training to come back from injuries or avoid them altogether. "First of all, there's less pounding of the legs on a treadmill than on the roads," says Sparks, Ph.D., an exercise physiologist at Cleveland State University. "That's because the treadmill belt gives when you land on it, unlike concrete and asphalt. Second, there's no side-to-side slope on a treadmill as there is on roads. That slope forces you to overpronate (your feet rotate too far inward on impact) and can lead to shinsplints, Achilles tendinitis, and knee problems. And third, on a treadmill, there's no lateral pressure on your knees and ankles as there would be if you were running around a track, and lateral pressure can lead to injuries."

Precise pace. Dr. Sparks also likes treadmills because they're precise. "They give you a much more evenly paced workout than running on a track," he says. "For instance, if you're doing 400-meter repeats on a track in 90 seconds, you might run the first 200 in 43 seconds and the second in 47. On a treadmill, you can't do that. Each 200 will be exactly 45 seconds."

Hills. Hill workouts are a special feature of treadmill running for McLatchie and 2:34-marathoner Joy Smith, Houston denizens who otherwise would have to drive 90 minutes to find an incline made by Mother Nature. Even Durden, a Colorado resident, prefers to run hills on a treadmill. "You can duplicate your hill sessions from week to week almost perfectly," says Durden. "If you want to do a 2 percent grade and a 1 percent recovery, you just punch some buttons. It's very precise and easy to do."

Race-course workouts. Computerized treadmills come with built-in programs that can take you up and down hills or increase the pace and slow the pace during your run. They also let you program your own courses.

Colorado's Matt Carpenter has trained on his treadmill to get ready for the Mount Washington Road Race in New Hampshire. Carpenter programs in the exact grade of the ascent and sets the pace at slightly faster than the course record. One year, Carpenter won the race but missed the record by 33 seconds on a day when rain made the footing slick. "You can't put mud on a treadmill," he says with a shrug.

McLatchie and Smith ran up and down hills before the 1992 Boston Marathon at precisely the grade and length of the Newton

Hills, including Heartbreak Hill. Ditto for the U.S. Women's Olympic Marathon Trials. Even though the Trials were held in Houston, McLatchie and Smith didn't want to beat themselves up running the mostly concrete course several times before the actual race. So they programmed their treadmills with the last 6 miles of the race—where freeway ramps provide the only hills on the course.

"We ran that workout on the treadmill once a week for three months before the Trials," says McLatchie. "We would run outside to fatigue our legs, then hit the treadmill for the 6-mile program. During the actual race, we felt that our legs knew those hills."

Avoiding the lonely road. Finally, treadmills come in handy for beginning runners and those who don't appreciate the loneliness of the long-distance runner.

"The treadmill, especially one in a fitness center or health club, provides a comfort because instead of venturing out on your own, you're surrounded by a room full of people," says Scott Kinzer, manager of several fitness centers for Procter and Gamble in Cincinnati. Similarly, treadmills are useful for runners who are wary of a solitary jog through the park.

How to Use It

Like a new pair of running shoes, a treadmill needs to be broken in—or, rather, you need to be broken in to the treadmill. "The first few times on a treadmill, start off slower than you think you should," says Durden. "You need to get accustomed to it so that you don't feel awkward or as though you're going to fall off."

Adds Smith, "You don't just do a 12-mile run on it right away. You need to get used to the rhythm of the treadmill. Most runners can get used to it fairly quickly, but for some, it's pretty tricky."

Take McLatchie's husband, Jim, for example. "Jim has been periodically banned from the McLatchie treadmill," says Carol with a laugh. "He just can't get the hang of it. He keeps falling off it and getting beat up. One time he fell off and was lying half-stunned, pressed against the wall, while the belt was whipping around and thumping on his leg. Finally, he reached over and unplugged it."

That's an extreme-case scenario. In reality, learning to run on a treadmill is like learning to ride a bike. Once you get the hang of it, it's easy.

Still, there are other things that you need to know about treadmills. "When I'm on the treadmill, I always have this feeling that I'm going faster than on the roads," says McLatchie. "I just don't have the visual cues, like scenery going by, and that throws me off a bit. Another sensation is that when I stop, my equilibrium is off.

Something is still moving. It's like I was out at sea, and now I'm on land again. I have sea legs for a few minutes. But you get used to those things."

Here are some other ways to make treadmills enjoyable and worthwhile.

Overcome monotony. The monotony of treadmill training is a big complaint among runners. And dedicated treadmill trainers won't argue with you on that point. Instead, they'll tell you how they've gotten around it. World-class marathoner Ken Martin blasts music by the B-52s on his stereo system while on his treadmill. Durden watches videotapes from previous Olympics. McLatchie's treadmill is next to a window that looks out on her backyard. Smith has a full-length mirror in front of her treadmill so that she can monitor her running form.

Another option is to schedule your treadmill sessions for peak hours at the health club—so you can socialize, or at least have something to look at. (But be aware that most health clubs have a time limit on treadmills, usually 20 to 30 minutes.) No matter where you are on a treadmill, don't look at your watch. "If I look at my watch, time seems to go real slow on a treadmill," says Carpenter.

There's one surefire way of avoiding monotony on a treadmill. You simply take your cue from Peter O'Toole in *Lawrence of Arabia,* who, after putting out a match between his fingers, explained that "the trick is not minding." And how do you not mind a treadmill workout? Throw in a little pain.

"I never get bored on my treadmill," says Dr. Sparks, who treadmill trains alongside garden hoses, rakes, and shovels in his garage. "That's because I know that when I step on my treadmill, I'm going to be doing an intense speed workout." Similarly, marathoner Don Janicki's treadmill sits isolated in his basement. "I know that when I'm going down there, it's going to be a tough workout," he says. "I actually look forward to it."

You can do practically any outside workout inside on a treadmill. Prior to his 2:09:38 second-place finish at the 1989 New York City Marathon, Martin logged all his long runs on a treadmill. "I'd just get into a nice rhythm and stay controlled," he says. "I also thought it was good because I had my drinks right there beside me, so I didn't have to stop to drink, and I could practice drinking on the run."

But Martin's may be a special case. Many runners can't tolerate a 2-hour easy run going nowhere. Other workouts, such as tempo runs, hills, speedwork, and specially designed race-course sessions, are more suited to the treadmill. Says British distance coach Brian Scobie, echoing Dr. Sparks and Janicki, "It's much easier to get through a workout on a treadmill simply by structuring it."

Run efficiently. Durden still remembers a structured tempo workout he did on a treadmill in 1980. "It was at a lab in Missoula, Montana, where they were testing shoes for Nike," he says. "In two days, I ran 14 workouts of 8 minutes in length at a 5-minute pace. I was extremely efficient on the treadmill. And two weeks later, I made the Olympic Team in the marathon."

Smith often covers 10 to 12 miles on her treadmill, but she breaks up the monotony by throwing in two or three 2-mile tempo runs (runs that start easy, build up to a steady speed, and then finish at an easy pace).

Coates likes to set the treadmill at a 5-minute pace and cruise for 15 to 25 minutes. "It's actually kind of relaxing," he says. "You don't have to check your splits, and you don't have to concentrate on keeping your pace. Because if you don't go a 5-minute pace, you're off the back of the treadmill."

Make speedwork count. Dr. Sparks has been running speed sessions on a treadmill since the late 1960s, when he was a graduate student for David L. Costill, Ph.D., director of the Human Performance Laboratory at Ball State University in Muncie, Indiana. "I didn't have much time back then, and some of my workouts would actually be jumping on a treadmill and running a 4-minute mile, then jumping off," he says.

Nowadays, on his homemade treadmill, Dr. Sparks clicks off 63-second quarter miles with a 1-minute jog in between. But don't try this at home—or at the health club. Most treadmills won't go faster than a 75-seconds-per-quarter-mile pace.

Therefore, you might want to limit your speed sessions on a treadmill to longer repeats, say, 800s or miles.

Choose your hill workouts. "Treadmills can really give you quite a workout," says Janicki, who does hill sessions on his treadmill. Most treadmills allow you to raise and lower the incline for both uphill and downhill running. You can very easily change the slope for short, steep repeats or set it at a particular grade for a long, steady climb. Also, many treadmills come with charts that convert miles per hour to mile pace at certain uphill grades, so you can determine your effort at different treadmill inclines.

A dirty, little secret—I've never done a long run on a treadmill. I think that 40 minutes is about my record. I'm sure that I could go much longer, but I just don't have the inclination. For long runs I'll still take the outdoors, even the frigid, icy streets outdoors. I just slow down. I'll go as slow as it takes to make the run feel safe.

Otherwise, I've grown totally addicted to treadmill running. Oftentimes, I find myself running on the treadmill on days when it would be perfectly easy to run outdoors. Why?

Because I like "going for the burn" on a treadmill. I do interval training—fast/slow running. Or I do 10 to 12 minutes of treadmill running, then an equal time on a stationary bike, then more running (or weight lifting or rowing or stair climbing). I enjoy the variety. I like exercising one part of my body for a while, and then another part. I keep running at the center of the workout but explore other possibilities.

My fast treadmill running serves a purpose, too. It helps me hold on to my leg speed. During the winter I don't do much (or any) fast running outdoors. So a few bursts of speedy running on the treadmill keep me in touch with faster running.

CHAPTER 31

MASTERS OF EFFICIENCY

Look to the Triathletes to Maximize Your Training

The theme of this chapter, training efficiently, highlights an important distinction that all athletes come to respect after they have spent a few years with their sport—the difference between shortcuts and focused training. Shortcuts rarely pay off, at least not for long. But focusing your training—that is, homing in on the workouts that really deliver—is essential. Without this efficiency, you waste hours and days of crucial time, often without realizing it.

When the running boom first hit in the mid- to late 1970s, for example, the people (like Jim Fixx) who wrote about it, often did little more than describe their own experiences. And what they had learned was that if you run a few miles, you get in shape. If you run more, you get in better shape.

But more often isn't better, particularly not if you have limits on your time (and who doesn't?). A better way to train is with workouts that have a targeted purpose, like hill training, speedwork, and long runs. You would get in better shape doing a few of these specific workouts than by spending much more time just running every day.

This chapter explains how several of the world's best triathletes learned to focus their training. These runner-swimmer-bicyclists probably train more than just about any other aerobic athletes in the world. They expect to spend hours and hours a day perfecting their craft. At the same time, they know they can't overdo it or they'll quickly become overtrained or injured. They look for limits—for the points of greatest efficiency—and then observe them.

The solution to the most pressing real-world problem that most runners face—not enough time to train the way they'd like—can be found in one word: *efficiency*. It's the art of maximizing the training benefits that you get from each and every run. And no other group of runners knows more about efficient training than triathletes.

Surprised? You think that triathletes succeed because they train all day? Hardly.

Triathletes achieve peak performance by making each and

every workout ruthlessly efficient. They can't afford to waste any effort, so they learn to make every minute count.

This is especially true when it comes to running—the triathlon's most important discipline. Its position as the final leg of the race means that no triathlete can afford to be a lousy runner. "The swim and bike basically just set up the run," says one of the sport's best runners, six-time Hawaii Ironman champ Mark Allen. "The run is where the triathlon happens."

How do top triathletes train efficiently to become great runners? Four of them reveal below their hard-earned secrets. The same approaches can also help you improve the efficiency of your training.

ALWAYS HAVE A PLAN

Mark Allen is generally regarded as the best triathlete in the world. His training year lasts from January 1 until he crosses the finish line at the Hawaii Ironman in October. By New Year's he has planned all 10 months, from base phase through endurance, race, and Ironman training phases. Allen believes that a detailed plan is a necessity, not an option.

Every workout has to have a purpose. "Over a year's time, you only have so much energy," Allen says, "so you need to use that supply wisely. Every year I look for tricks to streamline my training."

Allen does most of his hard training with a group, whether on the track or during a weekly 12-mile fartlek run. (*Fartlek* is Swedish for "speed play." During these runs, a runner will alternate between slow and fast paces depending on how he feels, instead of running for a set time or distance). Recovery days, however, are different. "I always run alone the day after a hard workout," he says. "If you run with someone else, there's a tendency to push harder than you should." If Allen doesn't get a full recovery, it can set his entire training program back.

His favorite workout is a slower-than-race-pace endurance run. Because of this workout, he was able to pull himself out of trouble in the 1993 Ironman. Ten miles into the marathon, Allen was struggling. His legs felt dead, he was seriously dehydrated, and he wasn't sure if he could finish, let alone catch the leader, Pauli Kiuru, who had a 3½-minute lead on him. "People are yelling at me, 'You're the best, you're the best,' " Allen recalls, "and I'm going, 'Hey guys, I'm almost walking.' "

A less-experienced triathlete would have panicked and called it quits. But Allen knew how to deal with the lead-legged feeling of the Ironman marathon because he simulates that condition in weekly steady-state endurance runs. The important part of the workout isn't pace, but duration. "At almost 3 hours, this run is just a little bit longer, timewise, than my Ironman," he says. "It gives me the confidence that I need to run the marathon."

It also helps him prepare mentally for the highs and lows that the body experiences during a marathon. Allen was able to rebound from his bad patch at 10 miles, and later he passed Kiuru for yet another Ironman victory.

QUALITY OVER QUANTITY

Karen Smyers, the 1995 Hawaii Ironman winner, could star in a training video for quality workouts. Before becoming a professional triathlete, she juggled daily training with a full-time career in computers. Her workouts were brief but focused. Here's a sample lunch-hour run: a quick warm-up, a series of intervals of 3 minutes fast and 2 minutes slow, followed by a cooldown. "If I had done the same workout at the track, it would have taken twice as long," she says, "because you spend all that time standing around and talking."

Smyers's training focuses on short but sharp workouts. Her usual weekly mileage is just 25 miles, down from the 70 she ran during her days as a pure marathoner.

"But I haven't lost anything," she says. "If anything, I'm a better runner now." She runs only four days per week: a track workout, a steady-state run (7 to 8 miles at a 6:20 pace), a race or time trial, and a long run. On recovery days she cycles instead of doing an easy run.

Smyers barely deviated from her routine when she moved up in distance for her first-ever Ironman in 1993. She increased her weekly mileage by just 10 miles per week and still ran a 3:21 marathon on her way to a fourth-place finish.

Her favorite workout is her Tuesday interval sessions with the Boston Running Club. The workout generally consists of 2 to 4 miles of fast repeats over a variety of distances ranging from 400 meters to a mile.

RECOVER AT A HIGH HEART RATE

Like Allen, Paula Newby-Fraser, seven-time Hawaii Ironman champion, believes that winning results from duplicating race conditions in practice. She achieves this with workouts that train her body to recover at an unusually high heart rate: 165.

"By training my body to rest at a high heart rate, I find that I can recover quickly during races," she explains. Newby-Fraser used this method to great advantage during the 1993 Ironman marathon.

Her main competitor, Erin Baker, ran at an 8-minute-mile pace and didn't stop at aid stations. Newby-Fraser maintained a 7-minute pace while running, but walked through the aid stations to get plenty of fluids and to allow herself a brief recovery period. This tactic helped her secure the victory.

Earlier in her career, Newby-Fraser often attempted as many as nine running workouts a week in addition to her other training. Then, in the summer of 1993, jolted by a stress fracture and the resulting forced layoff, she had to trim her weekly mileage by one-third. She settled for a more manageable 45 miles. Even on this reduced training, she ran a strong 3:16:24 and won her fifth consecutive Ironman.

"I found that over the years I was running more and more but getting less and less quality from my workouts," Newby-Fraser says. "It was increased mileage without increased results because I was so tired all the time." In the future, she believes, she will be able to run faster on less training because she'll be "willing to hurt more on the hard days."

Newby-Fraser avoids track workouts, favoring long fartlek runs that simulate race conditions. For example, she likes to do a 12-mile run that takes her heart rate as high as 172. For the recovery she will allow it to dip down only as low as 165. "I use these workouts to train myself to recover at a high heart rate," she says. "When I do these fartlek runs with other people, they often fall behind during the slower running, not during the fast running, because they haven't taught their bodies to recover at a high intensity.

TRAINING YOUR LEGS TO RUN FAST

Not surprisingly for a man considered to be one of the best cyclists in the sport, Mike Pigg focuses on a rapid cadence when he runs. Using the muscle-memory premise, he trains his legs to race fast by concentrating on a quick turnover. Even when he is warming up at a slow 8-minute pace, Pigg uses a short, choppy stride.

Pigg concentrates so much on using a fast turnover on all his runs because he used to overstride. That proved inefficient, as his hard heel-strike slowed forward momentum. Although Pigg came to triathloning from a running background, his overstriding caused him to lose races during the running phase, which should have been his strength.

To remedy the problem, Pigg used a combination of videotape analysis and stride drills. Essentially, he relearned his running stride by practicing a shorter, faster stride pattern. At one triathlon, Pigg ran a 10-K split of 32:20, just a minute slower than his best-ever performance in an open 10-K road race.

Pigg's favorite workout is a model of both efficiency and specificity. It combines strength and speed training, and he accomplishes the workout in a fairly short period of time. Pigg takes his bike to a track and mounts it on a wind trainer.

After positioning his running shoes on the infield next to his bike, Pigg hammers on the bike for 10 minutes, keeping his heart rate above 170 beats per minute. After 10 minutes he hops off, slips on his running shoes, and runs a hard mile, aiming for 5 minutes.

He jogs a slow lap to recover, then jumps on his bike and begins the whole sequence over again. Typically, he repeats the sequence five times. During this workout Pigg not only maintains a high cadence on the bike and during the run but also simulates the always-tough transition from cycling to running.

I learned one of my most important lessons about training after I quit training (well, not entirely, but just about). It was a lesson that I wish I had understood many years earlier. Here's what happened.

Shortly after my 30th birthday, I decided that I no longer wanted to run 100 miles a week as I had been doing for more than a decade. I would join the ranks of the recreational runners. I would put in about 20 miles a week, concentrate more on my job and family, and forget about racing.

I succeeded on the first several accounts but couldn't forsake races. I simply enjoyed seeing my old friends too much to stay away. So I continued entering the occasional race. Indeed, I ran well in a couple of races despite training only one-fifth of my former amount.

This was such a pleasant surprise that it inspired me to train a little more—about 40 miles a week. Suddenly, I began doing some workouts and running some races faster than ever—not all workouts and not all races, but enough.

My legs felt fresh, my spirits soared, and running was never more fun. All because I dropped a lot of junk miles and concentrated my training on workouts that produced maximum payoff, just the way the triathletes do.

TRAINING THE WHOLE BODY

Set Personal Records with This Unusual Mix

Nothing succeeds like success, and this is a major success story. Not only that, it's a story that I watched unfold up close and personal, as they like to say on TV. This chapter's author, Claire Kowalchik, works in the office next to mine at Runner's World *magazine. When she began the training program that she describes here, she was a middle- to back-of-the-pack runner.*

When she finished the program, she was a lot faster. Indeed, I haven't known too many veteran midlife runners who improved as much as Claire did over a six-month period. Part of her improvement came from pure hard work—the kind that's always capable of helping you lower your personal records (PRs).

But most of it comes from the fact that she decided to try a new training program and to stick with it even when the program made her feel slower and more tired before it eventually made her faster and stronger. The program was different, it was difficult, and it took time to adjust to—but it worked. It worked for Claire. And it can work for you.

In just 2 miles my workout would be over. A simple cooldown—something I had done hundreds of times before. Piece of cake. Or so I thought.

But after running 100 yards, all the strength and energy just flushed right out of me. My easy cooldown turned into a torturous 2 miles. This was my introduction to embedded circuit training, a form of training that draws its name from the circuit-training exercises that are sandwiched between runs. In the weeks and months that followed, I would grow to dread these circuit workouts. At least I dreaded them at first. Later, after I had set PRs of more than 4 minutes for the 10-K and 19 minutes for the marathon, I had a change of heart.

But before I explain embedded circuit training, let me back up a bit and tell you more about myself. For one thing, it has taken me years to get to the point where I can call myself a runner. I used to reserve that term for my friends and others who could run 5-Ks in under 20 minutes and 10-Ks in under 42. But not for myself. I didn't feel that I belonged.

When I started running in the early 1980s, I finished my first 5-K in over 27 minutes. But I kept at it anyway, covering 20 to 25 miles a week. By 1988 I was able to complete the New York City Marathon in 4:05—a glorious but painful experience. I didn't think that I would ever want to run another.

Still, I kept running and eventually got my 10-K time under 50 minutes. Then the Boston Marathon lowered its qualifying time to 3:40 for women in my age group. Boston . . . sigh. . . . I had to admit it: Boston was a dream, for me as for so many other marathoners. I decided to aim for the Portland Marathon, six months off, to qualify for Boston.

The Program

That was the easy part. The hard part was devising a training program that would get me to a sub-3:40. So I sat down to chat with Budd Coates, the Rodale Press (where I work) health promotions manager and an elite marathoner himself.

We began by going over my previous training and race times.

"What fitness activities did I do other than running," Coates asked.

None.

Had I been lifting weights at all?

No, not in a few years.

How much training had I done in the past two weeks?

I told him.

Coates never said, "Sure, you can qualify." Nor did he laugh and tell me to forget it. He simply said, "Okay. I'll write up a training schedule for you and get it to you in a couple weeks."

If he could write the program, I figured I could at least try it.

Which brings me back to where I began this chapter—with the embedded circuit workout. When my training schedule arrived, it included the usual mix of long runs, short runs, hill repeats, speed workouts, and so on. But my eye stopped when it came to an unusual entry. It read, "Run 2 miles easy, do circuit training, run 2 easy."

I called Coates to ask for an explanation. He told me that I should run 2 warm-up miles to the fitness center, and then do 30 minutes of circuit weight training. Coates had developed a special circuit routine designed to build strength in the leg and upper-body muscles that are most used in running.

Between each set of repetitions, I needed to do some aerobic activity for 30 seconds—skipping rope, stair climbing, stationary cycling, anything to keep my heart rate up. After completing the circuit routine, I finished my workout with an easy 2-mile cooldown run. Altogether, the embedded circuit workout would take more than an hour to complete. It seemed like a lot.

"But this isn't supposed to be a hard workout," Coates said. "The running is easy, the lifting is easy. Combining the two does make it harder, but doing the workout shouldn't kill you."

The purpose of all the circuit training, Coates further explained,

Embedded Circuit Training

This training offers the perfect way to use indoor facilities and equipment to build your strength and endurance. To try it, first pick two easy days in your current training program. Then complete the circuit exercises on each easy day.

Remember: Since you're adding a new stress—strength training—to your aerobic running, you can't expect fast results. In fact, you'll probably feel incredibly tired at first. But once your body adapts, you should run stronger and faster than ever before.

Here are guidelines for doing the exercises.

- Adjust the weights so that you are able to do 8 to 12 repetitions for the arm exercises, 12 to 15 repetitions for the legs.

- When doing leg extensions and leg curls, set the weights at 30 pounds for extensions and 20 for curls, or 20 pounds for extensions and 10 for curls. If you can only lift 10 pounds for leg extensions, then do not do curls at all until you become stronger.

- Between all circuit exercises, do approximately 30 seconds of some aerobic activity such as stationary cycling, stair climbing, or skipping rope.

- When trying embedded circuit training for the first time, you might want to forgo the aerobic activity between lifts, especially if you have never done any weight training before or if you are a beginning runner. Once you adapt to this training and feel ready for a more challenging workout, add the aerobics.

was to build upper-body strength that running alone couldn't give me. This would prevent my arms and shoulders from tiring during the latter miles of a race. With a better-balanced body, I would run taller, stronger, and faster.

Even more important, Coates said, the circuit training would help prevent injury. When the upper body tires, a runner tends to lean forward, which puts extra strain on the back muscles, causing the gluteal and hamstring muscles to become tense and tight. This can lead to lower-back and knee problems. With a stronger upper body, I would be able to maintain proper carriage and avoid injury.

- It's best to do these exercises in the order presented here. Exercises are paired according to the muscle groups that are worked (1 and 2, 3 and 4, 5 and 6, and so on), and the two exercises within a pair must be done in order.

- When you feel comfortable with this routine, you can increase the final 2-mile cooldown to 4 miles.

- Stop embedded circuit training a week before a short race, a month before a marathon.

The Workout

After running an easy 2 miles, complete the following circuit exercises.

1. Bench presses	7. Dumbbell presses
2. Dumbbell flies	8. Lateral raises
3. Lateral pull-downs	9. Shrugs
4. One-arm dumbbell rows	10. Upright rows
5. Leg extensions	11. Triceps push-downs
6. Leg curls	12. Dumbbell curls

Finish the workout by running an easy 2 miles.

The program certainly made sense, and I was eager to try it, though I still had some doubts. Could I do all this? My workout schedule had never before included anything like embedded circuit training.

DIVING IN

Coates pioneered the use of embedded circuit training himself in the mid-1980s. He had always done circuit weight training in addition to his regular running. He fit it in on his easy days. Since he also ran a few miles on his easy days, this meant that he had to cram in two workouts on what was supposed to be a relatively restful day.

Why not simply combine them? he asked himself at one point. So he did. And one day while running home after finishing his circuit training, he realized that the workout was more than just a time-saver: It was also a new way to prepare muscles for racing. The 2-mile cooldown in particular helped to achieve that.

Embedded circuit training isn't endorsed by coaches and athletes around the country. Its effectiveness hasn't been proven by researchers in controlled studies. But Coates has had success with it, running the second-fastest marathon of his life (2:13:48) at age 30. And a few other runners at Rodale Press have found it equally beneficial. "It's a great workout for the working person," he notes. "But you're all basically guinea pigs."

I know I felt like a guinea pig, churning away on various indoor exercise equipment in Coates's laboratory. I would be in the fitness center lifting weights, skipping rope, sweating, lifting, stair climbing, lifting, sweating. . . . Full of determination to get to Boston, I focused on doing all my training right—no skimping, no shortcuts.

Friends would look at me a little strangely as I would zip by—no socializing for me. They would come over to the stationary bike where I was pedaling as rapidly as I could and look at me in wonder. "Gee, you're really working hard," they would say. "Are you training for something special?"

"Budd's . . . (pant) . . . trying . . . (pant) . . . to kill me," I'd reply. Then I would run to the bench press: ugh, whew, ugh, whew, ugh, whew. Sweat beaded on my forehead. Grab the jump rope: skip, skip, skip. With the last lift of the dumbbell curl, I would dash out of the gym and head for the fitness trail, feeling all pumped up and powerful from 30 minutes of circuit training.

And then it would happen. I would hit the trail and crash.

Fatigue would rein me in and leave me shuffling along to the finish of another embedded circuit workout.

My routine called for two of these workouts a week: Tuesdays and Thursdays. I was always tired afterward. And they seemed to wear me down for intervals on Wednesdays. On the track, I would have to shorten 800s to 400s. At other times I would cut the number of repeats that I was supposed to do. I would finish a "speed session" and walk a lap with my head bent in discouragement.

This program isn't working, I thought. This is supposed to be easy. Only my confidence in Coates and my own stubborn tenacity kept me plugging onward.

I ran a few races during the spring but nothing very serious. Then, in midsummer, the time came to test my training in a more focused race. I decided on a local race, the Longswamp 10-K, with a course that rolled gently through Pennsylvania farmland.

Race day arrived unusually warm. About 200 runners showed up. I had no confidence, no goal, no strategy. I figured that I'd just go out and see what happened. In truth, I feared the worst.

A shout from the race director started us down the road. The early pace felt comfortable. In most of my other races, the first mile felt like hard work that would soon turn to agony as I inevitably slowed down.

At Longswamp, I went through the first mile in 6:50. Gads. That was much faster than my normal 10-K pace and it felt easier. I glided down the country roads, passing a few runners in every mile. This wasn't work, it was fun. The miles rolled on, and I felt good.

When I reached the final turn, I still had something left, so I sprinted to the finish. I crossed it in 42:20, finishing second in the women's division. More incredibly, I had improved my PR by 4 minutes.

The next week, I returned to my embedded circuit training with a new sense of confidence. Coates had promised from the beginning that my body would eventually adapt to this new training, and now it did. As I grew stronger, the lifting got easier, and I could run the 2 miles afterward without any difficulty. The Wednesday speed sessions started going better, too.

It was time, Coates said, to take embedded circuit training to a higher level.

Fortunately for me, this didn't mean a great leap in training— at least not on paper. I simply increased my post-circuit cooldown run from 2 miles to 4. It didn't sound like much, but it was. Once again, I struggled to finish these workouts and found myself more tired than ever. But once again, I soon adapted and got stronger.

WORTH THE AGONY

Finally, it was time to taper for the marathon. As the training loosened, my emotions tightened. I wanted so much to qualify for Boston. I had worked so hard to prepare. I had even seen the positive results. Still, with the marathon, you always wonder: Can I really run it at my goal pace, especially when that goal is more than 10 minutes faster than my PR?

The week before the marathon, I caught a cold. Depression. I slept. Cut back on running even more. Drank gallons of orange juice, swallowed thousands of milligrams of vitamin C, and plunged ahead with my marathon plans. I went over my race strategy with Coates. To qualify for Boston, I had to run an 8:20 pace or faster. We decided I should aim for something around an 8:10 pace.

Race day finally arrived. The weather was good—cool and overcast. Anxious and excited, I burrowed into the pack of runners. It was time.

The gun fired and we headed through the streets of Portland.

I ran the first mile nervously, not having a clue how I would feel or what the split time would be. I passed the 1-mile marker in exactly 8 minutes. The second mile went up a slight grade, but I never noticed it and hit the mile marker in 15:52. Whoops. Control yourself, Claire.

After the third mile, I relaxed and settled into my pace, which wasn't easy because I felt so good that I wanted to run faster. I had to hold myself back. The miles floated by. I felt more comfortable running the marathon than I had during any of my long training runs. At one point I thought, "Gee, I'm really running well. I'm a marathoner. I'm a real runner." And I started to cry.

As well as everything was going, I knew it couldn't last. In both of my previous marathons, the last 10-K had proved incredibly difficult. Yet I continued running strong through 20 miles, then 21, then 22. The runners around me were slowing down. Some began to walk. I passed dozens of them. Sure, I was getting tired. But somehow I kept running smoothly and rhythmically, working my way through miles 23, then 24, then 25. . . .

At last, the final turn and the finish loomed before me. I read the clock—3:33:45. Even after 26 miles, seeing those minutes pricked my desire to run as fast as I could. I reached down for whatever was left and quickened my pace.

I sprinted under the clock just as it turned to 3:34:00, beating my goal by 6 minutes. I had run a 19-minute PR.

And I was headed for Boston.

I have to confess, I have never tried Coates's embedded circuit training program, not even after watching Claire cut 4 minutes from her 10-K time and almost 20 minutes from her marathon time. But I've done somewhat similar programs, enjoyed them, and found that they worked.

One summer in particular, I became seized with the idea of making my training more fun, more varied, and more "organic." My training was organic, as opposed to mechanical because I didn't go into a gym and work out with weights and fitness equipment as Claire did. But I did do many of the same exercises, and I got very good results.

Basically, I spent two or three afternoons a week running on the pleasant, rolling green campus of a college near where I lived at the time. I didn't do continuous running, however. I did discontinuous running—that is, I would jog for a while, then do an exercise; jog, do an exercise; jog, do an exercise.

The exercises included short hill sprints, pull-ups on a tree branch, stretching, bounding, sit-ups, and other calisthenics. I probably never ran for more than 3 minutes at a time, but my workouts lasted 40 to 60 minutes. They were invigorating, they were difficult, they took place in a pleasant environment, and they provided a refreshing break from continuous runs.

Best of all, I raced well that summer and fall. Circuit training teaches us that there are many forms of interval training—not just classic, grinding interval training but also discontinuous interval training that includes different kinds of exercises to make the whole body stronger and fitter.

8

THE
MARATHON

GUIDEPOSTS FOR A MARATHONER

Follow These 11 Rules to Run a Great Race

Across the country in dozens of different cities and towns, marathon-training groups have sprung up to help runners train for the 26.2-mile distance. These groups prepare novices for their first marathons, help midpackers improve on their personal bests, and often set up special workouts for more advanced runners hoping for a big marathon improvement.

Here, Hal Higdon, senior writer for Runner's World *magazine, who ran his 100th marathon at the 100th running of the Boston Marathon in April 1996, gathers the best information from all the varied training groups. The result is a chapter that concentrates on key principles, or truths, as Hal calls them. He came up with 11 of these truths and, as any marathon veteran will tell you, each is essential to marathon success.*

Because of the emphasis on truths, this program can be followed by almost any marathoner, no matter what background. Keep the truths always in mind and adjust the training program as seems best for your needs. The result will be a self-designed, personalized program that's a good bet to lead you to better results.

Running a marathon doesn't have to be a painful and frustrating experience. In the two decades that have passed since the marathon boom in the late 1970s, a body of knowledge has emerged concerning how to train for a marathon, how to ensure that the completion of that marathon will be a joyful—rather than painful—experience, and how to strive for peak performance with a reasonable chance of success.

Dozens of training experts around the country have gradually assembled that knowledge and are using it to lead marathon programs for average runners. I've talked to many of these marathon coaches, including Bob Williams, who works with both advanced and beginning runners as they prepare for the Portland Marathon in Oregon; Robert Vaughan of Dallas, an exercise scientist and coach of elite runners; and Jack Scaff, M.D., a cardiologist who founded the Honolulu Marathon Clinic in 1974, through which thousands of runners are trained every year.

These coaches know their stuff, and their programs have helped thousands of runners achieve marathon success. I analyzed their training plans and extracted 11 essential truths crucial to the success of any marathon program. Then I incorporated these truths into an 18-week plan. It's here for you to try. I believe it will help you run a great marathon from start to finish.

Before beginning this program, I suggest that you should have been running for about a year and should be able to cover 20 miles a week comfortably. It also helps if you've run one or two 10-K races. Follow the training program for beginners if you currently run 20 to 25 miles a week. If you average 25 to 30 miles per week, use the intermediate program; follow the advanced program if your average is more than 30 miles per week.

1. Long runs get you to the finish line. The long run is the most important element of marathon training because it prepares you physically and mentally for the 26.2-mile distance. You don't want, however, to jump right into a 20-mile run in the first week of training. You need to increase the distance progressively throughout your marathon preparation.

   In the first week of the program, beginning runners should start with a long run of 6 miles, then add 1 mile to that run every week. On this schedule, you'll reach 20 miles (the longest run) three weeks before your first marathon.

   Intermediate and advanced runners who can run 35 to 40 miles a week may begin with a long run of 10 miles, also adding a mile a week. These runners will reach 20 miles in the 11th week of their training schedule and will do a couple more 20-mile runs during the remainder of their programs.

   Schedule your long runs on the day of the week when you have the most free time—Saturdays or Sundays for most people.

2. Rest days keep you healthy. Rest days are the second most important part of marathon training—they are essential to staying healthy. The mileage buildup required to run a good marathon creates stress. And while you need to stress your body in order to prepare it for the rigors of running the marathon, you don't want to overdo it.

   "The whole purpose of training is to break the body down so that it will rebuild itself stronger than before," notes Dr. Scaff. "It's when you fail to allow time for the rebuilding phase that problems occur."

The musculoskeletal system generally requires 48 hours to recover after hard work. Failure to allow your body time to recover can result in fatigue, muscle injuries, stress fractures, or upper-respiratory illness—all of which can hinder your training and ultimately limit performance.

For novices, I recommend two nonconsecutive days a week of complete rest—not days on which you jog easily or cross-train, but days when you don't work out at all. The best strategy is to bracket the weekend with rest days on Friday and Monday (assuming that you are running long during the weekend). If you need a third rest day midweek, take it.

Intermediate and advanced runners may want to do some jogging or stretching on one or both of the rest days or weave in some cross-training. But don't run hard. Even elite athletes must take rest days.

3. Cross-training lets you work while you rest. You can rest and work out at the same time by cross-training. This gives you a break from the pounding of running while you continue to train aerobically. Cycling and swimming are excellent cross-training activities, and you can add some stretching and strength training, too.

For beginners, schedule a cross-training session on the weekend, on the day that you are not doing your long run. For intermediate runners, schedule your cross-training on the day after your long run. Keep your effort in this workout moderate so that you don't compromise your long run.

4. Pace work is critical to race success. "Anybody can run 26 miles if he runs the right pace," says Vaughan. "But if you try to run too fast, you'll crash. If you run slowly enough at the start, you'll make it." Whether your pace is 6-minute miles (2:37 finish) or 10-minute miles (4:22 finish), you need to know how that pace feels to achieve it.

One way to fine-tune your pace is to do some training at marathon race pace. Picking that pace, however, takes skill. Vaughan offers two formulas for predicting your marathon time. Either multiply your best recent 10-K time by 4.65, or multiply your half-marathon time by 2 and add 10 percent of that total.

5. Speed training can help you reach a personal record. If you're a first-time marathoner, you don't need to do any speed training. Building up your mileage and running long runs is enough of a stress to your body; adding speedwork, which is a different physical stress, may lead to injury.

When you're aiming, however, for a second marathon or if you've reached a plateau in your performance and want to improve, speed training can provide that "something extra" that helps you to a breakthrough. Once a week, schedule an interval workout, hill repeats, or a fartlek.

It's also a good idea to do a tempo run once a week. This is a run during the middle of which you run 20 to 30 minutes at a little faster than marathon race pace—fast enough so that you are breathing somewhat hard but not so fast that you're out of breath. Advanced runners can schedule a tempo run on Tuesday and speed training on Thursday with an easy day of running in between.

6. Just plain running days are the staple of your program. Yes, there's still room in your training program for days of just plain running. One day a week, do a run that's approximately half the distance of your long run for that week and run it at the same pace you would your long run.

   Beginners should schedule this in the middle of the week (I've chosen Wednesday). Reserve the day before and the day after this medium-long workout for easy runs covering short distances. If you want to do some extra stretching or strength training, schedule it on these easy days.

   Intermediate and advanced runners also need to reserve a few days for easy runs; schedule them in between your hard workouts (the long run, tempo run, and speedwork).

7. Weekly mileage doesn't have to be mega-mileage. Total weekly mileage for novice runners should be about double the length of the long run. For example, in a week when your long run is 15 miles, your total mileage should be about 30. Intermediate and advanced runners will, of course, have a higher weekly total, but it should not exceed triple the length of the long run (such as 45 miles, given a long run of 15).

   Running more than this can lead to overtraining, signs of which include fatigue, "dead" legs, and a lack of enjoyment of running. If you notice these symptoms, you may want to take a few days of rest and then resume your training plan.

8. Stepbacks help you step up your training. Taking rest days is not enough to guard against the dangers of overtraining. Most successful marathon programs also include rest weeks. No, this doesn't mean that you take a week off (although if you need to for some reason, that's okay, too). During a rest week, you cut

back on your weekend long run.

Once every third week, cut the distance of your long run by approximately one-third. If your schedule calls for an 8-mile long run, cut it back to 5. The following week, resume your progression by doing 9 miles on your long run. The last stepback would occur four weeks before the marathon.

Even advanced runners need to do a stepback every few weeks for a physical and mental break from the intensity of marathon training. During these weeks, you'll relax and store your strength for a push ahead to the next level of training.

9. Racing builds experience. Doing some racing during your marathon preparation is particularly important for novice runners. "Running occasional races will help you get used to the race experience: how to warm up, what it feels like running in a crowd, how to take liquids, when and what to eat before and after, and whether or not your shoes will cause blisters," says Vaughan. "It's always best to make your mistakes in less important races so that you won't make any on marathon day."

Like most coaches, Vaughan warns against racing too often during the marathon buildup period. "Once every third or fourth week seems to be the limit," he says, "otherwise, you risk tearing yourself down."

Try to schedule a 10-K race two weeks before your marathon. From this race effort, you'll have a good sense of your level of readiness for the marathon and should be able to estimate your marathon pace.

At earlier points in your training schedule, you might want to try other distances: 5-K, 15-K, 10 miles or the half-marathon. On the weeks that you race, cut back on your mileage and eliminate your long run.

10. The taper is the time to recover and refuel for peak performance. "Too many runners want to train right up to the marathon," says Al DiMicco, who since 1984 has directed a training clinic for the Vulcan Marathon in Birmingham, Alabama, "but you need to let your body recover after all the hard training." DiMicco recommends a 50 percent cutback in mileage during the last two weeks, with very little running the final two or three days. This rest not only permits any damaged muscles to heal but also promotes maximum storage of glycogen (a complex carbohydrate that your body uses for quick energy) within your muscles.

Though mileage drops during the taper, the speed at which you run that mileage should not. The taper period is a good time to practice marathon race pace but at much shorter distances. One way to cut mileage is to convert easy days into days of complete rest. You may want to run some the day before the marathon to reduce nervousness and loosen up, but a few easy miles is the most you should do. The next day, you'll arrive at the starting line rested and ready to go.

11. Motivation holds it all together. Bill Wenmark of Minnesota has coached more than a thousand runners to finish the Twin Cities and Grandma's marathons. Described as someone who "could motivate a penguin to fly," he takes no credit for supplying motivation to the marathoners that he coaches. "The motivation has to come from within," he says. He feels that people sometimes underestimate the effort required to go 26 miles. Finishing a marathon requires courage, perseverance, and commitment, Wenmark says.

"If running marathons were easy, everybody would be doing it, but they're not," he adds. "You have to be committed to your training. If you're not focused on success, you won't be successful. You'll never succeed if you're not willing to prepare. If you want to succeed in the marathon, you need to be ready to pay the price."

Say what you will about it, but running 26 miles is one activity in which you get what you pay for. Runners willing to train properly and thoroughly will find that the marathon can be an experience that provides much more joy than pain.

THREE LEVELS OF SCHEDULES

Following are sample marathon-training schedules for beginning, intermediate, and advanced marathoners. Based on the principles and workouts described in this chapter, the schedules give recommended mileage for each day of the week except those days reserved for cross-training (designated "X-train").

Keep in mind that these schedules allow flexibility. If you're feeling fatigue on a particular day, shorten your run or don't run at all. Then resume training according to the schedule; don't try to make up for missed miles. You'll still run a great marathon.

(continued on page 260)

BEGINNER
(20–25 MILES PER WEEK)

	Monday	Tuesday	Wednesday	Thursday	Friday	Saturday	Sunday
WEEK #1 Type of Work Distance or Time	Rest 0 mi.	Easy 3 mi.	Medium 3 mi.	Easy 3 mi.	Rest 0 mi.	X-train 1 hr.	Long 6 mi.
WEEK #2 Type of Work Distance or Time	Rest 0 mi.	Easy 3 mi.	Medium 3 mi.	Easy 3 mi.	Rest 0 mi.	X-train 1 hr.	Long 7 mi.
WEEK #3 Type of Work Distance or Time	Rest 0 mi.	Easy 3 mi.	Medium 4 mi.	Easy 3 mi.	Rest 0 mi.	X-train 1 hr.	Long 5 mi.
WEEK #4 Type of Work Distance or Time	Rest 0 mi.	Easy 3 mi.	Medium 4 mi.	Easy 3 mi.	Rest 0 mi.	X-train 1 hr.	Long 9 mi.
WEEK #5 Type of Work Distance or Time	Rest 0 mi.	Easy 3 mi.	Medium 5 mi.	Easy 3 mi.	Rest 0 mi.	X-train 1 hr.	Long 10 mi.
WEEK #6 Type of Work Distance or Time	Rest 0 mi.	Easy 3 mi.	Medium 5 mi.	Easy 3 mi.	Rest 0 mi.	X-train 1 hr.	Race 10-K–15-K

BEGINNER—CONTINUED
(20–25 MILES PER WEEK)

	Monday	Tuesday	Wednesday	Thursday	Friday	Saturday	Sunday
WEEK #7							
Type of Work	Rest	Easy	Medium	Easy	Rest	X-train	Long
Distance or Time	0 mi.	3 mi.	6 mi.	3 mi.	0 mi.	1 hr.	12 mi.
WEEK #8							
Type of Work	Rest	Easy	Medium	Easy	Rest	X-train	Long
Distance or Time	0 mi.	3 mi.	6 mi.	4 mi.	0 mi.	1 hr.	13 mi.
WEEK #9							
Type of Work	Rest	Easy	Medium	Easy	Rest	X-train	Long
Distance or Time	0 mi.	3 mi.	7 mi.	4 mi.	0 mi.	1 hr.	10 mi.
WEEK #10							
Type of Work	Rest	Easy	Medium	Easy	Rest	X-train	Long
Distance or Time	0 mi.	3 mi.	7 mi.	4 mi.	0 mi.	1 hr.	15 mi.
WEEK #11							
Type of Work	Rest	Easy	Medium	Easy	Rest	X-train	Long
Distance or Time	0 mi.	4 mi.	8 mi.	4 mi.	0 mi.	1 hr.	16 mi.
WEEK #12							
Type of Work	Rest	Easy	Medium	Easy	Rest	X-train	Race
Distance or Time	0 mi.	4 mi.	8 mi.	5 mi.	0 mi.	1 hr.	20-K–25-K

WEEK #13

Type of Work	Distance or Time
Rest	0 mi.
Easy	4 mi.
Medium	9 mi.
Easy	5 mi.
Rest	0 mi.
X-train	1 hr.
Long	18 mi.

WEEK #14

Type of Work	Distance or Time
Rest	0 mi.
Easy	5 mi.
Medium	9 mi.
Easy	5 mi.
Rest	0 mi.
X-train	1 hr.
Long	14 mi.

WEEK #15

Type of Work	Distance or Time
Rest	0 mi.
Easy	5 mi.
Medium	10 mi.
Easy	5 mi.
Rest	0 mi.
X-train	1 hr.
Long	20 mi.

WEEK #16

Type of Work	Distance or Time
Rest	0 mi.
Easy	5 mi.
Medium	8 mi.
Easy	5 mi.
Rest	0 mi.
X-train	45 min.
Race	10-K

WEEK #17

Type of Work	Distance or Time
Rest	0 mi.
Easy	4 mi.
Medium	6 mi.
Easy	4 mi.
Rest	0 mi.
X-train	30 min.
Long	8 mi.

WEEK #18

Type of Work	Distance or Time
Rest	0 mi.
Easy	3 mi.
Easy	4 mi.
Rest	0 mi.
Easy	4 mi.
Easy	1–3 mi.
Marathon	26.2 mi.

INTERMEDIATE
(25–30 MILES PER WEEK)

	Monday	Tuesday	Wednesday	Thursday	Friday	Saturday	Sunday
WEEK #1							
Type of Work	X-train	Easy	Tempo	Easy	Rest	Pace	Long
Distance or Time	1 hr.	3 mi.	5 mi.	3 mi.	0 mi.	5 mi.	10 mi.
WEEK #2							
Type of Work	X-train	Easy	Tempo	Easy	Rest	Pace	Long
Distance or Time	1 hr.	3 mi.	5 mi.	3 mi.	0 mi.	5 mi.	11 mi.
WEEK #3							
Type of Work	X-train	Easy	Tempo	Easy	Rest	Easy	Long
Distance or Time	1 hr.	3 mi.	6 mi.	3 mi.	0 mi.	6 mi.	8 mi.
WEEK #4							
Type of Work	X-train	Easy	Tempo	Easy	Rest	Pace	Long
Distance or Time	1 hr.	3 mi.	6 mi.	3 mi.	0 mi.	6 mi.	13 mi.
WEEK #5							
Type of Work	X-train	Easy	Tempo	Easy	Rest	Pace	Long
Distance or Time	1 hr.	3 mi.	7 mi.	3 mi.	0 mi.	7 mi.	14 mi.
WEEK #6							
Type of Work	X-train	Easy	Tempo	Easy	Rest	Easy	Race
Distance or Time	1 hr.	3 mi.	7 mi.	3 mi.	0 mi.	7 mi.	10-K–15-K

WEEK #7 Type of Work Distance or Time	X-train 1 hr.	Easy 3 mi.	Tempo 8 mi.	Easy 3 mi.	Rest 0 mi.	Pace 8 mi.	Long 16 mi.
WEEK #8 Type of Work Distance or Time	X-train 1 hr.	Easy 4 mi.	Tempo 8 mi.	Easy 4 mi.	Rest 0 mi.	Pace 8 mi.	Long 17 mi.
WEEK #9 Type of Work Distance or Time	X-train 1 hr.	Easy 4 mi.	Tempo 9 mi.	Easy 4 mi.	Rest 0 mi.	Easy 9 mi.	Long 12 mi.
WEEK #10 Type of Work Distance or Time	X-train 1 hr.	Easy 4 mi.	Tempo 9 mi.	Easy 4 mi.	Rest 0 mi.	Pace 9 mi.	Long 19 mi.
WEEK #11 Type of Work Distance or Time	X-train 1 hr.	Easy 4 mi.	Tempo 10 mi.	Easy 4 mi.	Rest 0 mi.	Pace 10 mi.	Long 20 mi.
WEEK #12 Type of Work Distance or Time	X-train 1 hr.	Easy 5 mi.	Tempo 6 mi.	Easy 5 mi.	Rest 0 mi.	Easy 6 mi.	Race 20-K–25-K
WEEK #13 Type of Work Distance or Time	X-train 1 hr.	Easy 5 mi.	Tempo 10 mi.	Easy 5 mi.	Rest 0 mi.	Pace 10 mi.	Long 20 mi.

INTERMEDIATE—CONTINUED
(25–30 MILES PER WEEK)

	Monday	Tuesday	Wednesday	Thursday	Friday	Saturday	Sunday
WEEK #14							
Type of Work	X-train	Easy	Tempo	Easy	Rest	Easy	Long
Distance or Time	1 hr.	5 mi.	6 mi.	5 mi.	0 mi.	6 mi.	12 mi.
WEEK #15							
Type of Work	X-train	Easy	Tempo	Easy	Rest	Pace	Long
Distance or Time	1 hr.	5 mi.	10 mi.	6 mi.	0 mi.	10 mi.	20 mi.
WEEK #16							
Type of Work	X-train	Easy	Tempo	Easy	Rest	Easy	Race
Distance or Time	1 hr.	5 mi.	8 mi.	5 mi.	0 mi.	4 mi.	10-K
WEEK #17							
Type of Work	X-train	Easy	Tempo	Easy	Rest	Easy	Long
Distance or Time	45 min.	4 mi.	6 mi.	4 mi.	0 mi.	4 mi.	8 mi.
WEEK #18							
Type of Work	X-train	Easy	Tempo	Rest	Rest	Easy	Marathon
Distance or Time	30 min.	3 mi.	4 mi.	0 mi.	0 mi.	1–3 mi.	26.2 mi.

Note: Tempo runs are workouts that include 20 to 30 minutes of faster-paced running in the middle of the workout; you do not run all your mileage at tempo pace on these days. After a brief warm-up, you should try to run pace runs at your marathon goal pace.

ADVANCED
(MORE THAN 30 MILES PER WEEK)

	Monday	Tuesday	Wednesday	Thursday	Friday	Saturday	Sunday
WEEK #1							
Type of Work	Easy	Tempo	Easy	Speedwork	Easy	Pace	Long
Distance or Time	3 mi.	5 mi.	3 mi.	—	3 mi.	5 mi.	10 mi.
WEEK #2							
Type of Work	Easy	Tempo	Easy	Speedwork	Easy	Pace	Long
Distance or Time	3 mi.	5 mi.	3 mi.	—	3 mi.	5 mi.	11 mi.
WEEK #3							
Type of Work	Easy	Tempo	Easy	Speedwork	Easy	Easy	Long
Distance or Time	3 mi.	4 mi.	3 mi.	—	3 mi.	6 mi.	8 mi.
WEEK #4							
Type of Work	Easy	Tempo	Easy	Speedwork	Easy	Pace	Long
Distance or Time	3 mi.	6 mi.	3 mi.	—	3 mi.	6 mi.	13 mi.
WEEK #5							
Type of Work	Easy	Tempo	Easy	Speedwork	Easy	Pace	Long
Distance or Time	3 mi.	7 mi.	3 mi.	—	3 mi.	7 mi.	14 mi.
WEEK #6							
Type of Work	Easy	Tempo	Easy	Speedwork	Easy	Rest	Race
Distance or Time	3 mi.	5 mi.	3 mi.	—	3 mi.	0 mi.	10-K–15-K

ADVANCED—CONTINUED
(MORE THAN 30 MILES PER WEEK)

	Monday	Tuesday	Wednesday	Thursday	Friday	Saturday	Sunday
WEEK #7 Type of Work Distance or Time	Easy 3 mi.	Tempo 8 mi.	Easy 3 mi.	Speedwork —	Easy 3 mi.	Pace 8 mi.	Long 16 mi.
WEEK #8 Type of Work Distance or Time	Easy 4 mi.	Tempo 8 mi.	Easy 4 mi.	Speedwork —	Easy 4 mi.	Pace 8 mi.	Long 17 mi.
WEEK #9 Type of Work Distance or Time	Easy 4 mi.	Tempo 6 mi.	Easy 4 mi.	Speedwork —	Easy 4 mi.	Easy 9 mi.	Long 12 mi.
WEEK #10 Type of Work Distance or Time	Easy 4 mi.	Tempo 9 mi.	Easy 4 mi.	Speedwork —	Easy 4 mi.	Pace 9 mi.	Long 19 mi.
WEEK #11 Type of Work Distance or Time	Easy 4 mi.	Tempo 10 mi.	Easy 4 mi.	Speedwork —	Rest 0 mi.	Pace 10 mi.	Long 20 mi.
WEEK #12 Type of Work Distance or Time	Easy 5 mi.	Tempo 6 mi.	Easy 5 mi.	Speedwork —	Easy 5 mi.	Rest 0 mi.	Race 20-K–25-K

WEEK #13							
Type of Work	Easy	Tempo	Easy	Speedwork	Rest	Pace	Long
Distance or Time	5 mi.	10 mi.	5 mi.	—	0 mi.	10 mi.	20 mi.

WEEK #14							
Type of Work	Easy	Tempo	Easy	Speedwork	Easy	Easy	Long
Distance or Time	5 mi.	6 mi.	5 mi.	—	5 mi.	6 mi.	12 mi.

WEEK #15							
Type of Work	Easy	Tempo	Easy	Speedwork	Rest	Pace	Long
Distance or Time	5 mi.	10 mi.	5 mi.	—	0 mi.	10 mi.	20 mi.

WEEK #16							
Type of Work	Easy	Tempo	Easy	Speedwork	Easy	Rest	Race
Distance or Time	5 mi.	8 mi.	5 mi.	—	4 mi.	0 mi.	10-K

WEEK #17							
Type of Work	Easy	Tempo	Easy	Speedwork	Easy	Easy	Long
Distance or Time	4 mi.	6 mi.	4 mi.	—	3 mi.	5 mi.	8 mi.

WEEK #18							
Type of Work	Easy	Tempo	Easy	Rest	Rest	Easy	Marathon
Distance or Time	3 mi.	4 mi.	3 mi.	0 mi.	0 mi.	1–3 mi.	26.2 mi.

Note: Tempo runs are workouts that include 20 to 30 minutes of faster-paced running in the middle of the workout; you do not run all your mileage at tempo pace on these days. After a brief warm-up, you should try to run pace runs at your marathon goal pace.

In my own marathon training I've abused most of Hal's truths and paid a heavy price for it. Eventually, though, I learned a couple of additional principles: (1) There are no shortcuts, and (2) less is better than more. The crucial ingredient in a successful marathon is to arrive at the starting line strong, healthy, and well-rested.

The best way to do this, I've found, is through ample use of Higdon truth number 8—the stepback. Hal explains how to reduce the length of your long run every third week. When I'm training particularly hard, I'll reduce the mileage of an entire week of training, usually one week out of every month. In a three-month marathon-training program, I might have two stepback weeks and the taper week before the marathon.

Stepbacks work because they force you to take rest as part of the training. You plan for rest and you make sure that you get it. The wrong way to do a stepback is by getting injured or catching a cold. Both of these happen often during marathon training, and when they do, you have no control over the outcomes. When you plan stepbacks, on the other hand, you know when you're going to begin resting and when you're going to train again. What's more, it's all part of a plan, which is just the way it's supposed to be.

GUARANTEED RESULTS

This Simple Marathon Workout Really Works

During my 20 years at Runner's World *magazine, I have probably written hundreds of articles, some of them so encyclopedic that they could practically have stood alone like a book. The one that follows is the shortest that I have ever written—and also my favorite.*

I still remember the absolute delight that I felt when Bart Yasso first explained his "Yasso 800s" to me. I had been running and hanging around runners for a long time. I thought I knew, or had heard, just about everything, including plenty of crackpot ideas. But I had never heard of Yasso 800s.

Naturally, I had to put Bart's idea to the test. I'm a skeptic at heart; I don't accept anything until it has met my standards for scrutiny. Yasso 800s passed with flying colors. They have become one of the classic workouts of marathon training. I believe they're going to remain that for a long, long time.

When physicists discover a new subatomic particle, they claim the right to name it. Same with astronomers. Locate a new star out there in the way beyond, and you can name it anything you want: Clarence, Sarah, Mork, or even Mindy.

I think runners, coaches, and writers should be able to do the same. And I'm going to take this opportunity to invoke the privilege.

A few years back, I discovered an amazing, new marathon workout. Amazing, because it's the simplest marathon workout that I had ever heard. (And simplicity in marathon training, as in physics and astronomy, is much to be prized.) Amazing, because I'm convinced that it actually works.

In truth, I didn't find this workout. It found me, through the person of Bart Yasso, the race services manager at *Runner's World* magazine, who has run more than 50 marathons on four continents. But Bart's not much of a proselytizer, while I sometimes am, so I'm going to seize this chance to name the workout. I'm going to call it Yasso 800s.

Bart and I were at the Portland Marathon when he told me about his workout. He was training for a marathon later in the fall, so two days before Portland he went to a nearby track and ran Yasso 800s. "I'm trying to build up to 10 repeats of 800s in the same time as my marathon goal time," he told me.

Huh? Half-miles in 3 to 4 hours? I didn't get it.

Bart saw that he would have to do more explaining. "I've been doing this particular workout for about 15 years," he continued, "and it always seems to work for me. If I can get my 800s down to 2 minutes, 50 seconds, I'm in 2:50 marathon shape. If I can get down to 2:40 (minutes), I can run a 2:40 marathon. I'm shooting for a 2:37 marathon right now, so I'm running my 800s in 2:37."

Suddenly, things started to make sense. But would the same workout apply to a 3-hour marathoner? A 4-hour marathoner? A 5-hour marathoner? It didn't seem very likely.

In the next couple of weeks, I decided to check it out. I played around with lots of mathematical equations and talked to about 100 runners of widely differing abilities (from a 2:09 marathoner to several well over 4 hours), and darn if the Yasso 800s didn't hold up all the way down the line.

Now, this is a remarkable thing. Anyone who has been running for a few years, and, in particular, trying to improve his marathon time, knows that training theory can get quite complex. You have pace, you have lactate threshold, you have cruise intervals, you have tempo training, you have enough gibberish to launch a new line of dictionaries.

And now you have an easier way: You have Yasso 800s. Want to run a 3:30 marathon? Then train to run a bunch of 800s in 3:30 each. Between the 800s, jog for the same number of minutes that it took you to run your repeats. Training doesn't get any simpler than this, not on this planet or anywhere else in the solar system.

Bart begins running his Yasso 800s a couple of months before his goal marathon. In the first week he does 4, all in one workout. In each subsequent week he adds one more until he reaches 10. The last workout of Yasso 800s should be completed at least 10 days before your marathon, and 14 to 17 days would probably be better.

The rest of the time, just do your normal marathon training, paying special attention to weekend long runs. Give yourself plenty of easy runs and maybe a day or two off during the week.

But don't skip the Yasso 800s. This is the workout that's going to get you to the finish on time.

I was so enthusiastic about Yasso 800s that I wrote about them before I had a chance to use them in my own training. But believe me, I began using them the next time I trained for a marathon, and I have used them for every marathon since.

Okay, I cheat a little. The truth is, the most that I've ever done is nine. And I often reach only as high as seven or eight Yasso 800s. The fault isn't in the workout, though. The fault is in myself that I don't train hard enough for most of my marathons these days.

Even at just seven or eight repeats, however, I find Yasso 800s to be a great benefit to my marathon training. Basically, they build my confidence. I know that if I run them in the appointed time, my marathon goal time lies within my grasp. And you only need to do one Yasso workout a week. A form of tempo training, Yasso 800s provide a hard, solid, somewhat-fast workout but don't push you over the brink of fatigue. (If they do, you're aiming for too fast a time, and you should recalibrate.) They allow you to recover and run another good workout in two days.

Indeed, Yasso 800s and long runs now form the backbone of my marathon training. I do a Yasso workout in the middle of the week, a long run on the weekend, and fill in the rest of my training as best I can. A marathon training schedule couldn't be simpler.

EASE ON DOWN THE ROAD

Make Your Marathon Training as Smooth as Possible

The road to marathon success is never smooth and problem-free. Every runner, from first-timer to marathon veteran, hits a hurdle or two while preparing for the marathon: an injury, a cold, an unexpected extra project at work. If things came more easily than this, completing the marathon wouldn't be the major achievement that it is.

Although these problems may seem unique and uniquely troubling when they happen to you, they rarely represent anything new. The history of marathon training is a history of millions of runners encountering more or less the same sorts of hurdles. So don't panic. You can overcome and get to where you want to be: the marathon finish line.

In this chapter, Hal Higdon asks a number of marathon experts how to cope with specific problems. The questions (and answers) may not seem important to you until you encounter one of the very same hurdles. And, since the road to marathon success is littered with such obstacles, you probably will. When that happens, the advice offered here will help you continue down the road to the finish line.

America has rediscovered the marathon. Oprah Winfrey has run one, the 100th Boston Marathon has come and gone, and still the interest continues.

Why this renewed interest in racing 26 miles? No one knows, but some experts suspect that during the euphoria of the early running boom in the 1970s, many runners overraced then sensibly sought moderation, including alternate activities. But now those runners miss the achievement of completing the classic distance, and they have returned to the marathon.

Welcome back. Whether you're new to the marathon or merely reintroducing yourself to an old friend, you can always use some advice from running experts. Here is advice from the members of the American College of Sports Medicine (ACSM), the world's largest sports science organization. Based on the latest ACSM research, these 10 answers to your training questions will help you run a safe and successful marathon.

Q: **An injury has kept me off the roads, but I'd like to start training again. How can I build up safely for the marathon?**

A: "If you got injured once and don't modify your training, you will probably get injured again," says Russell Pate, Ph.D., director of the Human Performance Laboratory at the University of South Carolina in Columbia.

After following the daily training of 600 runners during a one-year period, Dr. Pate identified two major predictors for injuries: previous injury and heavy training. Subjects who prepared for marathons with frequent, high-mileage workouts became injured.

Start training for your marathon early and stay at your starting mileage level for two to four weeks. Then increase mileage gradually—no more than 10 percent per week. Don't try to resume the high levels of training you may have worked up to in the past. "Know your own limitations," warns Dr. Pate.

Q: **As I've gotten older, I've put on weight. Will that be a problem when I run the marathon?**

A: In a study of 350 women, ages 17 to 93, Rachel J. Stillman, Ph.D., assistant professor of kinesiology at the University of Illinois in Champaign–Urbana, found that as the body ages, body fat increased by as much as 5 percent per decade. But Dr. Stillman also found that the more active the subject, the lower the gains in body fat. "Even a moderate amount of activity helps," says Dr. Stillman, "but the difference between moderately and very active is significant."

Based on an ongoing study of 30 masters competitors, Michael L. Pollack, Ph.D., co-director of the Center for Exercise Science at the University of Florida in Gainesville, reports that subjects who have been able to maintain the lowest body-fat percentages included weight training in their running programs.

Since extra body fat equals dead weight in a race, you must trim extra pounds to maximize performance. You don't need to cut down to the levels of elite runners (8 percent for men, 12 percent for women). Instead, settle on an ideal weight at which you feel lean and strong.

To reduce weight, combine diet and exercise. Of course, your training regimen with its long runs and speedwork will aid in the fight against fat. "You reach your ideal weight by training down to it," says Paul D. Thompson, M.D., director of preventive cardiology at the University of Pittsburgh Medical Center. Be sure to include weight-training sessions, especially during the base-training period.

Q: **I've been training hard for a while, but I can't seem to improve my race times. What should I do?**

A: Many runners stagnate in their training. They run the same workout over the same course, month after month, and, as a result, never get any faster. To explore this syndrome, Peter Snell, Ph.D., and James Stray-Gundersen, M.D., both of the University of Texas Southwestern Medical Center at Dallas, collaborated on a study of 13 subjects who had been running for an average of 10 years. "Typically, they ran hard every day," says Dr. Stray-Gundersen.

The researchers began by putting the subjects through a six-week program of base training, involving long runs at relatively slow speeds. For the next 10 weeks, the runners added two hard days a week: interval training, fast-paced running, or a combination. At the end of the 16-week period, the subjects showed marked improvements.

In another experiment, David L. Costill, Ph.D., director of the Human Performance Laboratory at Ball State University in Muncie, Indiana, found that runners reported plummeting performances after training hard on consecutive days.

Dr. Stray-Gundersen recommends mixing slow base-training with speedwork for best results. Avoid identical hard training runs day after day. Dr. Costill advocates rest. "In order for the muscle to get stronger, it has to rest," says Dr. Costill. He advises alternating hard and easy days.

Q: **After months of training, I caught a cold just before the marathon. How can I avoid this next time?**

A: According to Gregory W. Heath, D.Sc., an epidemiologist at the Centers for Disease Control in Atlanta, runners have only half as many upper-respiratory infections as the general population.

But in the midst of heavy training, that protection dwindles, making prerace colds common among marathoners.

In a survey of 2,311 participants in the Los Angeles Marathon, David C. Nieman, D.Sc., professor of health and exercise science at Appalachian State University in Boone, North Carolina, found that 40 percent of them caught colds during the two-month prerace period. (These months, January and February, are the peak cold and flu season.) Training more than 60 miles a week, notes Dr. Nieman, doubled the risk of infection. Also, in the week following the race, 13 percent of marathon finishers caught colds, compared to 2 percent of runners who didn't race.

Save your high-mileage training for the spring, summer, and fall months when the risk of infection is lower. Get fit enough so that a week lost to flu won't be that serious of a setback. Taper early to prevent last-week problems. And make certain that you take postrace precautions against catching a bug since your resistance will be at its lowest then.

Q: **How can I motivate myself for a peak performance?**

A: In order to succeed in the marathon, you not only need to train properly before the race, but you must also push yourself during the closing miles. Exercise physiologist Linda Chitwood found that highly motivated, self-driven type A runners needed no encouragement to achieve high oxygen-uptake scores during a treadmill test. Type B runners, however, performed an average of 15 percent better when cheered on.

If you consider yourself a more laid-back type B runner, pick big-city marathons where you'll thrive on support from the crowd and other runners. A training partner also provides motivation. Even talking to yourself helps. "The year I ran best at Boston," says Dr. Thompson, "I placed 16th by telling myself, 'Keep going,' and, 'I'm a tough dude.' "

Q: **How can I minimize the wear and tear that my body undergoes both in training and in the marathon itself?**

A: Damage displays itself in many ways. Randy Eichner, M.D., professor of medicine at the University of Oklahoma Health Sciences Center in Norman, analyzed the blood of 25 endurance athletes and found that 90 percent showed red blood cell destruction. The force of the foot striking the ground during fast training or racing is to blame. "Blood destruction occurs more in high-mileage runners who have slapping or stomping gaits," says Dr. Eichner. Other Oklahoma studies showed gastrointestinal bleeding in one out of five runners and cyclists following races.

That's only part of the problem—add muscle glycogen depletion that lasts several weeks, microscopic muscle tears that contribute to extended soreness, and the effects of dehydration that occur during a marathon performance.

To minimize damage both in training and in racing, keep your weight low, wear shoes with plenty of support, and run with a shuffling style to lessen the pounding on your legs and feet. When possible, run on soft terrain. Says Dr. Eichner, "Man was born to run on forest trails, not to go pounding down the pavements."

Q: **How much should I taper before an event?**

A: Dr. Costill believes that runners often train too hard in the weeks immediately preceding a marathon. "They do one last butt-busting workout and tear themselves down," he says. To test the less-is-more theory, Dr. Costill tapered the training programs of a group of runners beginning three weeks before a track race. During this period they ran only 2 miles daily, "just a warm-up." When it came time for a time trial, the runners were so rested that they went out too fast and faded. But in a second trial, the group relaxed and ran their fastest.

Start your marathon training early enough so that you can afford to taper two or three weeks before the event. Realize that your most important workouts are the ones that you do months before, rather than weeks before, the race. Since you will be burning fewer calories during the tapering period, modify calorie intake to avoid adding weight.

Q: **Most marathons start early. What should I eat the night before?**

A: W. Michael Sherman, Ph.D., assistant professor in the department of exercise physiology at Ohio State University in Columbus, fed very large amounts of carbohydrates to a group of trained cyclists 3 hours before exercise testing. His results showed that the cyclists increased both power and endurance after these late feedings. "The cyclists were able to maintain a higher output for a longer period," says Dr. Sherman.

Another study showed that athletes performed better if they ate 4 hours before exercise. "We can safely say that if you have a carbohydrate feeding 3 to 4 hours before a marathon, you can enhance performance," summarizes Dr. Sherman.

A large prerace meal may be hard to stomach, so Dr. Sherman advises runners to eat pasta late in the evening the night before the event or to rise early for a breakfast that could include pancakes or toast washed down with orange juice. Liquid meals featuring high-carbohydrate drinks may work best for races near dawn. Dr. Sherman warns, however, that runners should try this routine first in practice or for minor races before going to the line at a major marathon.

Q: **How much should I drink during a marathon? Which fluid is best?**

A: Leonard A. Kaminski, Ph.D., assistant professor of exercise physiology and cardiac rehabilitation at Northeastern Illinois State University in Chicago, monitored the fluid intake of five runners during an ultramarathon. One participant running a 62-mile race consumed 14,000 milliliters of liquid; another who ran only 26 miles, drank only 280 milliliters. The latter, not surprisingly, showed the most loss of vascular fluid, resulting in thickened blood plasma and impaired performance.

Experts agree that you need to drink enough to restore lost fluids. The weather, the distance, and the intensity of your effort will all determine how much you should consume. In shorter races on hot days, water works fine as a replacement drink. When the distance exceeds 10-K, you should probably switch to a sports drink that will replace burned carbohydrates as well as fluids. Again, don't drink anything that you haven't tried in practice.

Q: **As fatigue sets in at the end of a marathon, my stride deteriorates. How should I compensate?**

A: When studying the mechanical efficiency of male and female 5000-meter runners, Keith Williams, Ph.D., assistant professor of physical education at the University of California at Davis, found that fatigue toward the end of a run caused the runners to change their stride mechanics. Most frequently, they lengthened stride.

Other scientists have noticed that late-race stride changes as well. While counting strides-per-lap for competitors at the 1984

Olympics, Jack Daniels, Ph.D., assistant professor of physical education and an exercise physiologist at the State University of New York in Cortland, noticed that as runners dropped off the pace, their stride lengths shortened.

Dr. Daniels believes that you can use high-mileage training to improve efficiency. Marathon training should include runs at varying paces and at varying levels of fatigue. If you know that you'll need to break into a survival stride to complete those tough last miles, try that stride in practice.

Dr. Williams adds that the practice is worth it. If you concentrate on form during the final miles of a marathon, you should be able to run faster.

In the final weeks of my marathon training, I have one major goal, and it's not to get stronger or faster. It's much more basic than that. The goal: not to catch a cold. The first time I caught a cold just prior to a marathon, I thought it was both trivial and a simple twist of fate. But over the years my friends and I have so often caught colds late in our marathon training that I now recognize it as something to which I should pay particular attention.

Prevention should be a relatively simple matter: Don't overtrain, taper early, stay well-hydrated, and get plenty of sleep. Also, I finally acknowledged the wisdom of washing your hands often. This, I have found, is particularly important in the last several days when you may be attending a marathon expo. These expos bring together thousands of runners, often from countries around the world, into one crowded location and provide a too-perfect germ-swapping pool. I go to the expos because they are fun, but I wash my hands often throughout the day.

It seems ironic that you should be most susceptible to colds when you're in peak marathon shape, but there you have it. Given the amount of attention that you're focusing on nutrition, stretching, and long runs, it only makes sense to extend your vigilance to the common cold. Training for the marathon isn't simply a matter of increasing your weekly mileage; it's a matter of getting stronger and healthier in every way possible.

COUNTDOWN TO THE BIG RACE

A Close Look at the Two Weeks before Your Marathon

Preparing for a marathon is at the same time both simple and complex. The simple part is the training. If you follow any reasonable schedule for several months, you'll probably get yourself in shape for the distance.

Putting all the other pieces in place, on the other hand, often amounts to a considerable challenge. You have to eat right, get enough sleep, avoid injuries and colds, pick a good marathon, travel perhaps to a strange city, and then negotiate all the ins and outs of number pickup, meals, getting to the start on time, and so on. Marathon morning, by itself, is often a graduate-level course in logistics and deployment.

With all these things to consider, it helps to have a plan and a checklist. That's the purpose of this chapter by Gordon Bakoulis. Here is everything that you have to think about and how to handle it. With this plan, your marathon success is practically guaranteed.

The marathon is a gamble. Over its vast distance and time, anything can happen. And you can't control the weather or the course. So the object of the game is to focus on those things that you can control. And we're not just talking about long runs and pasta. The well-prepared marathoner looks after every detail of proper physical and mental training, nutrition, hydration, clothing, and equipment.

In the last two weeks before your marathon, you should focus on these matters even more as you fine-tune your training and your diet and put all the last-minute details of your race in order. In general, you shouldn't introduce new elements into your training or—if possible—into your life during these two weeks.

To help you in your final preparation for the marathon, here's a daily checklist of things that you should do in the last two weeks prior to your race. Grab a calendar and a pencil and get ready for your best-planned marathon ever.

If you have done the training and can check off every item listed here (or most of them), you're virtually guaranteed success on marathon day. You've taken control of everything you can; the rest is up to fate. With reasonably good weather and a decent course, you may have the race of your life.

Saturday, Day 15

Training: This is the day before your last long run, so you want to run lightly. Either take a day off or jog for 30 to 45 minutes easy. Stretch in the evening.

Mental preparation: Mentally prepare yourself for your last long run. Remind yourself that the hard work is nearly over, but that you want this final long training effort to count. Do something relaxing and inspiring, such as listening to your favorite music.

Diet: Eat a high-carbohydrate dinner to top off your stores of glycogen (a complex carbohydrate that your body uses for quick energy) and drink plenty of nonalcoholic beverages without caffeine.

Sunday, Day 14

Training: This last long run should not be your longest. (Most experts suggest doing that no later than three to four weeks before your race.) Run at a comfortable pace, saving your best effort for the race. Include surges only if you have done so previously in training. A good last long run will give you a tremendous mental boost. But don't let a subpar effort discourage you. Remember that the race is what counts.

Mental preparation: Plan some visualization exercises for the next two weeks to help you relax and build your confidence. Find a quiet place, close your eyes, and relax. Imagine yourself running well at various points in the race.

Diet: Weigh yourself before and after your long run and drink enough to make up for any lost pounds. Or drink until your urine is plentiful and clear. Also, you should replace carbohydrates within 2 hours after your run, when your muscles are most receptive.

Equipment: If you haven't bought the shoes that you plan to wear in the race, do so now. If your current pair has more than 400 miles on it or is worn or frayed in any way, you should replace it. Train in your new shoes during these next two weeks. Never race in brand-new shoes and don't change models, either. Stick to the shoes that you've been wearing throughout your training.

Other details: This is your last chance to experiment with the food or drinks that you may eat before and after the marathon. You can test, for example, whether a bagel eaten an hour before a long run sits well in your stomach. If you think that you might take a sports drink during the race, find out which beverage will be available on the course, fill up a few water bottles with it, and plant them along the course of your long run.

Monday, Day 13

Training: Run or do some form of cross training (if you have been cross-training) for 30 to 45 minutes, or take a day off to recover from your long run.

Mental preparation: Shift gears to think "countdown" from here until your marathon. Rather than building up your training, you're backing off. Visualize the race start—standing on the line feeling relaxed, confident, and eager to run.

Diet: Evaluate how you handled yesterday's food and fluid intake. Eat extra carbohydrates if you're hungry and drink more if your urine is still sparse or dark. It can take 24 to 48 hours after a long run to restore fluid and glycogen stores.

Tuesday, Day 12

Training: Run for 45 to 60 minutes. After the first 20 minutes, do eight 30-second hard efforts with 30-second recoveries between each. This workout should shake your legs out but not drain you. Include the pickups if you have been doing intervals throughout your training.

Mental preparation: Visualize the first 5 miles of the race. You're holding back, letting other runners go because you know you'll pass them later. You feel fresh, alert, even able to chat with those around you.

Travel: If you're traveling a long distance to your marathon, call your airline and hotel to reconfirm your reservations.

Wednesday, Day 11

Training: If you usually do a midweek semi-long run, run 60 to 90 minutes today at training pace. Otherwise jog for 30 to 45 minutes.

Equipment: This is a good time to make a list of clothing and equipment that you'll need to take with you to the marathon such as petroleum jelly, tape, extra shoelaces, a key holder (attaches to your shoe), plastic garbage bags to wear at the start if it rains, containers for water and food, and clothing for before, during, and after the marathon. Purchase any items you need now. Don't count on being able to buy them once you get to the race.

Thursday, Day 10

Training: You should do your last hard speed workout today. Do 3- to 5-minute intervals 10 to 30 seconds faster than your planned marathon pace with 30-second to 2-minute recovery jogs.

Mental preparation: Congratulate yourself on another hard workout well done. Visualize miles 5 to 9 of the marathon. You're settled in, running comfortably, recording even splits and taking plenty of water. You feel well-trained and rested and know that you're going to have a great marathon.

Diet: Plan some of your favorite tried-and-true high-carbohydrate meals for the next 10 days. Don't try unfamiliar foods, but don't eat the same thing every day (even pasta). Choose from a variety of high-carbohydrate foods such as potatoes, vegetables, fruit, bread, rice, and other grains. And don't neglect protein. Figure low-fat meat, poultry, fish, legumes, egg whites, and low-fat dairy products into your diet as well.

Friday, Day 9

Training: Take a day off or cross-train for no more than 45 minutes. Remember, nothing new now.

Equipment: Go over your marathon shopping list and make sure that you have everything you need.

Travel: Make sure that you know exactly where your airline tickets are and check on your passport or any other travel documents you'll need.

Saturday, Day 8

Training: Many marathoners do a semi-long run (no longer than 2 hours) or a race of 10-K or less a week before their marathon. Either way, this is your last hard effort. The semi-long run keeps you in a pattern of going long without overtaxing you close to race day. You should finish feeling refreshed, not drained. Afterward, you may want to schedule a massage to work out any kinks and help move lactic acid out of your legs.

Mental preparation: Visualize miles 10 to 13 of the marathon: You still feel great, although you're starting to work a little harder. You hold a steady pace. No one's passing you, and you're looking forward to the half-marathon point.

Diet: Are you obsessing about carbo loading? Contrary to popular belief, if you have followed a high-carbohydrate training diet, you don't need to change your pattern very much this week. You may want to increase your carbohydrate intake by roughly 10 percent in the few days before the race by eating extra servings of bread, fruit, pasta, or rice. Vary your diet, but don't add unfamiliar foods.

Sunday, Day 7

Training: Run easy or cross-train for 30 to 45 minutes.

Mental preparation: Listening to music or inspirational words before the start of a marathon can get you psyched. If you think it may help you, prepare some tapes to bring along to the race.

Diet: Continue to follow your high-carbohydrate, low-fat diet and make sure that you're drinking plenty of fluids.

Equipment: If you're traveling to your marathon, make a packing list and start gathering the clothes and items that you'll need.

Monday, Day 6

Training: Run for 45 minutes. After the first 20 minutes, do 8 to 10 pickups of 1 minute each with 1-minute recoveries between. Stretch thoroughly afterward.

Mental preparation: Visualize miles 14 to 17. You are working hard, running steadily, feeling calm and confident. You have taken plenty of water, and your muscles are relaxed and loose. You're on pace for a personal record.

Travel: If you're flying to your race and have to cross time zones, plan, if possible, to arrive a few days before the marathon so that you have time to adjust to the new environment. The air in planes is especially dry, so drink extra fluids. And eat lightly; airline food is generally high in fat. Or, better yet, bring your own low-fat, high-carbohydrate snacks. Once you reach your destination, get on the new time schedule immediately.

Tuesday, Day 5

Training: Jog for 30 to 45 minutes.

Mental preparation: You may feel restless at this point and be tempted to add extra last-minute miles. Don't! Extra training now will hurt rather than help your performance by tiring you and preventing your legs from saturating with glycogen. Relax once you get to the race site, but don't spend days lying around your hotel room. Just avoid excessive walking and standing, and get plenty of sleep.

Diet: Don't worry if you gain a few pounds between now and the race. It's extra water and carbohydrates that you'll need for the marathon.

Equipment: Check race-day forecasts and start to plan your outfit. Make a list of any items that you have forgotten and need to buy.

Wednesday, Day 4

Training: Jog or cross-train for 30 minutes. If you like, do four to five pickups of 30 seconds each after the first 15 minutes of running.

Mental preparation: Visualize miles 18 to 21. This is a tough segment for many people. You have been running for at least 2 hours, yet you still can't smell the finish. See yourself digging down, working hard, holding your own, and starting to pass others.

Other details: If friends or family have come to watch you race, make arrangements to meet them near the finish.

Thursday, Day 3

Training: Take the day off or jog for 30 minutes. Remember, the less you run now, the more stamina you'll have on race day.

Mental preparation: You're likely to feel keyed up and irritable in these final days. Do what feels right for you: Spend time alone, hang out with a group, or visit with one or two friends or family members.

Diet: Your carbohydrate intake should be at least 65 percent of total calories. You should feel comfortable after each meal, not unpleasantly stuffed.

Other details: Plan to have two working alarm clocks. You never know when one will fail. Don't rely solely on a friend or a hotel wake-up call, either.

Friday, Day 2

Training: Jog for no more than 20 minutes. Some advanced runners throw in a few light pickups to remind themselves that they still have leg speed. This isn't necessary for most people.

Mental preparation: Visualize miles 22 to 26. These miles are usually the toughest, but you'll be ready because you have trained hard and raced smart. Imagine yourself running strong and steady toward the finish, passing all those who started too fast.

Diet: The food you eat today will help you more in the race than the food that you'll eat tomorrow. Keep up your pattern of ample carbohydrates and fluids. And especially now, don't try anything new or exotic.

Equipment: Race-day weather forecasts should be detailed and accurate at this point (although surprises can happen). Plan your race-day outfit, and if you need any last-minute items, visit the marathon expo. Pick up your race packet as early as possible to avoid the last-minute rush and carefully read all the instructions.

Sleep: A good night's sleep matters more tonight than the night before the race. If you can't sleep, don't worry about it—lying down for your usual sleep period is still beneficial.

Saturday, Day 1

Training: If you run at all, jog for no more than 30 minutes. Many runners like to run the day before a marathon to get any kinks out. Just take it easy, no matter how good you feel.

Mental preparation: Visualize the finish: You have made it, and you're exhausted but triumphant as you run the final few hundred yards feeling strong and steady. See yourself raising your hands as you cross the line to the cheers of thousands of spectators.

Diet: Try to make one of today's meals a special event with family and friends who will relax with you and share your excitement. Contrary to popular belief, what you eat today will have little effect on your marathon as long as you stick to the usual—plenty of carbohydrates and beverages. Eat dinner early so that you can get a good night's sleep.

Equipment: Lay out everything that you plan to wear or bring to the start: racing singlet and shorts, tights and a short- or long-sleeve shirt if appropriate, mittens or gloves, hat, headband, bandanna, sweats, rainsuit, whatever you will need. Pack a separate set of warm, dry clothes for the finish. Your equipment should include your bag, running number, extra shoelaces and safety pins, bus ticket to the start, car key, beverages, containers, food for before and after, money, petroleum jelly (to prevent chafing and protect exposed areas from wind and cold), sunscreen, music tapes, a headset, and a plastic garbage bag if it's raining.

Other details: Make fail-safe plans to get to the start and meet someone at the finish. Have a backup plan for every possible disaster such as your car failing to start, missing the bus, sleeping through your alarm, or breaking a shoelace. Go to sleep confident that nothing stands between you and getting to the starting line feeling calm, strong, and ready to go.

Sleep: Marathon-related anxiety dreams such as missing the start, losing your shoes, or running the wrong course are common. So don't worry if you don't sleep well. If you're generally well-rested, one night's poor sleep won't hurt you.

Marathon Day

Diet: Wake up at least 2 hours before the start. Give yourself enough time to eat something light but high in carbohydrates. Drink water or a sports drink, stretch, and get to the starting line with time to spare.

Mental preparation: Mentally, you want to achieve a state of optimal arousal. That means that you want to be eager and excited but not crippled by nervousness. Think back to other races to recall this feeling. If you feel too keyed up, sit or lie down, close your eyes, and breathe deeply. Visualize the race or simply think peaceful, happy thoughts. On the other hand, if you're not "up" enough, walk or jog and talk to other runners, but don't tire yourself.

Equipment: Keep warm and comfortable until the last possible minute before the race. Many runners wear old sweats to the start and discard them just before the gun. Otherwise, standing around in the cold can cramp your muscles. Apply petroleum jelly to areas likely to chafe, such as underarms, nipples, and inner thighs. Mark your bag so that you can find it easily at the finish. During the race, discard layers if you feel too warm, or you'll lose precious fluids through perspiration. Keep extremities covered if it's cold.

Warm-up: It's not necessary to warm up extensively for a marathon, but try to do some walking and a few minutes of jogging to loosen your legs and raise your body temperature.

Racing: Running a successful marathon is an exercise in holding back. Ideally, the hard work shouldn't begin until 20 miles. Then your training and willpower will get you to the finish. During the race, remain calm and focused. Note your splits, and take encouragement from a steady pace early on, even if others are passing you. Break the race into segments, and work through each part rather than attack the full 26.2 miles.

Other details: Don't eat or drink anything on the course that you haven't tried in training. If you do, you may suffer digestive woes. Take water early and often. If you feel cramps or stomach upset en route, walk until the problems lessen.

Finish: When you come through the finish line, keep walking and take fluids right away. Pat yourself on the back—you made it. Find your friends or family and go celebrate.

The last two weeks before a marathon are often an unsettling time. You begin to train less but think about the race more. You get cranky. You lose sleep. You start to feel aches and pains in your legs at the precise time when they should be feeling their best. After all, you're tapering off and giving them a break after weeks or months of hard training.

This chapter tells you how to deal with almost everything but the strange and disconcerting feelings a marathoner often experiences before his race. Suddenly, all self-confidence vanishes.

He begins to wonder if he hasn't bitten off too much. The closer the race gets, the worse he feels and the more he obsesses over his many doubts.

I can only tell you one thing: The doubts will pass and race-day magic will take over. Race-day magic is the heady phenomenon that makes virtually all marathoners feel better during the race than they ever imagined possible. It's the magic that helps you run farther and faster than you thought you could.

And you'll never have the chance to enjoy it unless you get to the starting line. So don't let the doubts deter you. Stick to your plan and reap the rewards.

CHAPTER 37

A TIP FOR EVERY MILE

Let the Marathon Man Be Your Guide

Doug Kurtis looks like a regular guy. He's not particularly big, not particularly strong. And he's a regular guy in other ways, too—wife, kids, mortgage, full-time job.

Until he steps up to the starting line. Then he becomes the Marathon Man. Mr. Consistency. Mr. Sub-2:20—he ran a dozen of them in 1989 alone.

Very nice, you say. But what's in it for me? Lots. Because Doug Kurtis is also Mr. Nice Guy. He's willing to share his marathon secrets, all 26.2 of them, with you. Best of all, you don't even have to catch up with him between training runs.

Doug Kurtis strides smoothly beneath shady trees and past emerald lawns through the streets of Dearborn, Michigan, a suburb of Detroit. He is on his lunch hour, running his usual 8-mile route near the Ford Motor Company, where he works as a systems analyst. Accompanying Kurtis are two friends, both sweating heavily on a humid day, though Kurtis seems barely damp. Later, after work, he will run another 8-mile route from his home—just part of his regular training week.

Kurtis is between marathons. Two weeks earlier, he ran the Revco Marathon in Cleveland and finished ninth in 2:19:32. Three weeks after this workout, he will run Grandma's Marathon in Duluth, Minnesota, and finish sixth in 2:17:59. These are his 117th and 118th marathons respectively, also his 59th and 60th faster than 2:20.

"Doug breaks every rule," explains Dennis Quenneville, a 2:50 marathoner who trains with Kurtis. "You're not supposed to run marathons back to back; he does. You're supposed to rest for a week afterward; he doesn't."

Kurtis smiles at Quenneville's comments. Though he may break a few of the so-called rules of smart marathoning, Kurtis abides by, and indeed has invented, several. Otherwise, he couldn't race as often and as well as he does. "Everybody has to learn what works for them," says Kurtis. "I couldn't run a dozen marathons a year if I hadn't established my own rules." And here they are.

1. Consistency. At 5 feet 7 inches and 130 pounds, I'm built to run marathons, but the key factor in my success is my consistency. I run the same mileage (105) week after week—no downtime, no uptime, no breaks. I recover well and rarely get injured. I could probably run more, but I would have a much harder time avoiding injuries. When you're consistent with your training, you have a much lower chance of entering a race undertrained or overtrained—two reasons why people get hurt or run poorly.

2. Mileage. I have a strong incentive to train twice daily because my high mileage permits me to run sub-2:20 marathons. But everybody has a mileage level that's best for them. Each person has to decide what's important in life and use that as a guide to dictate training levels.

3. Intensity. Many people believe that they have to train hard all the time. They feel that they're not getting anything out of a workout unless they're running race pace. But I often run 2 minutes per mile slower than my marathon race pace—even 3 minutes per mile slower at the beginning of a workout. If I ran any harder, I would burn out and get injured.

4. Speedwork. If you expect to run fast, you need to do some speedwork. My favorite is a workout that I read about in *Runner's World* magazine and adapted for myself: 8 x 800 meters with 200-meter jogs between. (For more information on this workout, see chapter 34 on page 261.) I average 2:24 for the 800s, faster on a good day, slower if it's hot or windy.

    Another favorite workout is mile repeats—four of them at about the same pace as the 800s. Sometimes if someone runs with me, I'll do his workout, often 400s. Usually, I prefer to train at a track where something is going on, even if it's only soccer practice and nobody's watching me. I feel more comfortable with people around. It's hard to run with nobody there.

5. Diet. With my high mileage and double workouts, I burn an extra 1,500 calories a day. To maintain my energy level, I need to pay close attention to my nutritional needs. I eat at least three good meals a day, plus a snack sometimes. I'll start with a good breakfast: a mix of several cereals with fruit, toast with peanut butter, and a tall glass of orange juice. I'll have a solid lunch and a dinner that varies from Italian to Mexican to Chinese to good old American meat and potatoes. I drink plenty of fluids. I never pass a water fountain at work without stopping.

6. Rest. I'm not afraid to take days off. Usually, I average 15 to 20 rest days a year. I don't plan them in advance but take them when something comes up—travel or illness or a family outing. Rest days are good for me, and I probably should take them more often. One of the advantages of training consistently year-round is that when you do take a short rest, you lose very little of your training edge.

7. Training routes. I don't train just to race. I run because I enjoy it. I do my first workout during my lunch hour, picking scenic routes along streets near my office. In the evening, I often run from home along a parkway. I like to find pleasant places to run and to see the sights. I enjoy being out there day after day.

8. Goals. I go into marathons very relaxed. People worry about the weather or their competition, but I worry only about myself. I'm fortunate to have as a goal running more sub-2:20 races than anyone else, catching Kjell-Erik Stahl. I can place 10th or 15th, it doesn't bother me. If race circumstances prevent a fast time, I don't worry because there's another marathon three to five weeks later.

Marathoners also need short-term goals, other races leading up to the marathon. I'm amazed when I meet people whose first race is a marathon. It's hard to keep up your enthusiasm for a marathon that's two to three months away. Focusing two to three weeks ahead on a 10-K can help keep you motivated.

9. Travel. I usually run the *Detroit Free Press* Marathon every year because I've won it four times and it's held in my hometown. It's convenient. But I recommend that you use marathons as an excuse to travel. Plan a vacation around your race and make it a festive occasion. Spend a long weekend or a week. Bring the family. Do some sightseeing. See the museums. Take in a show. Relax and get comfortable. I love walking around expos, looking at the equipment, and seeing and talking with other runners. It's fun to hear everyone else's stories.

10. Tapering. The hardest thing for me to do is to taper for a marathon. I have a tendency to overtrain right before a marathon, not back off early enough. Often, when I run marathons back to back, I run the second marathon better. Part of that is because I taper for two weeks: one week before the first marathon and a week of rest between the first and second. I enjoy running so much that I find it difficult to eliminate any of my workouts before a race.

11. Confidence. You can talk to runners before a marathon and know whether or not they're going to have a good race based on their confidence in their training. If I've invested a lot of time in training, I go into the race with more confidence because I know I'm ready. The same is true if I have performed well in short races leading to the marathon. Inevitably, a high level of training builds a high level of confidence and leads to success.

12. Equipment. After a blister problem almost forced me out of my first marathon, it took me a long time before I found shoes that fit. I now tell people that the time to experiment is not during the race, yet I still see runners show up at the starting line with brand-new shoes. I won't even try new socks. I break in everything: socks, shorts, singlet, shoes. I do track workouts in my racing flats to make absolutely certain that they're comfortable at racing speeds.

    Sometimes I'll put in only a few miles, but I'll know those shoes work for me. One good way to work out the bugs and test your equipment is to enter shorter races before the marathon.

13. Fate. Things sometimes happen that you cannot control. For example, early this year en route to Arizona, I got snowed in at the Chicago airport, and I didn't get as much sleep as I would have liked to Friday night. On top of that, it was a warm day for the marathon, yet I placed eighth in 2:24:31.

    How do you cope with the misfortunes that come along that you can't control? You adjust your goals. You try to think positively. Many people tend to dwell on the negative rather than the positive. Inevitably, those people wind up beating themselves.

14. Prerace meals. Usually, I eat my last meal the night before the marathon. Rarely will I eat anything the morning of a race, unless the race begins late, such as Boston's noon start. I'd rather lie in bed an extra hour than get up just to eat. Some runners can eat and be ready to run an hour later. I find that I need 3 to 4 hours to digest my food before I feel comfortable running. I've experimented with eating 2 to 3 hours before a race, but it didn't work. Again, it comes back to what you feel comfortable doing.

15. Prerace sleep. The general rule is that the most important hours of sleep are those that you get two nights before the race, not the night before. I find that to be true. If I get a good sleep Friday night before a Sunday race, the amount I sleep Saturday makes little difference. Before most races, I have no problems

sleeping, but sometimes I'm nervous or have to get up early to go to the starting line. In Honolulu, the race begins at 5:30 A.M., so you know that you're going to come up short on sleep unless you go to bed right after dinner. But everybody seems to survive. As long as I'm in bed relaxing, I don't worry whether or not I'm actually asleep.

16. Prerace fluids. Once in a while, before a cool-weather race, I'll have a cup of tea to get some caffeine into my system. But when I've tried that before a hot-weather race, I felt nauseated. Most of the time, I drink only water in the last hours before a race. I'll drink whenever I'm thirsty, regardless of how much time remains before the start.

17. Warm-up. I like to get to the starting line at least an hour before the race. That way, I don't worry about little things going wrong, such as getting caught in traffic or not finding a toilet. Usually I find a quiet, cool, shady place and sit relaxed. A half-hour before the race, I start walking briskly. Then I'll jog. I used to think that I needed 4 miles of warm-up, but I do fewer now, usually 2, maybe 3 if it's cold. I mix that with walking. I do a little bit of stretching but not too much. Then I wait for the starting gun.

18. Race start. You need to run intelligently. When I see the early leaders go out hard, my first reaction is to want to go with them, but I start slow. It's hard to hold back and be patient. But experience has taught me that this is my best strategy.

19. Race pace. I don't pay much attention to splits. I think of the course and the weather conditions. If it's hot, you don't want to overheat early. If the course is hilly, you can't run fast. A lot of runners go out too hard and die later. I pass many runners in the last 4 to 5 miles.

20. Focus. During a marathon, I do my best to concentrate on the race: how I feel, the weather, how my competitors look. I try to stay as comfortable as I can. Sometimes you have to push it but not for the whole race.

    My mind wanders at times. I like to look around and check the scenery, but not for long. On out-and-back courses, people usually wave at me coming back. I'd like to be friendly and wave back, but I can't. When I run Detroit, I appreciate the cheers that I get as a local runner, but I need to think about what I'm doing. I particularly try to focus late in the race, especially when I know a sub-2:20 is on the line.

21. Race fluids. During the race, I drink only water. Sometimes I find that I drink too much, so I don't always stop if there are water stations every mile. Once in a while, late in the race, if I feel tired and think sugar will give me a boost, I'll take one of the replacement drinks. But if you have never tried replacement drinks, don't start at mile 3 of the marathon. Experiment on a few training runs first.

One trick that I use to make drinking on the run easier is to squeeze the top of the cup as I drink. You spill less water this way. During hot-weather races, I'll also pour water over my head, but I try to dump it toward the back so that it won't leak into my shoes. I try to keep them dry.

22. Bad patches. Often in the middle of a marathon, I'll go through a bad patch where I don't run well. I lose the rhythm for a couple of miles. It happens to every runner, no matter how well trained or how experienced. Unless you ran too hard at the beginning of the race, you can usually work through a bad patch.

I simply back off a bit. If I'm running with somebody, I let them go and hope to catch them later. I try to avoid negative thoughts and think positively instead. I focus on relaxation. I adjust my stride. I check my breathing.

23. Rehydration. After I cross the finish line, I usually want something other than water to drink. It helps me bounce back more quickly. I prefer soft drinks to beer, which is a diuretic. Diet drinks don't work as well for recovery, because they don't contain sugar. I'll drink as many as 10 cups of fluid, if not more, right after a marathon. The only problem with drinking a lot is that you begin to lose your appetite and may not eat as well.

24. Refueling. I'll start with bananas and oranges, but after I get back to the hotel and shower, I'm ready to eat something more substantial. The stress from a marathon often causes me to lose my appetite temporarily, but once I start seeing food in front of me, I get hungry again. I watch what I eat, but I'm not fussy. One year after the Twin Cities Marathon, I craved hamburgers, french fries, and a milk shake.

25. Recovery. I bounce back very quickly from marathons, usually by the next day. Some people say that you should take a week off, and that's probably a good idea if you have really sore muscles. But because I like to train consistently, I start running right away. Also, if I have traveled to a marathon, after sitting in a plane or car, I need to walk or jog to loosen up my muscles. Usually, I can limp through a 5-mile run the first day. By the second day, I start to feel okay. By day three, I can go out and do 15 miles without a problem. That's one of the advantages of high-mileage training. You don't necessarily run that much faster, but you recover more quickly.

26. Learning. I tell all my training partners that they have to find out what works best for them. They look to me for advice, but I still make mistakes. With all my experience running marathons, I've simply learned to minimize the mistakes. I come back to certain races year after year and know what to expect. But you have to take each marathon as a whole new race every time you run it. What worked one year may not work the next. I've finished more than 100 marathons, and I'm still learning.

26.2. Fun. At the Barcelona Marathon one year, I went out too hard on a hot day and faded to eighth. Afterward, the winner from Denmark asked me, "Was that one fun?" I had to admit it wasn't, but if I didn't think running marathons was fun, I wouldn't run a dozen a year. Often the enjoyment is the training beforehand and the memory afterward.

In my first marathon more than 30 years ago, I was amazed to find that I could feel good (at the beginning), good (in the middle miles), terrible (at 19 miles), and then good again (at 22 miles). I had imagined that running a marathon would be like climbing a nearly endless mountain: It would just get harder and harder. I figured that once I began to feel bad in the last 6 to 8 miles, it was part of an inevitable and unstoppable deterioration. Things would gradually get worse and worse.

Instead I learned, as Doug says, that you go through bad patches that are often followed by a return to feeling good. This is an important phenomenon for every marathoner to understand. It means that when you start feeling bad, you haven't fallen off a cliff. You're not going to crash and burn. You can get it together again.

How? That's not easy to say because it differs for every runner and every situation. But here are a couple of good tricks: Slow down drastically (or even walk) and have something to eat. Slowing down just a little won't work; it will feel good for a moment or two, but then you'll get tired again. Slowing drasti-

cally, however, gives you a complete change of pace and an opportunity to recover. Don't worry about losing precious moments. The truth is, you won't lose much, and it will give you the chance to start running strongly again.

All marathons provide as many water and aid stations as they can, but I have often found that solid food helps me more during the late stages of a marathon. In fact, one of my favorites is simply a piece of hard candy that dissolves slowly in my mouth over the course of a mile or two. Other runners favor the many bars and gels that are now available for marathoners. Be sure to try them on training runs before deciding to carry several with you in the marathon (in a pocket or small hip pack).

CREDITS

"Unexpected Pleasures" on page 23 is adapted from "Passages" by Hal Higdon. Copyright © 1991 by Hal Higdon. Reprinted with permission.

"Fueling Up for a Peak Performance" on page 31 is adapted from "Seven Days and Counting" Applegate, Ph.D. Copyright © 1994 by Liz Applegate, Ph.D. Reprinted with permission.

"The Lowdown on Fats" on page 36 is adapted from "Fat as Fuel?!" by Liz Applegate, Ph.D. Copyright © 1994 by Liz Applegate, Ph.D. Reprinted with permission.

"For Men Only: 10 Truths" on page 42 is adapted from "Real Men Eat Right" by Liz Applegate, Ph.D. Copyright © 1994 by Liz Applegate, Ph.D. Reprinted with permission.

"Tomorrow's Beverages Today" on page 47 is adapted from "Futuristic Fluids" by Liz Applegate, Ph.D. Copyright © 1993 by Liz Applegate, Ph.D. Reprinted with permission.

"Say Good-Bye to Meat" on page 51 is adapted from "Going Meatless" by Liz Applegate, Ph.D. Copyright © 1993 by Liz Applegate. Reprinted with permission.

"Buried Treasures" on page 56 is adapted from "Buried Treasures" by Liz Applegate, Ph.D. Copyright © 1993 by Liz Applegate, Ph.D. Reprinted with permission.

"The Big Five" on page 63 is adapted from "First Aid" by Dave Kuehls. Copyright © 1995 by Dave Kuehls. Reprinted with permission.

"To Dare, to Create, to Dream" on page 129 is adapted from "To Dream, to Dare, to Create" by Joan Samuelson. Copyright © 1991 by Joan Samuelson. Reprinted with permission.

"Time-Tested Advice" on page 135 is adapted from "25 Great Training Tips" by Joe Henderson. Copyright © 1991 by Joe Henderson. Reprinted with permission.

INDEX

Underscored page references indicate boxed text. **Boldface** indicates illustrations.

Underscored page references indicate boxed text. **Boldface** indicates illustrations.

Underscored page references indicate boxed text. **Boldface** indicates illustrations.

<u>Underscored</u> page references indicate boxed text. **Boldface** indicates illustrations.

Underscored page references indicate boxed text. **Boldface** indicates illustrations.

Underscored page references indicate boxed text. **Boldface** indicates illustrations.

Underscored page references indicate boxed text. **Boldface** indicates illustrations.